Elaine Randell

Collected Poems & Prose

Books by Elaine Randell

Songs of Hesperus
Telegrams from the Midnight Country
Untitled
Seven Poems
A Taper to the Outward Roome
Early in My Life
Long Hair for Birds
This, Our Frailty
Larger Breath of All Things
Hard to Place
Songs for the Sleepless
Beyond All Other: Poems 1970–1986
Gut Reaction
Selected Poems 1970–2005
Faulty Mothering
The Meaning of Things

Elaine Randell

Collected
Poems & Prose

Shearsman Books

First published in the United Kingdom in 2024 by
Shearsman Books
P.O. Box 4239
Swindon
SN3 9FN

Shearsman Books Ltd Registered Office
30–31 St. James Place, Mangotsfield, Bristol BS16 9JB
(this address not for correspondence)

www.shearsman.com

ISBN 978-1-84861-956-2

ACKNOWLEDGEMENTS
The books contained within these covers were originally published
by The Curiously Strong, Black Suede Boot Press, Sceptre Press,
Transgravity Press, Laundering Room Press, Permanent Press,
Oasis Books, Spectacular Diseases, Pig Press, North and South
and Shearsman Books.

Contents

THIS, OUR FRAILTY

BEYOND ALL OTHER: POEMS 1970–1986

UNCOLLECTED POEMS

III. PROSE

GUT REACTION

PROSE FROM *THE MEANING OF THINGS*

UNCOLLECTED PROSE

*This collected work is dedicated to my husband, Ian,
and our daughters Phoebe, Beatrice and Naomi.
It is also offered to the publishers, writers and friends
who have supported me across a lifetime
to whom I give my lasting thanks.*

Autobiographical Prose

The publication of a collected volume is significant and one which I often speculated might happen after my death, if indeed at all. The work in this volume has been set out largely chronologically and the autobiographical context is set out below.

My Mother

My mother was always in a hurry; everything she did was at double speed and with a unique and unforgettable amount of style. An example of this was, coming home from school one day, I found that she had painted everything in the kitchen with Household brown paint. My mother liked change and became bored quickly and so painting everything in the kitchen, including our large American second-hand fridge, in Household brown paint certainly gave it a new look but rendered the boiler unusable for some time until the paint had burnt off it, with attendant smoke and smell for months. The budgie, who sat on top of the fridge, was saved from transformation. Household paint was made by Woolworths: enough said.

My abiding recollection is of running next to my mum as a child, and later as an adolescent, as her walking speed was so fast. Keeping up with her was a task of its own. On reflection, I can see that moving quickly got you out of danger. She had endured the London Blitz as a child and often slept in the underground stations near Crouch End. The damage to North London had been terrible and was still there when we visited my grandfather in Drylands Road, and where we lived in south east London bomb-sites were common.

Mother's favourite phrase to me was "Buck up, Elaine"; I have been doing that for over 70 years now. My parents started married life in Hilly Fields near Catford, My birth at the Charing Cross Hospital in WC1 was reportedly accompanied by the sounds of Ava Gardner in *Showboat*, which was playing next to the hospital. My parents could not afford the rent in Hilly Fields and so moved to Drylands Road to live with my grandfather for a while until finances improved. In 1953 we moved to Southall, Middlesex, at 156 North Road. This was so my mother could be near to my grandmother who had divorced my grandfather some weeks before my birth. My grandmother had become a housekeeper to an extraordinary man, Charles Tordiff, an inventor of many electrical devices including the wire recorder, an early forerunner of the tape recorder. The house, in Morland Gardens, was a haven with sunken garden and huge greenhouses, where I played with my grandmother's button box. She had been a tailor and dressmaker, having made the fleecy lining of airmen's boots in the war, and endless garments, plus the red velour velvet cape of an allegedly notorious and significantly hunchbacked woman. This job was said to have nearly killed her, getting the hunch covered properly and seamlessly. My first school blazer was handmade by my grandmother and, while it was lovingly done, including the embroidered school badge, it did not look anything like the ones the other children wore; but off I went without understanding the implications of being ridiculed for being different. At that time, Southall was becoming a significant Sikh area. This was fascinating to me, as the landscape changed and shops became emporiums of different encounters, colours and smells.

My first school, Dormers Wells, was for only a short time as we moved not long after. I didn't mind it much but my dislike of school and education in general came later. Two things amazed and astonished me at the age of five. One was when a little boy was asked to go to the front by our teacher and was slapped on the back of his legs very hard, for what seemed an age, with a ruler. I remember the boy, even now, his red raw legs and face in a knot. The second was the sight of my friend, Yvonne Fletcher, who was allowed to sit on the back, in her own little seat, on her mother's bicycle. Mum had a firm and clear anxiety about bikes and I was always told that I would never be allowed a bicycle; so the idea of an adult who allowed their child to sit in this very wonderful position on the back was remarkable. Going home to tea with Yvonne Fletcher one afternoon, her mother perched me on the back of the bike under my mother's strict instructions that I must only be wheeled along the pavement, so the thrill was not quite the same.

When I was six-and-a-half-years old my parents moved to Lee Green in South London to 71 Horn Park Lane. This move again was made by following my grandmother, who had moved to Exford Road in Grove Park. This was a far better and more gracious house, semi-detached but with a long garden and a pond. I was to attend the Horn Park School, to which I walked every day; this involved crossing the busy A20 of

Westbourne Avenue and then going up through the council estate until the school was reached. Often I would go with other children: my friend Jennifer White who lived across the road, or Keith Bloomfield, a little lad who had started his journey from the bottom of Upwood Road. He must have left very early as he was only six and, being fascinated by all insects and leaves, his journey to school would take him twice as long as everyone else, as he inevitably had one foot in the gutter and the other in the hedge. Looking back, it's a miracle we arrived at school alive.

Growing up in Horn Park Lane was interesting. My friend Jennifer White, across the road, had the kind of lifestyle that I longed for: she had ballet lessons. My mother was an inveterate jumble-sale addict and together we would visit every church hall looking for bargains. On one occasion I found some ballet shoes. I was in seventh heaven: they were maroon and an adult size 4 while I was a child's size 8. This didn't deter me and, with elastic bands and cardboard at the back, I wore them all over the house. Jennifer White asked why I was wearing them and I told her that I too was having ballet lessons. She informed me that they were the wrong size, but that didn't matter to me. It was a lie, but I was now a contender.

Jennifer's father was a photographer on the *Daily Sketch* and my envy of Jennifer White was further enhanced as years later she had tickets for *Top of the Pops* and her father took regular photos of pop stars. I couldn't compete with that as, by then, my social life was at the Methodist Church Hall in Burnt Ash Lane. My father ran the Sunday School, a continuous sore point with my mother who loathed the church, after being raised in a Salvation Army background. Her life and interests were film, film-stars, notorious criminal trials and crooks, a passion which remained with her until the end. I remember well the look of the Sunday School leaders when my prize for good attendance, chosen by my mother, was *Film Show Annual*.

When I was eight my mother became depressed. This was very frightening and marked the start of my anxieties over going to school and leaving her at home. Several times, I walked home from school during the day to check that she was all right. I rarely returned, feigning a sore throat. When my mother had her nervous breakdown, a familiar turn of phrase in those times, I thought the world had ended; she became very thin and her hair started to fall out. She had always looked smart and fashion had been a great thing for her, albeit that my grand-mother still made many of our clothes. Mum became afraid of going out, agoraphobic; she wasn't sure what she was afraid of, but knew she didn't want to leave the house. My father went to prayer meetings where they prayed for my mother's health. This made her worse and she particularly hated the Methodist preacher who, I well recall, once gave a sermon on the perils of young men who wore elastic-sided boots. He was Welsh and emphasized the gravity of this depravity with his sonorous tones. It took years for my mother to recover but not before some of her problems were identified as being linked to acute thyroid disorder. Many of her insecurities had started in childhood when her parents would argue, and their divorce many years later continued to affect her as an adult. Trying to please both parents was complex for her and I learned much from her in appreciating the plight of children managing parental separation at any age. Years later she became depressed again and was hospitalised. It was a distressing time for me as a child and the impact of a parent's mental health upon children has been a factor I have borne in mind throughout my working life.

When I was ten I suffered a serious accident while horse-riding with a child of my parents' friends, the Maynards. They lived in Bexley and the stable was near to them. My anxiety about being killed outright by almost anything, particularly bicycles and horses, probably did not make me the easiest rider and doubtless the horse knew this. I was riding a horse called Pinky – he had a brother called Perky. The girl leading me on a lunging rope had possibly never done the job before. Pinky saw Perky and took off with me on his back. The result was serious, leaving me with a leg shattered in several places. The event bought me to one of the first of many significant events of my life – separation from my parents. As a much-loved only child, cosseted and having worn a liberty bodice from the moment I could breathe until I was sixteen, the idea of being away from my parents' influence and their tender loving care brought its own challenges. We had a family car but it didn't work well and in those days Lee Green was some distance from the West Hill Hospital in Dartford, where I was an in-patient, placed in traction. My mother would often make the journey by train, and it would take her all day. Being in traction for three months was a disturbing experience, but for once I was immobile and therefore a captive audience. I had no schooling for almost a year. Studying the other children around me, I was amazed by their different lifestyles, their situations and how they coped with their chronic illnesses. The girl opposite to me, Monica, was almost blind. Surgeons worked hard to restore her sight but by the time Monica was discharged, having been a patient for over six months, she still only had some peripheral vision. I remember Monica's visitors, her mother with dyed red hair who came to see her every three weeks with a number of different men friends whom Monica called Uncle. My eyes were opened yet further by my closest bed-mate, Rosanna, who told me all about the facts of life and her own experiences of having been sexually abused by her brother from the age of four; she never told an adult. Rosanna had unexplained chronic stomach pain which, looking back, was understandable.

It was during this time that I resolved to become a doctor. My surgeon was a Mr Hulbert, who, at that time, seemed to me to be a very elderly man. I was enthralled by the skill of doctors who could turn our lives around with their expertise. I wanted to change the world and make people better. But more of that another time; it was, after all, 1961.

My mother's sense of humour was legendary and remained, luckily, despite her illness; it was something she had inherited from her father who always had the funniest slant on the world. Their habit of talking to everybody and anybody who stood next to them for more than a second continued and is doubtless a genetic family trait. My mum's warm and humane style continued throughout her life but her fear of being alone remained. My grandmother had a Victorian interest in death and the afterlife; she was a medium and had been a famous speaker in spiritualist churches in the 1930s. My mother would say that she was fed up with hearing about death, and that life was for the living. She would always buy flowers for herself, professing loudly that they were no good to dead people.

Mum did not enjoy cooking; she was a fastidious housewife and in fact a good cook, but having people come to the house worried her and was one of the sources of acrimony between my parents; that and the church. My mother worried about what she would give people to eat, about them staying too long – longer than three minutes – and importantly, their potential for making a mess. I remember once when someone came to the house to see us, unannounced. We were in the middle of our lunch, but my mother gathered up the four corners of the table cloth, complete with plates knives and forks and the contents of the meal and placed them in a cupboard, much to the amazement of my father and me. Mother did things that were expedient and, in the ancient Tudor house she later shared with my father on Romney Marsh, before his death, she would throw her tea-bags out of the window as it was quicker than using the bin. For her it was out of sight and out of mind, to which many of our cupboards bore testimony. As the cottage bordered the churchyard I often wonder what anyone made of the pile of tea-bags accumulated over the five happy years they lived there.

Mum spoke often about her childhood in Crouch End, about enduring the war under the Morrison table-shelter they had in the kitchen, and her friendship with Peter Sellers who had moved to Muswell Hill in 1935, just up the road. My grandmother's origins were half Polish-Jewish, a long story in itself. One of her sisters had married an Italian who was interned during the war; she died of TB and so her son was raised with my mother. He was a sad child who later started a famous hi-fi shop in Hampstead. Peter Sellers brought him famous customers who all wanted hi-fi equipment. Grandfather's house in Drylands Road had four floors and during the war – and indeed after it – was full of tenants. One such tenant was Miss Green who, it was strongly rumoured, was a spy. One day she just completely vanished, leaving a flat full of belongings, later removed by "some men". Stories of the tenants at Drylands Road and their antics throughout the war were legendary, including Mrs Dealy whose daughter Maureen was said to have tried to stop the house's iron railings from being taken away for melting down at the munitions factory by tying herself to them with a silk stocking.

My mother's propensity for quick movement was at its peak in cafés. At Lyons' Corner House, Charing Cross, looking for a table with our tray, no tables were vacant. My mother, seeing a plate of food, knives and forks on a table with no person in attendance, swept the lot into the nearby food waste trolley and told me to sit down. A puzzled man was seen soon after searching for his place, holding his glass of water. My mother insisted we should not make eye contact but "just buck up Elaine and carry on eating".

Mrs Scott was our neighbour. Her driveway, which overlooked our kitchen door, was several feet higher than ours, perhaps because our house was slightly further down the hill. Mrs Scott was a tall, well-built person so she made a considerable impact when she loomed over the fence as she was then a good two feet above us. My mother liked Mrs Scott, who had a lot of hair that she would put into a French plait. She was also a piano player. Her favourite tune was *Fleur de Lys* which she played repeatedly.

In common with my mother, Mrs Scott was very expressive in her views about people. These were both interesting but often puzzling to me as a child. The coal-man's son was in my class at school so it was a surprise to hear from Mrs Scott that Mr Morley was, "so strong and honest, but placid as a golden sloth". The arrival of Mr Morley with coal on his back to either household was always an event. He would place the sacks across his back, usually two at a time, crouching almost to the ground as he staggered up the driveways until finally off-loading the Home Glow and anthracite into the coal cupboard. Mr Morley was always covered in black dust and his black leather cap, which he never removed, was greasy and waxed. The cap had a flap which went across his neck and onto his shoulders. The milkman Mrs Scott believed to be as secretive as a pearl, making it clear that she didn't trust him and thought he had plans to "bump us all off". People often spoke about others "being bumped off" as I recall. A term first used by Hemingway in 1920, it seems.

Mrs Scott spoke a lot to my mother about Scotty, her husband. Poor Mr Scott had been wounded in the war, and he had retired as a police officer at Shooters Hill Police Station. It was a second marriage for them both because, "the first Mrs Scott couldn't cope, dear, not after all that". Mrs Scott's voice would trail off at that point or dip to a lower register while I played with my hula-hoop or the dog. I was a lonely, only child, constantly trying to gauge the mood of adults. Mrs Scott also said in even lower tones, "Scotty couldn't manage in the bedroom department, not after all that…". Mrs Scott made it clear, "I have other fish to fry, dear, in Hither Green". To my knowledge they had no children, and there were certainly no visitors to the house, but Mrs Scott would go out shopping most days, waking quickly with her umbrella and diaphanous raincoat, with an immaculate French pleat.

Mr Scott was a tall man with a most terrible limp; he had to drag one leg behind him as he walked. However he was always active in the garden. I could see him sometimes if I was on the swing and got up to some height. He was always in and out of his greenhouse. He never spoke to me once that I recall but I was terrified of him for no reason other than that he was there. I never understood what the bedroom department was which was spoken about so quietly by Mrs Scott, and I once asked my mother when we were in Chiesmans, in the furniture department, whether Mr Scott came here. She had no idea what I was talking about.

When Mr Scott died it was no surprise; we'd been expecting it for years. Mrs Scott materialised over the fence saying, "the creaking gate lasts longest they say, dear, but I did not expect it to be this long, dear. I stuck with him though, poor Scotty". Mrs Scott moved away soon afterwards and went to live in Hither Green. My cousins lived in Hither Green so I knew it a little. I looked out of the fish and chip shop to see if Mrs Scott was there, frying fish, but to no avail.

My Father

My father, Harry, was one of six children born in Lewisham, south-east London, in May 1919. He was the middle child, having two younger sisters, one younger brother and two older brothers. At one point in the family history another boy was adopted into the family when his parents died, making them a group of seven. In common with so many at that time, the family were extremely poor, but they had a home at 13 Mercia Grove, Lewisham and, importantly, love and affection. There is a photograph of which my father was most proud. It is of him with a small bicycle, at about seven years of age. In the foreground his sister Florrie wears a torn dress, a familiar sight in those days. The picture is important because owning the bicycle made the family proud but it was short-lived; the bicycle was sent to the pawn shop the following day to pay for food and never returned.

My paternal grandfather was a munitions worker at the Woolwich Arsenal but was often without work. He was involved, I am told, in the hunger marches of the 1920s and joined the Jarrow Crusade in October 1936. He endured a hard life and, in common with all members of the Randell family, he died before receiving his pension. My paternal grand-mother, Florence, was born in Greenwich; family myth says that her father traded in diamonds, but sadly there was no evidence of this. She was uneducated but I remember her always doing the crossword whenever I saw her in the basement, where she would sit, immovable, by the coal fire. Nanny Randell, as she was known, enjoyed a drink, something that my father particularly loathed, and she was often found in the Sultan pub in Lewisham, having drunk too many pints. She had endured a hard life but managed to keep the majority of her children in close proximity. Auntie Win and Alf were at number 15, Auntie Florrie and Fred at 17 and Uncle Bob and Jean were upstairs at 13. Visiting the family was an all-day event, being entertained from one house to the other. Uncle Fred and Ivy lived in Hither Green where they chain-smoked Kensitas cigarettes, furnishing their home with goods bought with the Kensitas coupons. The more you smoked, the more goods you could acquire. Uncle Arthur and Ann lived in Plumstead; along with ourselves, they were the out-of-towners. We were known as "posh" because Harry had made good and was rich. Indeed, for years, my father supported his mother financially; it was what you did.

A major part of my father's entire life was his involvement in the church. As a small boy, he joined the Sunday School and the Boys' Brigade at the local Methodist Church in Lewisham. They were his role models, and likely his main support growing up. Dad left school at the age of 14 and the July 1933 school report from the headmaster of the Hither Green LCC school describes him as having a "well-earned place at the top of the class. He will develop to be a diligent and earnest employee."

In 1934 my father found work at the Oil Well Engineering Company, in Moorgate, as an office boy. He remained working there for the following 28 years, save for the period when he was in the army. When war broke out he signed up with the Royal Engineers, which became part of the infamous Forgotten 14th Army that was in Burma to fight the Japanese. In common with those who served in, and survived Burma, he spoke very little of the horrors and atrocities that he and others had endured. Enough was said, however, to give us to understand that the experiences were traumatic and the effects lifelong. When finally he was demobbed from the Army, sometime in 1945, Dad returned to his old job in Moorgate, where he met my mother Daphne, who was working as a secretary; my father was 8 years her senior. They married in 1949. Having little money, my father often walked from Hilly Fields near Catford, where they lived, to Moorgate. He was stick-thin and remained so throughout his life, since, like my mother, he never stopped moving. In hindsight, Dad was involved in too many things. Certainly, the church used up a great deal of his energy, as did amateur dramatics and, once we had a proper home, gardening. He was a hopeless DIY man: "I'm no Barry Bucknell," he would say, as shelves were put up at angles and pictures fell regularly from the walls.

Dad would encourage me to make miniature gardens placing soil and moss in a seed box, making a miniature pond from a mirror, a tiny seat from plasticine, and tiny trees from twigs. It was perhaps a precursor for my later sand-tray work with troubled children. My father adored my mother and they made a good team. He never returned from a trip abroad, or even to the shops, without a gift or a bunch of flowers. Dad loved socialising and having people to our home. Mum hated this, as she would become anxious that people would need something. It was the one bone of contention between them.

As a teenager, I joined the Peace Pledge Union and CND. Dad had not been a conscientious objector in the war and he enjoyed nothing better than long, heated debates with my friends, many of whom he persuaded to read Albert Schweitzer, someone he quoted often – much to my deep embarrassment at the time. "The only way out of today's misery is for people to become worthy of each other's trust." My friends loved debating with my dad and envied me that I had that possibility. Fathers in the 1950s and '60s were not always as easy with their role.

Our house in Horn Park Lane had previously belonged to a wealthy local motorcar mogul, who had several showrooms. Mr Penfold of Pen-fold Motors had put in a chrome-and-white tiled bathroom that was the envy of the street. The bath was rarely used, however, as my parents believed that too much bathing caused illness. Years later I found a letter from my mother sent to my grandmother warning of the dangers of bathing, taking a protective layer off the body. In fairness, it was cold living in homes without central heating, and simply being grateful for having survived the war was doubtless key for many at that time. Once, while fixing the immersion heater at our home, my dad found a loaded revolver and £100 wrapped perfectly in newspaper at the back of the airing cupboard. He smartly and carefully took both to Lee Green Police station and the previous homeowner, Mr Penfold, was doubtless contacted about the gun. My all-too-honest father was worried about the £100 and donated it to the church.

To my knowledge, I disappointed my father only twice. The first time was when I was truant for two days during my first year of grammar school, where I had been granted a special "Governors' place" due to my having missed a whole year of schooling with my broken leg. I had been terrified of the French teacher, Miss Barnes, who had thrown my book across the room towards my head every time she saw my homework. It had been worked on – by me – so many times in my efforts to get it right, using an ink eradicator, that holes had been worn right through the pages. I was worried about going back for more and so went with a friend to Greenwich Park instead of school. So far, so good, except I tripped while running downhill towards the museum and broke my toe. On arrival at home, the offended toe swelled and was painful. I said that I had injured myself playing lacrosse. The next day my father telephoned the school to express his concern that I had not been treated by a doctor. They, of course, confirmed that I had not been in school. The balloon went up, but with good results. Miss Barnes was told to calm down. My mother confided to me her significant upset with a needlework teacher who had distressed her so much that she had smuggled her embroidery home in her knickers so my grandmother could do it instead. My father said he was disappointed that I had not been able to tell him my worries. I was grateful for my place at the Kings Warren Grammar School, even though it meant a long journey of two buses, changing at the Woolwich Arsenal, getting the 53 bus outside Manze's Eel Pie shop to Plumstead Common, but I wasn't in the Latin stream and knew I wasn't as able as the others. Over the past twenty-five years I've been a school governor, knowing how important educational opportunity is for children and the need to further understand the normal, frequent anxieties and perils of childhood.

The second occasion I disappointed my father was years later and my one and only foray into the Juvenile Court as a criminal. I had evaded my train-fare going to London to meet a boyfriend who lived in Balham, and was prosecuted by the Transport Police. My dad was clearly distressed that I had possibly embarked on a life of crime. Sadly, he didn't live long enough to see the thousands of reports I have written over the years on behalf of, and about, children and young people in trouble, in an attempt to improve their lot.

Dad also had a very keen sense of humour and was well known for being careful that no jokes or comments should ever be used against anyone. This made him popular with those who knew him; they felt they could trust him, which was unusual in the cut-throat oil industry of the 1960s. If anyone ever behaved badly or was criticised by my mother or me, he would always say, to know all is to forgive all. He was keen I should understand why people did certain things and behaved in a certain ways. It's no wonder that social work was a career possibility. My father left the Oil Well Engineering Company to become self-employed in the late 1960s at the time of oil and gas exploration in the North Sea. He was responsible for the erection of the first fixed, concrete oil platform; he was rightly proud, but feared the long-term impact upon Scotland, a place he loved both as a walker and fisherman. Dad in fact enjoyed, and was involved in, every sport he could, excelling at tennis, being well respected by the Rye Tennis Club, and he was also an excellent cricketer. Our holidays were always based on rivers in the UK so that he could fish. I would have my own rod too, set up between watching my mother trying to sunbathe on the riverbank with her movie books beside her. Mum hated sport of all kinds and watching dad fish was a double purgatory.

My father's family had all their lives feared being sent to the work-house, a reality they had doubtless narrowly avoided, since it was not until 1929 that local authorities had the responsibility to change work-houses into infirmary hospitals. The anxiety over seeking medical help was deep-seated and, despite his intelligence, Dad resisted seeing a doctor when he had chest pains and so he, like all his siblings, died before his sixtieth birthday. When he died in 1979, over 300 people wrote to my mother and me, saying how much he had affected their lives for the better. I only found it bearable to read some of the letters recently; people spoke of his kindness, his generosity, his constant and genuine interest in the welfare of others and of his diligent work, in addition to his tireless energy and, importantly, his quick sense of humour. Over £8,000 was raised in lieu of flowers at his funeral and the roof of Snargate Church, next door to where my parents had lived and where the tea bags had been thrown, was able to be replaced. A fitting tribute, tea bags and all.

My Maternal Grandmother

Helena Sawicki was born in 1900 at Great Portland Street where the family then lived. They wisely changed their name to Francis and lived in fear of their Jewish heritage being disclosed. My grandmother's father was a tailor with a shop in Foubert's Place near Carnaby Street. His father had been a professor of languages at Krakow University. Family members who remained in Poland were exterminated in Auschwitz; their photos can be seen at the camp. My great grandmother was British; she was a staunch Catholic who had a love affair with a Catholic priest, leaving him all her money and belongings with an agreement that she would be buried at Buckfast Abbey. My efforts to trace her grave indicate that she is buried under the car park.

Despite her preoccupation with spiritualism, my grandmother had a broad outlook and approach to life. In her youth she had joined the Communist Party; she told me they arranged great hiking trips at the time, which was her motivation for joining up. I never met my great-grandmother who was perhaps living with the priest in Torquay at the time of my birth.

Helena's marriage to my grandfather Percy was an unlikely match. He was a painter and decorator, one of eight children, and his parents were Salvationists. I recall attending services with him. The chapel was full of homeless people who shouted out rather spectacularly mid-service, and with some effect – "shut up preaching, now we'll have a hymn". Grandpa played the piano well, but he was not keen on spending his money and this caused friction in the marriage. At 16, having lied about his age, he had been sent to the Somme as a soldier; he was lucky to return and knew it. In his twenties, he suffered from TB and was sent

to convalesce for a year, shortly after my mother was born. He lost a lung but survived into his 70s. My grandfather never remarried and lived alone in his large house in Drylands Road, Crouch End. He was a good man, extremely humorous, who loved nothing more than to speak to people, strangers particularly, as he was curious by nature. In common with many, my mother felt constantly torn in her allegiances between her divorced parents throughout her adult life.

My grandmother did remarry, a merchant seaman, Alfred, a lovely man who was away for long periods so I had her all to myself, which suited me well. She was always on my side, I felt, a great thing to impart to a child. She was, to me, the kindest, most magical person, with endless patience, time and energy. In later years she would wrap money in her handkerchief and pass it to me with a whisper not to tell anyone in that way that grandmas should.

Jobs and moves

In 1966 I had a Saturday job in the bridal and silk-flower department of Chiesmans, the department store in Lewisham. The supervisor told me never to get out a veil for just anyone on a Saturday, as it was usually silly girls wanting to try them on with no intention of buying. The supervisor was right; wrapping the net train back up again, perfectly, without my sweating palms marking it dirty, was not easy and I was caught out more than a few times. The 21 bus journey from Horn Park Lane to Lewisham didn't take long. I usually stopped off on the way back visiting the second-hand record shop next to the King of Lee pub to buy ex-jukebox records. These were singles with no centres, which I made at home from cardboard with a range of success resulting in some different interestingly distorted sounds at times depending on the glue quality or my cutting accuracy with the homemade centre. It was a far from perfect solution. The bus conductor would always ask if I was selling programmes at the Coronation when I asked for a ticket to the King of Lee. I was pleased to own Brenda Lee, singing *I'm Sorry*; Bobby Vee, *Rubber Ball*; Jimmy Jones, *Handy Man*.

My first real job in 1968 was at Sylvester's Silver Antiques in Chancery Lane. It was a tiny shop, crammed with priceless silver objects which it was my job to clean without denting the sometimes fragile items. This was done with Vickie who lived in Kensal Rise; she had a boyfriend, something I was in awe of. Vickie encouraged the boyfriend to cut his hair short as then no other girl would fancy him because, like most men in my view, he looked far more appealing with his hair longer. Mr Sylvester had health problems and he would sit by his oxygenator, a contraption which allegedly changed the air to improved oxygen which made the whole shop smell terrible.

Mr Sylvester was proud of his son-in-law, Frank Marcus, who had just written the stage play, *The Killing of Sister George*, which had premiered at the Duke of York Theatre in town to a great rumpus. It told the story of two lesbian women, or did it? Frank Marcus said he had written the play as a farce in order for it not to be banned. Mrs Sylvester saw her role as shop manager and protector of Mr Sylvester; she would scream orders at the top of her voice to Vickie and myself, shouting out that time was money and we must clean faster. Often we would be close to tears. Mrs Sylvester would then apologise and say she was worried about Frank who had just developed Parkinson's disease; his infamy as a playwright had put a strain on her, she told us. Mrs Sylvester shouted at me once too often and I left, never to return. I recall her standing on Chancery Lane with a silver polish cloth in her hand, shouting at me to come back as I legged it to the tube station.

In those days interesting jobs were easily found in the *Evening News* classified ads section; alternatively *The Stage* or *Melody Maker* would have some tempting offers. For a brief time I worked for *The Spectator* at 99 Gower Street. Auberon Waugh was the heart of the building and the magazine. It was an education in itself. Auberon's son, Nathaniel, had been born in 1968 and had been given the third name of Biafra, thus marking the terrible civil war in Nigeria which had killed an estimated 3,000,000 people. Nigel Lawson was the editor, who subsequently fired AW following a prank that allegedly backfired. Such times.

To fill in some time before I went off to study Art Therapy at Goldsmiths, I was asked by one of the editors of *International Times* to do some secretarial work. *International Times* was a full-on underground newspaper of some alternative repute. David Mairowitz had me come to his swanky apartment in Holland Park for my instructions. I had letters to type to extraordinary characters such as General Westmoreland – known at the IT offices as General Waste More Land. General Westmoreland, of course, had a key role as Chief of Staff for the US Army. He was a much-loathed figure given his strategy in the terrible war in Vietnam. Soon after I travelled a little in Holland where there were many young men from the USA dodging the draft.

The Arts Lab was in Drury Lane, run by Jim Dine. I was a very frequent visitor. Once, on the stairs, my tea was knocked over by John Lennon, rushing to get to Yoko who was doing a thing at the time. I was totally unaware of being in the crucible of such huge social shifts but that's always the case; we never appreciate the importance of where and who we are at the time.

In 1969–1970, I took a job cataloguing rare books at the Covent Garden Bookshop, Long Acre. It was run by Dr Nothmann and his wife. My colleague, and subsequently chum, was Tony Rudolf. Mrs Nothmann ruled the business with a rod of iron and, as employees, we were not permitted to speak while working. It was tough. I had by then started *Amazing Grace* poetry magazine from my bedroom floor in Horn Park Lane. My bravado in contacting poets for contributions at that time knew no bounds, and the generosity of people like James Kirkup, Jeff Nuttall and Michael Horovitz brought it more attention than it deserved. James Kirkup was later subject to great public attention when his poem 'The Love that Dare Not Speak Its Name' was published in *Gay News*. Mary Whitehouse successfully prosecuted the editor under the Blasphemy Act. Tony Rudolf introduced me to Barry MacSweeney who also contributed to *Amazing Grace*, in addition to rather changing the direction of my life. We married in 1973.

Working with Dr and Mrs Nothmann became all too difficult and I moved to work for Foyles rare and antiquarian book department where the regime was easier. My wonderful colleague Reg Read and I had interesting scrapes delivering priceless books, including, memorably, a first edition of the *Seven Pillars of Wisdom* and *Audubon's Birds* to a rather well-known artist then residing at the Coach and Horses pub just down the road. Reg was always in fear of arrest given his gay status, and his stories of notoriously outrageous antics were renowned. Reg was hugely knowledgeable about rare books and our weekly meetings with the Foyle family ensured there was never a dull moment. Lee Harwood was at that time manager of Better Books in Charing Cross Road. It was a good time.

For a while I worked a florist shop in Wigmore Street. The shop arranged the flowers for Brian Jones's funeral. Mick Jagger sent one rose with a message, "Fly High, Love Mick".

My first job as an art therapist was at a hospital called Mabledon in Darenth, near Dartford in Kent. I ran an occupational therapy group alone for 20 mentally unwell patients in a hut 50 yards from the main building. Patients' ages ranged from 16 to 80 years. Many were very unwell, with psychosis and schizophrenia. The hospital was run by Dr. Bram, a wonderful Jewish psychiatrist from Poland, who had set up the hospital originally to care for ex-soldiers and Polish people who had been traumatised in the war and were unable to return to Poland. Many staff were Polish and had also suffered trauma in the war. My manager was a woman who, along with her friend, a nurse, was a survivor from Auschwitz. Her number was tattooed on her wrist. She was a marvellous, courageous woman whose empathy for the patients knew no bounds. She had endured more than I could ever contemplate at that stage of my life.

The Polish patients were skilled and creative and taught me how to weld stained glass for windows they were making for the chapel. Some patients were very unwell, and helping them manage their feelings onto paper or pottery was deeply challenging at times. Barry and I were living in Sherard Mansions in Well Hall Road, Eltham, above a greengrocers and then later in Ramillies Road, Blackfen, near Sidcup. At that time, Barry was working at the Greenwich Museum, and later as chief reporter for the local *Kentish Times*. His skill as a journalist was phenomenal but his enjoyment of alcohol at lunchtimes did him no favours.

For a year I was drawn back into journalism myself and acquired a job as Assistant Editor of a free fashion-magazine, *Sophisticat*. Millions of copies were handed out at tube stations. It was hard work and one which brought me into contact with the tacky world of advertising but also with wonderful journalists such as Antony King-Deacon; Barry wrote the book reviews. The three-day week was in operation and driving to the splendid office in Pimlico in the Morris 1000 was a challenge. The building had been owned by the Sitwells originally and much of their furniture remained in the huge sprung ballroom where the editorial work took place. The Poetry Society wars were in full swing at this time and much energy was spent in Earl's Court battling over whether Arts Council funding should be accepted or not.

During the early 1970s Ed Dorn's stepson, Fred Buck, invited Barry and me to stay with him in Massachusetts. New York brought memorable meetings with Joel Oppenheimer and Allen Ginsberg, with a memorable but fleeting glimpse of Bob Dylan and Roger McGuinn who were at a very cramped party at the latter's flat.

Returning to social work for a local authority and on night duty, attending to mental-health and child-and-family emergencies while managing some of the more awful times of Barry's drinking – rages with accompanied violence – was difficult. The period coincided with my parents being involved in a serious car accident on the A20 at Wrotham. It left my mother with a life-long leg injury and my father with a chest injury. One of the perils of being an only child is that there is no one with whom one can share concerns and compare notes. My mother's propensity to move with speed had to be tamed and she found this very hard indeed. There was no more bucking up to be done as she slowly recovered, while getting increasingly depressed along the way.

My parents moved to a remote ancient house on Romney Marsh after recovering from their accident and Barry and I moved to Folkestone for a short time before moving to a smallholding in Lyminge. Barry was news editor for the *Kentish Express* while I worked for Kent County Council. In 1979 my father died very suddenly, aged 59, and I then made the decision to leave Barry. The drinking, the violence and Barry's own fragile emotional health meant that it was not sustainable for me to remain. Barry later found happiness and great love with Jackie, where his ability as a poet went from strength to strength. He died on May 9th 2000. Living alone at Spot Bungalow in Warehorne was a welcome, necessary, healing period for me.

From 1980 to 1983 I trained as a child and family psychotherapist but continued as a social worker and children's *Guardian ad Litem*, working primarily in care and adoption proceedings.

In 1982 I married Ian Rose; we moved to Snoad Hill in Bethersden, and our three lovely daughters followed soon after. Moving our Soay sheep, English setters and the children, plus my mum, with us to our current home in Aldington in 1993 was a good decision. My own career has continued in social care and mental health, working with children and families. Writing continues.

Twelve Poems from a Letter

by

Barry MacSweeney & Elaine Randell

Well now,
          I am at work
       my boss comes back
    hastily   into oblivion

The letter
my desk

Well
down
electric

The letter was
         35
   _____think about
          clinging

in you too"

                        people moving
Had to stop there. Call
            On a blue fjord.   So
        Touched
In Amsterdam I listened
                In London I

Was discovered

                It is
My dear old mum
                    every weekend.   I'm going
on Sunday
                    singing sweetly
    I can see all the people moving

                    This afternoon I feel
                            her in the National
                Beckenham tonight
        coming over
him
                before
Did I tell you

                              I've
tried
Did I tell you
                    saying
                              as the boat
left
            "I wonder if those concrete
      in the rain
a loud and wonderful voice
                    of the Gods"

a sheep
of the Hook,   if I lived
Enclosed
              because you drink
      I wonder,
                    maybe
someone
out as Barny
                    I really have to eat.

I must tell
someone

Right, now I really have
                    it's strange
                              "if I run my hand"
I've always loved
              I feel I should
          maybe not—— perhaps I'll
      have guessed
      what you know

we'll have to
      forget

                    we'll spend some Friday night in a real
Monday
      but it isn't so I
fright
Away to Beckenham and back

                back to try on
angels   over
Barnet tonight

some poems

                Can I look
outside
            the sanity

I get
A small bird

In winter   snow

            on the trees

We
slot
your voice
       my dog
moves
    the salt

We leave

First Publications

1972–1974

Songs of Hesperus (1972)
Telegrams from the Midnight Country (1973)
Untitled (1973)
Seven Poems (1973)
A Taper to the Outward Roome (1974)
Long Hair for Birds (1974)

Songs of Hesperus

I

This is like sitting
in a railway tunnel.
"what is this phantom
of the mind
this love, when sifted
and refined?"
All birds in a patient forest
are mute – this
room is full of rocks
and if there's any choice
left I'll take the white.
This man has vision for two.

II

Voice
Eyes
Longing hands
Weeping trees
in tremble.

III

We swallow earth.
It is a warm room.
How do you ask a
carrier pigeon to return?
Leaves fall.
I have almost
lived a season with you.
We graze too much
(in passing)
to recover.

IV

Soon.
Without
what need to
rattle on.

V

This morning
I am sweet Poll of Plymouth
"And have they torn my love away"
Crimson apples grow on the tree
            next door.
It is twenty degrees above
            laughter
        in this keyhole.

VI

Spirits melt.
Why is this square always
        so holy
    I read your letter
    I read your letter
    I read your letter
    I read your letter
What is this strange procession
        of animals.
There aren't many saints left
        to talk to.

VII

You are going home.
I wonder how you lie at night.

VIII

            – there are no trees
left in the North Sea   now
just this
            splintered sun
and human loss.
There is so much salt
            stretched.
Sweet bliss   (gulls)
pump wings – there is a tired pain
in his heart.

Loss.

We too fly home alone.

IX

Bells sang out of the blue sky.
Trees burst.
Heaven now seems lighter.
This night holds
no scream
just the tap
as you approach
come
as a tetrachord.

As a letter unsounded – silent.

X

To reach the top
you've got to climb.
Soft grief.
Chime.
Stratum of tree.

52

Song for Each Man in Rain

Tread the continuously perfect
smell of wet grass – how easy
it has all suddenly become.

Always corrugated roofing.
Children inside school. Come
to believe in what we know most of.

Verse is a bull of the lunatic,
this natural rim of the kingdom.
Applaud life and birds.

Allow everything to wander
Find each still item beneath a
quiet crisis.

He walks back again past the house
kicks at damp earth.

Waste the heart out over gravel.
The clouds reassemble like orphans.

Park

Light behind two dozen trees.
Bear bounty of notion.
A fine life of the painter
his hard shirt of frozen bleach.
Light spate of aloof mild
dew.
Vacant park
the only thing we may leave intact.
That shrapnel of independence
we find will not hold air.
(Certainty barks us hollow limb from bough)
Imitate sap.
No
thing can be dis grace ful, it is all agile
as it seems.
Earn every survival.
Frequent the treasure to hold this
your utter love.

For You — Today

See how the tree comes to
ward.
A heavy wind here pesters
loose wood.
Sky steps are light.
The birds fly up ec
static.

Tonight telegrams from the Midnight
Country may soothe grain pulp.
Air.
"How goes it with you there below."
The newsboy runs down with flooded eyebrows.
Waking and it was already night again.
Receive the bird's feather
                the parked cars,
Child wakes the mother's sleep,
Frost on the sky/roof
Now sleet catches hold of the careful miner.

Irenical Song

Observe how the eye has
heard of so many frightfully
poisoned sources.
The owl is a perfect remedy
his phonetic nocturne.
I could not demand it from you.
Adorn ink into celebration
of nights alone in a tower
with her. This untidy venue. A
spherical stem in my wild mid
drift of Forest Law paradise for any
bored Morris dancer.
Oblique incipient winter
here already is the bus is a
burden of small boys
capped with brief
cases
of last term's addition
al step.
Leave your clothes to soak.
Walk into
familiar delirium.

Stem and Root

Find the field as a fatal idea and
septic palate of the cauterised heart.
Step outside to watch
translucent cloud question the gardener
and his option.
Go alone to
snatch bleak stars. Late vehicle
your hair parting that sepa
ration.
The body is a house, delicate canopy
of certain humble service.
Die from malnutrition, of an embrace,
turn the used bus ticket over & over
in your velour pocket.

In Relation to

the wet face of the world
folds,
Kindness we remember. Ever
y woman walks around. This
onus populi.

Important.
Sudden cold.
Eternity spits on our new shoes.
Refuge of each bulb.
A house would not hold us
its hard outer lips strut –
no one will travel to see it.

The radio is quite still / it
plays while
you stand at the window to watch local
bird life.
Another jerky film from Asia.
We all go home
and talk about each other.

Song

Our feet work the
earth
is a changeling is a message
is something to contend with
brought
here on florid brow
lines crease up the whole idea
of it
as something more simple than watching
heat rising in the shadow
contagious field
let me in.

More Than

Stars perpetuate silver.
Belief.
Yet not enough
we make demand to
trouble air
contend with nothing.
Delight
simple
as catching your face
half turned toward
street light.
The heart is a trellis
work of many.
I would not walk away now.
The tree astounds my
prospect into breath.

Poem

I look at my two hands
the complete strata.
Capable of it all
& to be
is surely without
dull clap of sound
or
another rude awakening
to the bud.
And now it's already yesterday.
As if
I was nothing but the
wood to which
the bow is strung.
Flowers
are buds
turned inside out.

Song

Caught in the cyclopean bus
which would shake your arms
off
raw.
Spread in the barnlike winter
with you.
Lou sings Skater's Waltz
in the kitchen.
Again
the giant gamble of Monday.

Here the Horse

for Robert Bly

Aerials stream upward into cloud.
The tree gets surprised into
camouflage.
A numb light, bulb of a morning, me
I'm here watching goatish flames
in the yard two doors away.
The horse draws closer, licks
grass, his great legs move up.

Snow on
concrete outside.
    A
friend's address.
Hollow air
          from
the open door.
There are two oildrums
by the railings.

"It weighed more than I"

who taps to glance at
thread and wave love as it
were a certain emblem.
Trees are our silver
from the window I watch
bodies lean forward against the
hail / We are
wind and bright blue.
The field is dark
& draws skin taut to
flesh / An old man walks
out of the door to stand.
He cannot think why he came.

In Praise of Daylight

for Barry

You looked at me,
Almost a year since we watched stars – certain
tears brief us, wind still pesters
loose wood in the building & I'm here
walking around until tonight when you
will woo me without knowing.

It's nearly 2 p.m. Fog and light rain and
no one agrees with my solemnity.
All day I hear slamming doors and angry feet,
the light sparks on and off
along the ward. Treetops are giant lungs
their massive tips hang straight up.

And sometimes when you talk I fear my
breath would disrupt the delicate paw
of you. Time and long branches are no
longer ornaments to me. I do not pass myself
easily, my plans are finite and quite bleached
by your light.

Untitled

Our feet work the sallow
earth
is a changeling is a message
is something to contend with
brought
here on saline brow
lines crease up the whole idea
of it
as something more simple than watching
heat rising in the shadow
contagious field
let me in

Seven Poems

Only a handful of leaves
left on the tree   and here
listening to the flux
inside the white night

Stave spread on glass
Mercury of a cooling pearl

A crippling in the gore
where the seams of the heart
make a join in the raft
– and it's back home–
Tall as a bear in the sierra
and we learn the steel gauge of
the head
I watch you often
still in the nest
between lip and teat
and the stars make good on your brow

Brush the willow

A spreading acorn
in the chestnut of the breast

Grapple in lilac, down along
beside the vital
stream under the walls

Lilt over the sway
by the bridge and the elemental lesson
"the space between three violins"
The child with the heavenly
document in the back pocket
of his jeans.

'A Taper to the outward roome'

The stars shall be comfortable
in all their drifts of patience at us
as we
wink at the stellar fancies above our
cold nights and warm flutes of conscience.
My heart heaves into what we are
tonight
as close as the earth that beats
alongside the rabbit's quick paw.
Our savage discontent, tooth of sheep,
bracing the kiss of fox
as each brown shrew counts the blessing
of being nourishment·.

'When you're lost in the rain'

A need to be rocked forever and assured
in the warm sleeve of love.
The pavement could be any man's blues
that some misdemeanour throws up to
land between the smudge of self and
myth of the redwood.
Outside the slow chime of the street acrobats
plausible smile
as though
all mankind were as alone as the
events and hours that sway him
into the compulsion of love.

Poem

I sit sewing your jeans while you
sleep on the single bed and the
cat murders my cotton.
Often now I sink beneath my reason
worried at your apparent discontent
– have no argument with any creature
it is only a different arrangement of
yourself –
I marvel the tree, how it laps the
air, untitled. Damp love and whipped
hearts are warmed by the veined life
of hands, the advice of a pine cone.

'I could never throw love out of the window'

Fear is cowering against my hope and ideal
when alone.
Standing upright next to anything so set upon
death is not valour with a mouthful of grit
and hollow spear.
The evening folds down, the trees stay complete.
I can only walk to the edge of explanation to
watch its bitter acidic sound force me onto the street
where I examine my reasons for staying to find that
love has thrown me from the window.

Yet

Another small closed tired day,
spring and its great green
perfection indicates grass, the
flower, our limbs so
wrought with unworship
we can barely stand.
We are not merely this.
The patients talk behind me –
'do you fee I better?', 'got
to get through to Friday morning
and I haven't the energy'.
Their obvious pleas.
I turn toward them now, the window
is open, the spring comes in
drawn tight against human fear.

Upon watching an upright leaf

If I seem to have come this far
without pausing
it's not for lack of exercise that
love extends its bugle
to play the tarantella.
I sit here, able as an echo
walking home, evening squeezes
my arm.
Consider the lilies.

How I demand time to be my schooner
for the river to approach to be
scalded into the hour and kiss
of forever. At ground level
the trees can only get greener,
the light rain feeds buttercups
who shrug at us in their yellow hats.
Birds fly up in series against all
who dare to curse this.
Nothing can possibly clash.
The Gull its Sea
The Wrapper its Street
The Sun its Moon.

"The hen can hatch her eggs
because her heart is always listening"

Tend the human frame,
touch dangerously in
the quiet street of patience.
People and animals die in winter
their old arms rise
according to the state of cloud
              the easy bay of horizon.
Constant tilling ear of this age
covers the world with pollen.
Pull the heart into shelter
for we can barely limp back into
the yard our heads bowed in relief of tears.

Bass Notes

for Jack Kerouac

You're right Jack
life does finally get tired
of living or anyhow
ends up putting paid of the attempt
to observe the street signs, hairline,
death, cough and promise as sacred.

And if I were to put out my hand
would it snap at the wrist?

Dank air today, my dog dead for two weeks
now. The sanguine bird takes flight
and it's no longer much use in knowing
we're all angels because only
the dead are angels and then its because
we've half forgotten them anyway.

Morning Mist Fine Sunset

Touching the grain dust of misuse
under the gates of our palm we all
squat beneath pain, wrinkle with ease
as great Egyptian eyes of trees
smile and hoot.
We rise, young miracles, patient
animals of the world clambering
over chunks of fraternity, chancing
the bright froth to understand its
glow.
We lunge toward death suctioned with
love.

For a declaration of need

Will I always be hungry and helpless for love,
reaching out for the warm arm of local comfort.
Here, the line of hills require your touched backbone,
– the air alive with the verge of some larger thing.
We drive up to watch the sun dip and rise over
the mad
yes
tic hills   O clime of tree:
O strata of halo.
Will you always remember me by this.
Devout under trees the horsefly hangs stuck to the
water-clogged window.
The sky is close to tears
I wear your jumper for warmth.

Last Sad Note

It's five thirty
driving down the High Street I
watch the late shoppers being late
O envy of walking couples and their
embracing hands.
Where will you be
standing in rain or cement under orchard
and simple ideal?
And now later still it's no longer the
finger that points to the moon but the moon
I am watching and all who stand under.

And if I am found bleating for love under
some stained thrown anger will I be less
than woman if I hold my heart against
cut glass and attempt reason.

So take these arms
they are used for balancing sullen air.
Knee deep in leaf
I mean in lost dream, for the eyes – they
are loaded with waiting.

Poem: Before Breakfast I

And to never wish for you to be without this.
Morning, eyelid of the valley space and pine
beneath the knuckle of warm air /
Nothing to clamber for.
Each blade a sheath of its own home,
nature and her tidy woman strength.
Silence and vision are bright green leaves.

Poem: Before Breakfast II

You are.
Feet down in the valley mild spring
we swell into age and fruit.
A man ploughs the field, cold breath
and dry earth fly up behind.
How warm the sun is when we stand still.
River, knowing something else
runs clear quickly.

Poem: Before Dinner

What does not see is seen.
The mountains are not glass
nor is the earth ashamed of
time and its ailment.
Gulls hover to whine at juice
and promise.
Don't worry.
The air is there
very innocent and certain.

I get up to collect wood for the fire. Mike and Barry
are chopping it in the yard, swinging the axe down with
great strokes and definition, bringing the axe up again
with the log attached, down and up, finally snatches
the wood in two, grey and cream knots and grain smooth
pine. I take the wood to the fire, it glows amber and
ash, falls to the bottom keeping the new alight.

❖

Walking down the drive to the bridge, go to the left
and along the edge of the river. I startle a ram
which, not waiting, jumps
16 maybe 18 inches into the river, stops midway, then
paces across the stones, quick great heart beating against
the sand, races faster under a barbed fence leaving
his long hair for birds.

Early in My Life

Too Late

for stars
and barefoot I return home.
Growing pains.
The trees are covering the streetlights,
my hand on the far side of your wrist
and all that with-stands-pain.
People in bus queues, they lean and sway
and put down bags and take them up again.
Death steals us back.
And tonight someone is whistling as they
walk along the pavement
is taking stride after stride with air in
their lungs
is wearing clothes that fit and move
is carrying objects dear to them
is walking home never the same again.

"You Wait a Long Time"

Rose, marigold, tomato leaf
a strand of Timothy grass
crushed between the fingers,
how the hands pull back
never to be amongst street trees
so innocently again.
I water the indoor plants, wipe
greenfly from the shelf, disturb earth,
clean the leaves. A man at midday.
A long afternoon   we turn it in our palms
the cats move about the house, city light
above traffic
I am home again. Do you wonder…
the air, the afternoon as it is
return me.

Three Poems

1.

Heart overbeating
I pace tired ground
moved to light tears
and heady distraction
by the look of a woman
carrying bags standing
in a doorway
some miles
from here
her bent hand
resting as it did
on her forehead
if only for that
I am grateful.

2

Trying to build homes
rain-soaked women
walk the High Street carrying lino
           prepacked vegetables
           bread.
Rain on every inch until after five
when, the men with long strips of wood
corner home together.
In the graveyard opposite
two children up to their thighs
in long grass
on the street a woman walks by in
lace hat and gloves.

3

There are fingerprints
on the glass of the television
shop where the men stand around
watching cricket at lunch time
and the women wander past in jeans
and lightweight raincoats with
midweek shopping.
The bus crews come out of the pub
red-faced and argue. Another hardware
sale in the High Street selling chrome
taps and fittings.

Early in My Life

So we
are left with action
that device we only know the
carriage of.
The clouds reiterate.
I give up the chase.
Late love   early in my life,
pressing as it does leaving me
exquisite fine shadow of hair
the rush of wet road
daily life despite this.
Skilled storage, shelving
of obligation and all too often
the night goes on by and girls
hover in doorways with tattoos –
O rain-damaged heart.
The shadow passes over itself.
Dark hot evening a dog barking,
church bells.
These;
cliffs that we drown upon,
your arms unfelt.

Larger Breath of All Things

As if
it were given
night appeals
if only to lone sleepers

non sleepers

who worry the sky
and are caught between
bright tragedy
and taut mornings.

Dark sleep
the lightest mist
on your arm
as it rests
among a spate of aloof
birds where suburban streets
become alive
with an appeal of night

and lone sleepers
non sleepers

who worry within a tearing
that is available to early
dawn birds alone.

"Like prisons, hospitals were considered a last resort. Nobody thought of them as tools for administering therapy to improve the inmates." —Illich

Greed
We enlist others and as
the seasons shift
our heels become a ladder to remorse.

Grief
Our hearts blood.
Burning stubble sterilises the soil,
we look away quickly although fascinated.

Guilt
Not knowing at that moment
we retort anxiously.
The flint in the fields remains so for years,
calcifying naturally without our concern.

Gall
We swallow and present
such a picture. Eyes burn up
so vulnerable with the contest of it.

Gentility
Can we ever lay claim to such as this.
It is in doing,
this death of all else.

Routine

How many times my hands
go to the sink
performing some duty
of the house.
Fingers stretched
      related
      stern, promised.
"take my floured hands
in your entire step"
And if I ask for constancy in my life
do I really suggest solidarity
or boredom or the ability
to learn the agility of others faith
in me.
Too often I am glib with the grief of others,
      I am a creature of flight and earnest
I make my life a belly of people
worn by routine
    by the consistence of stars.

Suddenly it becomes sordid

Suddenly it becomes sordid
the way death
brings itself onto itself

The queueing people
prepare for the unexpected,
reiterate their good intentions.
Coaches filled with workers from the pit
laugh and climb down in the cages
to the coalface.

Suddenly it becomes sordid
as if I could do nothing
but watch heavy eyed and turn away.
Women meet one another in the street
and laugh at their broken hearts and scuffed shoes.
Later they talk about each other and compare crises.

Suddenly it becomes sordid
to argue over what the dead have said
to consider that barter between life and death.

The pink chestnut blossom is here
by the window
– simply it shouts.
How could we be left with ashes of the dead
to fertilise what remains
but we are and how sordid the taste
is any wind that ruffles our smallest preparation.

Until the Gardens are Drenched with Rain

Alarmed
Disarmed
by light
vulnerable
I have seen you
misty wet
misty wet
with rain.
You watched
from the window.
There is nothing
but the air
the very air
the seagoing vessels,
the early tourist,
field upon field
ploughed, levelled, waiting.

Greenwich Park — February 1977

for my parents

Walk within the warmth of you
           joy of you.
Squirrels sleep in Winter,
come out for the occasional nut you say.
Ducks swim without effort
perfect webbed feet scan the pond. Surprised by early
blue iris
we remark how fine
how very fine it has been together again
as if
it could ever be otherwise.

Covering Poem
for a letter

I would be
always ready to accept
that you were too busy
to write or telephone.
Never consider making demands
or suggest that we take a few hours
together or sit with the sun on our backs.
Always the way
it seemed
the possibilities, the speculation.
O the idea of it would leave us
the skeleton of a perfect day.
You see
I am forever welcoming
forever
out of danger.

Whether she could take his arm

and hold it casually so
close to her ribs as if
in walking that way
no matter how temporarily it
would lend itself some
how to memory
yes now it is already remembered
'If you insist' he had said impatiently
and allowed her to hear him
touch the keys of the piano. The art
of caring; that facility she felt in him.
Earlier he had listened to the heart of
a sick man observed the giant Blakean muscles.
What else is there she thought but
the touching of others however brief
tight between fear.

Drought 1976

          To what can the heart be blamed
empty buses wind up hill and dry pavements
          where local dust has remained now
for weeks. Loud, as unfettered as a lion
          I make my roar silent as bush fire
that creeps here in South London to take hold
          of kerbs and sidings until they
belong elsewhere. "I don't mean to abuse the
          water but it cools and cleanses and I
cannot resist." To what can the heart be blamed
          golfers strain their muscles in the heat
and arrogant schoolgirls hover in ones and twos.
          If the night were only the night
and darkness confined to dark shapes that are
          seen to be birds. Three-quarter moon
the larger breath of all things. Blond beyond
          blue your eyes, we change and are as frail
and soft as a crayon.

Notation

1.

Alone.
Debussy loud in the room
I return from the garden –
mottled hydrangeas that change daily,
red tipped roses, the last of the
Michaelmas daisies, spinach for dinner.
The cats trip me up to get fed quicker,
your shoes in the hall, pens on the desk,
such luxuries as these.

2.

Anxious children walk to school,
preoccupied mothers
leave them at the gate and shop
in the supermarket for a quick dinner
to ease their overcrowded, harassed
and loveless lives so full of
injunctions, separation orders, bailiffs,
Valium and nights alone.

3.

Travelling by car the grass hedgerow
is a different green on the offside than
the nearside. Wind tunnel caused by the cars
travelling in opposite directions makes the
grass turn. Watch for it.

4.

Vulnerable. We are.
We speak of it easily, take our turn in
offering what we know of our lives so far.
Out on the beach the skyline tips and falls
as clouds move off suddenly.

5.

Burnt stubble.
Slow moving Harvesters glance up at
my passing car.
Sugar Beet almost four foot high now.
Fruit pickers lean their ladders against
one another, sit among the
boxes and eat the produce.

"Which Is Neither Mine Nor His But in Common"
for Barry

And how much do you know
of being my main concern.
The sun at its zenith as the
'Orphanage of the Tender Tiger'
is with us for another year.
As if
it were only I that was meant to be
still, dark,
listening at time devour its
useless motions to what the personality blames
itself for; small to be afraid that tomorrow
we will not be seen in winter.
Ripen trees.
The lake at ice point.
Just a hair's breadth away, this we measure by.
Someone has placed a lost glove on the fence.

Morning teeters on the fine edge of sparse trees.
I intend to be early, bright and credulous as
'looking forward' is the key to eternity.
So tell me how much do you know of being my
main concern.
"It's not catastrophes, murders, death, diseases that
age and kill us; it's the way people look, laugh and
run up the steps of omnibuses."

Robins arrive in the bleak climate.
His red turn.
This,
love, for you, in winter,
brightly blue.

This Time of Year

As when daffodils are on the turn for
bees to suck at pollen before rest, to what
can the heart be blamed.
Women in the road make Bank Holiday shopping
lists and children eye chocolate eggs.
This warm open air on our necks as we loosen
a tangle in the hair or readjust a scarf.
In the street the backs of people as they
sniff and exhale and move off in cars and are
gone; sky changes are not observed.
The sun rose up again today as it does this
time of year. On the verge of leaning against
tears I watch the early tips of trees through
 a square of glass; take this life towards it,
outside there are rooftops and eaves.

This, our frailty

This, our frailty

Hands which follow clay
touch skin:
the heart young again.
Beige reeds on the river
   this wintered place.
A water rat moves across the river,
we mark his course. A flurry of
migrating birds, the disarming of you.
The life of creatures and plants below
water. Seeing the hours of you move
   through my hands.
On a night wrought with storm, sealed by gale
– we exchange this our frailty, love.
Stealth, constancy, take the urgency from my
body for "I squandered the summer away without
love." Woodsmoke, warm flagstones beneath
the feet, a simple measure of our hearts' smallest
hope.

In Winter

How the sun has moved
while we sit
and men all over Kent in bars
discuss the events of another day
below ground.
You move
and take air again and scan the horizon
for an end to this strange absence that is
marked strongly by the need of a certain vulnerability.
A man at midday.
Found to be / in loss / the hands of him / moss and lichen /
Wintered leaf / mark this as a day / take fright as a gazelle /
hunted wolf like / the need for small birds who fly off
As we
make our mark on the pebbles and disused
perimeter of the golf course.
Early November bonfire
who could resist
to set a match to so much
dried driftwood.
So many areas of your
heart's wooded climb.
The afternoon wears down, cloudless Autumn. How we should
think of it, slow, quite breathless, without breath.
Winter wheat you tell me but I question you just because it seemed
so supple and young / too tender for exposure to
Winter air. Meantime the air becomes slow, quite breathless /
without breath in Winter.

The Mating Call

for Edna O'Brien

Soft as a crayon warm air rises
        surrounds a woman
She swoons into daylight
we cannot insist on her effort. Above all
one is stolen   at best solemn with pleasure
at the half light / an interlude of gaiety.
"People laugh and come late at night and flop
onto…"
Love and unity.
The whole valley at night   great clouds
move and the trees remain   only I fear
for them now that they will stay and be
shown to those I love.
That pleasure of leaning against someone /
not merely the attitude of leaning
but that of terror and the
ceaseless need to touch it.

This restlessness: this ache

Our chipped hearts!
Your forearm across my body; at night
the gift of one another
how it holds me to this temporary axis of living.
The luxury of breath
that brings the idea of you,
talking in bed, a movement of hair
falling across your neck
causing my life to shift with this
restlessness: this ache.
The divine family of light
Vivaldi's Winter Song.
38 hours of solid rain, how the unlikely warmer
air of summer haunts me. Here the cats
asleep on my desk, a solid rushing of air / high
hard wind along this coastal town where off-
season waiters lean in doorways and old people
shudder to the Post Office.
Your head on the pillow, waking from sleep
before a working day – this restlessness; this ache.

"For the sight of myself"

A pain across
    my body.
Often I am the
    entire gaunt
fear of myself.
Startled heart
will you remain
    so or
gulp back
without enduring
    surprise.

    Amber ferns
    waist high.
The light in the
    sky!
Just look how it
makes this moss
    and bark
start apart and
    belong
to those who see
each detail for
that which it is.
    A frosted day
bright sun set too
soon and saw us
mysteriously certain.

Dog with Man

His collar is turned
turned up to hide that piece of the neck
that area of the shoulder so tender to the
world so telling, so open.
It rains heavily on his head his hair clinging
to the skin he appears thinner than he is.
They move quickly together – the dog and the man
quickly across the pavement.
The dog stops for no reason just to smell the
air; the man gets wetter standing like that
for almost nothing but he waits looking over
his shoulder at the dog,
patient, exposing that area of the shoulder,
that piece of the neck so tender to the world,
so telling, so open.

Bitten by it we conjure by touch

A late bird across the
darkening sky sky
as if
it were
shaking me
these thistles so
fill of seed
disturbing
these ginger trees
high road above
valley, shadow
these alert me
youth and large
night
we are truly
young in the
centre of force
the courting couple
touching swooning
It is this fear
this total fear
of nothing
permanent
that leads me to this
ache for
it is seen
quick longing

And above in the
high road
leading down
to the valley
where the courting couples
touch and swoon
the air
is alive
with an urgency
that is
found in
folds of dew where
now it twists
even over what
seen as urgent
as a man's wrist
this which
touches upon
others' lives
so carefully
so
so
so
urgent
your hair
a handful of leaves
autumn

Dusting

I sweep the floor and dust
the furniture.
O dust full of earth, leaves,
branches, stones, chalk,
cardboard, tyres, rain.
Particles of bird, mouse,
flower, vole, bee, cat, tree,
chair, curtain, eyelash, postman
and moth.
O dust of shop, wellington, paw,
mouth and starling.
O dust carried in the air from
the fire, from a car, from a foot,
from plane, from lip, from speech,
from a bus, in coal, in wood, in paper.
O dust brought from miles away coming
here to rest in this kitchen only to be wiped up,
moved on, taken hack.

In all things it is this tenderness which holds me

Learning how to work hard is freedom // Later he shows
me his garden where the plants flourish under his care
as they have no demands and are plain and tender. //
Trees shake their fists in the wind where long-tailed birds
hop in the edge of the field and shout at the darkening sky //
Both knowing how well suited they were but left just the
same. // Does the mind retain its own identity independent
of its biological origin and its involvement with society, or
does its fundamental nature consist in the elaboration of
new structures in the course of constantly changing constructive
development. // A perfectly rounded pebble; the safety of
it. I am dazed by the strength of my pleasure and the process
of all things healing without our concern. // Children
dart in front of the car across the road to buy fish and chips
shouting to one another above the wind and traffic their
shrill voices carry into the car. //

On Sighting the First Bluebell

My eye is my heart
I cannot go further
Bluebell
breaks
the sticky sap heals
At once a dream of waking
the bell it has a safe place
easily sliding between showy shoots
Blue present of early May
I smell the blueness of it
quite returned

I am touched by your fear

as we walk out from the coast
into these rural villages where
the women become bored and wait
for buses back into town.
I am troubled by the idea of the moon
and how one year comes upon another
leaving me here with the cows who
never sleep but lean against the field
to rest.
You chance into sleep, the white limbs
of young trees behind your head.

To see who you might be

Holding ourselves up to the light
              our lined palms
The way one life crosses through another.
All hope is investment.

"A lone quiet life
still she held it closely
as though it would cure her of any malady."

A whole season has shifted in on me
              tired sparrows see us move off.
These heady years!
A stray hair of yours on the pillow
my heart is the whalebone of me.
Skin and earth you track me down to
a patch of land which burns as I sleep.
I astound myself by my misused strengths
solemn at my nakedness at all times.
Urgency utter urgency.

Songs for the Sleepless

This book is a celebration of the work of Elizabeth Smart. Each poem title is a quotation from *The Assumption of the Rogues and Rascals*, published by Jonathan Cape and the Poly Tantric Press, 1978.

"The womb's an unwieldy baggage. Who can stagger
uphill with such a noisy weight"

O frantic surgeon
on the blister of us all
in our vain attempts to reshape
our survival driven frames.
The clatter   the frippery of womanhood
it is impossible to do without it.
Will this person be seen winding wool
            be seen putting coats on children
            be seen being seen
            be lost among the loud others.
All the wasted worried hours.
The person does return safely
eternity spits on our new shoes.
Drunken pitfalls.

*"She is fearful in case there will be no next time
and the future suddenly cease."*

So many deaths in one month
endings bitten with shock.
The mist comes down despite any tragedy
                       any plan.
Out of the corner of her eye the map alters
– a gradual growth of trees, cutting down of shrubs
    lick of tarmac across the heart.
"helpless animals and men have difficulty learning
that responses produce outcomes."

"You were too busy being. And you are too busy now. You couldn't spare the time to note down a few facts: how the sun and silence poured into the big room with the yellow curtains; how everything was never-ending and expendable."

Tomorrow I shall.
Tomorrow time will be used as soap, to be spread
cleansed with.
Crying spells.
Perhaps soon the day will be an agonising howl
as the donkey in the next field screams out at all human suffering
and ceaseless need.
I have almost given up hope of using the moment for that which it is
to take in sensually the second the open heart the open heart.

"But the body, the body, the perishable instrument through which all work and visions have to trickle."

My futile legs!
They won't take me out this door across the lawn and up into that field and down the other side again!
Women sweat as their special pelvic bones grind apart during childbirth as endlessly hands are wet from wiping down tables, children, men, their own bodies. Keep crevices clean that no one will see, yell secrets to one another to improve bonding.
Bonding/sweat is the common result of vision.
Ache body swoon O sweetness laughter.

"The greed of plants doesn't seem at all disgusting."

Male interest in food is also understandable.
A shift in the skyline.
Holding my mother's hand, that contact between inner and outer.
A sharp pain across the body.
Is rain simply water?
The history of human endeavour
Men hover on bridges quite abashed with wonder at the
reproductive process.

"Once you start speaking, of course, the agony lessens."

Helplessness
Helplessness against what appears to be fate
Yours to swallow up
is instantly lit
into the way of the world.
Is my voice really so shrill
are all these actions so meaningless
in the face of tragedy everything
is wiped dry and put away.

"All you can learn is ecstatic surrender."

Reassure me that dark will follow light
that sleep will rock us back into wakefulness
the anger in your heart will turn to something
for the moth banging fruitlessly at the pane.
O level my fears into something useful
mould my tears into a harmless gesture
for the end isn't really the end only getting to
know our love better.

"Nothing is known. It is merely a comfortable deadening to think anything's familiar; it is an expedient blotting out of an inherited estate that's far too big for you."

Even the walk through your arms is new
although the anticipation of it led me to feel that
I would have remembered it after so much hoping.
Bright red rosehips across the river walk
as we discuss how many shades of green or is it brown.
I shall sew my heart with these webbed cob dewy autumn
ideas. The revelation of a new town is like the seduction
of a strange man.
Walk out   walk back   no one pair of hands
entices me so as the quick earth with its easily forgiving
deaths.

"Anything noted while alive? Anything felt, seen, heard, done?. You are here. You're having your turn. Isn't there something you know and no body else does. What if nobody listens? Is it all to be wasted? All blasted? What about pricey pain."

I wish I could say.
I wish I could say something about the way you looked
that day. I wish I could say something of the lamb as
it came out with your hand into the world and your face
your face.
But perhaps the silence is enough to remind us of the smack
of nothing and how tortured we are and so afraid for ourselves
and how empathy and love is our only tool.
Thin twigs of beech chance the heart into a hope of
fresh mistakes
O caution and anger could breathe great fools of us all.

"They tell me that the endless repetitions of life and death are soothing, rhyming lullabies, patterns in the jibbering void."

Heartbeat.
A growing up and a bearing down.
Shall we rid ourselves of the same muddy pitfalls
in relationshipwrecks.
The day comes up and we all go down again upon ourselves
with an ear to the soil and a hand on someone's arm.
Love is a repetitious dancer whose terms swoon us into
impossible demands and expectations.
O female cycle patience blame allocation.

"Well keep your eye on the object then. And keep your hand moving."

Accept no replica.
Go after that idea of yourself.
Most plans get torn up or rearranged and passed
on in one shape or another; generation to victim.

The window
the outside
It's air and rain
air and rain
"there are some things beneath and too
powerful than grief"
The clear vase of nasturtium leaves.
Look at the others in such agony as they walk along
the street.

"Maker accept no rest. Listen tonight. Above the autumnal winds there's that possibility so wild with hope battering at the shrugging shoulder and the pooh-poohing diffidence."

So was that love no more full of intent than
to pass it by with a turning down of the palms,
a turning over of bodies and new leaves.
Brave men read other people's letters.
We always do it. We always seek out with feet like
limpets any encouragement.
Give yourself leisure and stop wandering around; give yourself
some good things.

The families go on and on shopping, piling groceries into bags and
bags into cars and cars into garages and garages
into driveways and driveways into plots that are alongside
other plots and other driveways and other bags
but don't let that depress you.
It is such a fright to remain within anyone for very long.

We were together when we saw the little lights of the
town below us
come out of the darkness and shake us hollow with the
alarm of others' lives.

"Everything you are this minute flows away faster than a breeze. It takes pain to burn through time, to turn a spot on the wall into the centre of the world now and hereafter."

But then there is all that attempt
all the effort of non-doing
all the sitting around and hallo
and see you
but then the moorhens gather together each morning whatever
and the frosting trees are gladder than ever.
A pianist breaks his hands on the chords
but it's only a temporary arrangement
like death it comes and it goes.
It goes away and without realising it
we are back again with our lips in shreds
with nothing to say but that it's gone and we're alone
with the weather and the remarks of the trees
are but efforts to make the
trembling slower.

"What is it? Glimpses, flashes in the medley sudden revelations impossible to recall, except for their absoluteness – the rock revealed by lightning."

Nothing shameful or spent.
Composers and painters are
poets are
shot to pieces
at the cool tablet of reflection.
Male tiredness is of such,
the bark of young trees
gentle objects roused by their dream of leaves.

"The cheap sparrows peck about in the dust."

What else is there to do
but to go after a special index of passion.
Praise the long limbs of young men
and the downy hair on their brown forearms
and the edges of fresh white shirts
covering the sides of strong capable chests.
Knowing becomes loving.
It's not who you are but whose you are.
Local means safe means close.
On the motorway sparrowhawks loom over litter
bins and foreign trucks pass on the inside lane.

I can't settle this
I can't sleep.

"Everything would delight because it would have no con-
notations, no history, no meaning but its looks"

I was waiting for someone to overwhelm me
but the light went on being
the light.
We have come to the end of this then.
A strong storm
water everywhere
bleaching it out
bleaching it out.
No one comes.
Shaping ourselves
cutting on clay on unions   bonding
learning what we bargained for.
All these couples making do with one another
tearing up their hope with loathing.

"Owls are about. A cat complains. Children murmur with bad dreams. The walnut tree sways in a burdened way. The cats tracks wander suggestively off into the horizon. The pigs bang about in their pens."

So much contact in a day. Ways of making the shaking bearable.
We will never know the way we think of one another.
Neither all that goes in between the talking and the seeing:
it all goes by with one great yawn and a little sleep,
we recoup overnight and time does it
sparrows do it
the wet grass of the field does it
the light in the sky manages it.
All spent all spent all given up to the
misty evening
all this and the evening light
no one else nothing.

"But I could have told you it would be like this. You should have said to death "O death, it is better to keep you in mind remembering every moment how short time is, and what a concentration is necessary to get you where you're going or where you hope to go."

To look and find that the palm of your long white
fingers and hair curling was only the light from
the car headlamps as you turned the other way and the
fear of falling is
the idea of waking is
the ideals of hope are
only the light from the houses
soft trees as if warm liquid were
the line of a man's lip
the idiot heart
china heart.
What it all seems to amount to is a ceaseless agony to know
that all is well,
forgiven accepted and known
full face on. The rest is a grid of controllable text.
I was with you when you said that I had presupposed on our love.
I shook the tree and nothing came but the wind falling through
arms O empty arms.
All these agonies making do with grief.
It passes
yes goes so fast and the place where you stand can only be your
own. I have no idea what's coming next – I can only hazard at the
movement in the trees.

"Women with gusty voices pound pianos in pubs. Impossibly happy against great odds. More ravaged and more successful by far than you, they know how to back-slap life with a greeting of gratitude."

Across the fields here I lose my heart
where the mushrooms come up in seconds
with the damp and the sun and the watching out for.
Hunger for another
is part of this growing into
after that it's just a falling into patterns
but until then I suggest that women walk alone into
the arms of one another.
I wish all this would go away
all this watching and waiting for no reason.

"Other people must know more, I think. Who? Who is whirling on in virtuosity and can throw a brilliant sudden torch into this obscure bog where I don't even jog on?"

None of them appear to clatter on and on
they all seem so damned happy.
If the nights get any darker I shall need
more than the sun to get me up.
Do I tell people about myself or do I
let them find out? What is essentially required
– is it already on my face? Can this be that easy?
Almost everyone has met someone else.
Is it only the newborn who aren't alone, is it the
cutting of the cord that sets offal! This separation.
Is this the information that the others have.
Is that why they look.

*"Can love keep us from need? Needs are bolting in my garden,
lanky and green irresponsible with unsuitable conditions."*

Who's to say where we go and where we've been.
We go knocking on the wombs heavy door and out again
into the waiting kerb of sweltering knowledge.
Others have been here sick with ideas and no feet.
Love saves us from ourselves, spins its
chaotic fuse into our mouths.
Outside the cows never lift their heads intent on their
function.
It's so humiliating to be caught so with all this
gaping envy hanging between our legs for no reason.

"Those to whom the day is a weight to be borne and dropped for relief at night. Those who come nosing into the evening like dogs kept back too long."

On the boxed estate the pubs
are billions with the street.
Under stone pavement slabs drains
and sewers pulse about with black
causalities.
In the morning the first paperboy clanks a gate
stirs a woman lying face down in her bed already
awake and watching his shadow move across the
room as he dresses to leave.
Why wait for it to
happen
go out and dig at the
suckers in the garden.
Your body – its angle
just keeps me hanging on
waiting for you.

"This endless exterior is your remedy. Wrinkle out every ounce of life. That is the work in hand. It's a sweaty excavation"

Experience is a clammy joy.
We stood in the garden that night
and heard the children's voices singing
in the dark two miles away at the Guide
camp.
A few days later we drove past them
as they stood between the fields and the
edge of the road.

The nightingales   The nightingales   it seems
have somehow left off singing to us these last few
nights and instead   I'm finding the small dead
frames of tiny bats and the larger soft bodies of
moles.

I wish the seagulls would stop hammering this
sense of loss into the memory of that first day
we came to this town – the damp and your sad lungs.
My running from it and the ache the ache
the impossible sick ache of it all.

"But here you must go to your office looking sprightly with a sparkle even if synthetic in your eyes. For who dares to stand up and say, We are weary O Christ but we are weary."

Of all things and their celebration.
In the photograph my father's long-
boned hands hold my entire frame as
a newborn baby. His face is that of
an angel.
But you must go out on the course again.
Keep loading the shots
for to be in danger is to look
and not wait but pass back across
the waste where the sleepless lay waiting.

Beyond All Other

(1986)

Poem

I look at my two hands
the complete strata.
Capable of it all
& to be
is surely without
dull clap of sound
or another rude awakening
to the bud.
And now it's already yesterday.
As if
I was nothing but the
wood to which
the bow is strung.
Flowers
are buds
turned inside out.

More than

stars perpetuate silver.
Belief.
Yet not enough
we make demand to
trouble air
contend with nothing.
Delight
simple
as catching your face
half turned toward
street light.
The heart is a trellis work
of many.
I would not walk away now.
The tree astounds my
prospect into breath.

Songs of Astraea

I

Strike in the nest
reek into a certain pool.
How do you seal the
corners of the heart?
A wheelbarrow stands full
of cut grass.
Lip to lip, breath to breath
we divide the zealous,
confirm the boring.
Outside this blown semaphore
night – (if I should fail
tell me) – it's more than
travelling it's like living
inside your magnificent airplane
heart.

II

"If I could sing only one
song, I'd sing of you"
Perhaps tonight in the high
brick tower you are wounded.
Morning – a bird was born in
the eaves of my house;
I heard new wings move
in folds against
the peep of day.

III

Like Midas you waited
to lick life into the
branches;
help a trapped salmon
to its river.
This evening I wept for
you – with joy of walking
through leaves.

IV

Only the sacring bell
heliostat for breath
        in the
  dark blue woodland.
Carry this heart around
the batteries won't fade.
I shall not make the morning
    without you.

V

Of you
being
the father
to my child
the songster in the
woodshed,
sower of seed, vein
of leaf,
Message of Sepal.

Watching Women with Children

1.
Wood (and all else) by the sink.
Frozen winter clothes
moss on the path outside,
her veined life.
"Will you know me tomorrow like this?"
lines on her chapped hands
the storm of yesterday.

2.
The day
she woke early
bright sharp dawn.
Eyes that broke the floor
with anger spilled at the child the night before.
"The prism of mere life is unbearable,
plants and animals in their secular change,
eaten up with will power.

3.
The fall of winter has attended with sorrow
concrete and iron steps from the basement
– you could fall so easily –
she thought, watching the child totter and smile as she
held out her hand.

4.
His quick tears
swift as a balanced balloonist.
He cried bitterly – heard their shout
and anguish from between the banisters.
Ajax on the flannel and all over the
bathroom floor.
Life, it is known of love
so roughly tested and beaten across
the table.

5.
Woke to find him stirring beside her,
his slight warm body had crept in
in early light.
He who turns to look at moon and
name it space beyond all other value
to draw back the curtains and smile at
the stellar desire so gently regarded
as time.

6.
Often walking across
the green square
she would pull the oak towards her
and they would feed the ducks,
wander home by the library
intent as the hospital steps where
she first heard him cry.

7.
Cleaning the offices
her stern legs
and tired arms   men stand around
in their shoes watching tightly, guilty.
She met him from school
by the wire-mesh gate.
He ran out, the last child.
"I wet my pants" he cried so hard.
Picked him up, the cold air and his wounds
whipping her heart.

8.
They are laughing together at the back
of an old distant photograph.
A key at the door, he is home,
anxiously worn,
snapping at her for some small mistake.
Shipwrecked we are on so faint a seizure
of reality.

9.
He caught her hand.
The weather, time of year, youth
and its ready soul
– how her mother had laughed when
later she told him she would not see
him again as he'd almost a limp he'd
received as a boy in the Blitz.

10.
"Seed Propagation" – the teacher told him
to underline it and read aloud from the book.
"Birds are responsible for a great many seeds, they
carry them in their beaks and feathers and drop
them as they pass." He ran into the playground
kicking at a tennis ball.
"Come in right now" the teacher called from the
window "come along quickly". He ran, his heart
sinking; she had found the torn book.
"It's your Mother" she said "she's not very well.
Now I'll take you home to your Dad."
He was not certain of tears, put his coat on and
the teacher did not mention the absence of his cap.

11.
'As if pulled and gripped by pliers
the spine is severed and tortured, the
blood comes and the womb is drained.'
We're going to save your baby – the nurse had said.
But she knew it was helpless,
felt the warm pulse slide between her legs.

12.
Maternal scream
spirit of Leithia damned into salt
unable shadow of trees.
Dreary the belly of cold sheep
scream of even air.
Death whips us from each other
long before we are ready. Hot iced sleep.

13.
Cut grass, creosote, tar and urine
in the phone box. She called him.
"I am barren, sterile, empty. My heart has
broken like a robin's egg. This wreck and
all unborn reach the horizon of all finite tears."

14.
"What are you doing?"
"I am listening to the moist cave where all
things begin."

15.
Along the High Street a woman slaps
her child. Livid at sound.
The lonely assault struck her ribs with clay:
heart broken as a robin's egg.

16.
Leap, don't jump.
They caught her by the coat.
Dangling
moth-
like
eighteen storeys up, clothes
limply between the legs.
Shopping list falling from a pocket.

17.
"Hello Mum, I'm home."
He ran into the house.
"Yes, I can see that" she said leaning
away as he tried to kiss her.
"You haven't a cold have you, we don't want
anything spreading."
He ran out into the garden as far
as the lawn would allow.

18.
"The fate of the world today depends
on the common understanding by the
whole human race of what a human being
really is and on enlarging the common notion of man."

"A Flame in the Darkness Is the Pilot of My Loss"

The improbability of chance!
A songful thrush in the garden.
Your mother's death dips its already bent head
onto our shoulders.
We cannot talk of it now
and speak in whispers
waiting, so grief may find
its cleaner way.
"Love, faith and flesh alone"
We will not forget.
In the playground the children have left
a clean handkerchief
folded on the tarmac.

Distant Tender

for my Father

Your last sight of snow
brought the end to a life that gave that gave.
Now the first white hairs on my mother's head
come as I show snow
to my daughters
their tiny hands take hold and ask
"What are we going to?"

Upon the earth
wind, sleet, snow, gale.
There is much coldness amongst the world
we learn to warm the fears of others
on our loss.

"Tell them how easy love is"

how the light mist comes up and across
the marsh in late afternoon
how the big trees are so big.
If I was a man the love of a good woman
would keep me safe and wear me out.
Tiny flowers in the wood tonight
I picked a few and brought them home.
Crow and sheep share the same water trough
just the way the light rises
up drawing together the day and the voices
of the people warm in their homes.
O tell them how easy love is.

Waking up in America

Mass., U.S.A. 1975 for Fred Buck in whose house it was.

"Is that Spider Man, Daddy?"
asks Ketty, I turn over and ask
Barry to move over – "For crying out loud"
he says. Outside sirens and machinery
bright sunlight and boats.

Boats in the harbour
herring gull shrill

sore eyes. Salt wounds
men at midday.

Under the sky   rolling lobster rock
and wail and loose their souls,
too easily for my liking.

Children learn by kindness
we touch their smaller limbs.
Yowling items in the kitchen, but
still they grow and turn and breathe
and ask nothing.

I am finding it easier to be casual
perhaps it is the way of my body
changing as it does
daily
casting off all kinds of ailments with ease
and mercy. Yes I find it easier to be lighter
soon I shall blow away without
any bother at all.

Case Note

The first hot days of the year
girls move about the town in last year's
summer clothes and the men with rolled
sleeves or bare-backed paint houses and thatch
moves in the villages.
I admit into hospital a woman who calls me
the devil's advocate and Princess Anne, her
delusions hallucinate her dry.
Later an urgent phone call sends me to the
caravan site where Jim, out on bail, tells me
that if I don't give him money for his wife
and child he'll rob a bank. I tell him to rob one for
me too while he's there. On his arm is tattooed
'born to lose'.

I prepare myself for the sight of myself

As in territory alone
fear is encountered
and once looked at
        realised for the hollow air
that it is.
That stance we have and see
in passers by
        like the face as it
contorts
as it moves up the hill
in friends
        the sight of ourselves.

Open Letter

My dear
I would be
as it were
caught into action of non-action,
drawn as I am
to the pavements of this town
the low ploughed fields of Kent.
And missing you, as I do,
there is nothing
but space
and I walk into rooms
and study the plants again and span
the length of raw days with my palm
"and a sob comes
simply because it's the coldest
thing we know."
So you leave
and the climate is holding
I long for silence
and thin air.
Often we are vague and small
at the end of a day.
Briefly encountered
who sees him as to
feel him
it is in dying,
apparent sunlight
so often we
prospect after dark.
Streetlights grow old
ghosts on my sleeve.
Autumn could find me out,

running my hand along the cut edge of
Kentish flint.
The purr of your teeth
along my lip,
tender
it haunts
and I fall in.
Youth sketches the horizon
alone in cloud.
For so long now I have spoken
of touch without fertility.
I have used up the sepia of afternoon
my hands are numb.
Wounded water, it rains
teeth within another's mouth.
Taut against circumstance
meet daily gall of human tears
that are ribbons of attempt.
Wood-sorrel. The dream is tender.
Will you flash your fears at me.
Rubbing the hand brings blood to the surface.
"The trivial rain, its sparkle on grass"
Laurel Nobilis
I would give you this
to mark the things you love.
Velvet magnolia tree.
It's that simple.
The things we admire in others we own in ourselves.
Of us all in our better moments.
Arms linked in sleep
anxious wakers that we are.
Rooks on the Marsh making their nests high
in the trees about the tiny grey churchyard.
My dear
the evening moves on. The swans flay themselves into the

telegraph wires.
Tight buds of hawthorn
I am below surface again.
Bitten by it we conjure with touch.
My dear,
you are day-worn at the end
of demands.
You fall asleep almost instantly
male tiredness it is of such.
Warm bones and young stubble.
Bells prompt
us of lives firm within this peculiar electricity
we call hope.
When stars cease to be light giving and take in all
that is around them they absorb without giving.
We must
"remain worthy of fire
like a poet growing older."
The wagtails on the green at Wookey
a late afternoon
I have befriended myself yet again.
"She was looking for reasons to unlove him"
Air so solitary it could only be likened
to the Hepworths in the park. Her heart like
a robin's egg.
The years are getting shorter
certainly they press for some
fine line within me for
I have seen the evergreen replace itself
and the pink stones by the waters edge
but my dear I am drawn to the
chalk hills of Kent and the pink orchards
will find me knee deep in autumn leaf
alone.

To see who you might be

Holding ourselves up to the light
        our lined palms.
The way one life crosses through another.
           All hope is investment.

"A lone quiet life
still she held it closely
as though it would cure her of any malady."

A whole season has shifted in on me
           tired sparrows see us move off
These heady years!
A stray hair of yours on the pillow
my heart is the whalebone of me.
Skin and earth you track me down to
a patch of land which burns as I sleep
I astound myself by my misused strengths
solemn at my nakedness at all times.
Urgency utter urgency.

Diary of a Working Man

His arm is a brace
of pigeons.
Shouting across the yard
the figure darts forward
slumps back, drops.

A bird tears his eye
Panic and night
his son was born on the
horsehair settee – later
he mopped the floor with towels.

The instrument was obviously
power
less all else.

Spat down the tunnel
with a scream of fluid on
his tongue.
Singing with such belonging
at the match.

Again the yellow madness.
Light cloud –
early shift
across the track.

Coal, sweat, oil, pay
that's how it was
falling out of the tight throb
at 11.15 and still two hours left.

Like turning a wet
shirt inside out
the room was inside his overall.

Bird song from a long way off.
Exceptional death.

The sky has run out of ink and
awful hatred for her skin.
He goes out to the corner
past the ironmongers and the men
carrying trade plates.

Blackened aspic hell – shrill
light in the aviary above tears.
Even this is shown to be free from
an emblem of chance
up against the bar.

"Shrivel" the doctor said
"you are a cloudy apple" (spit at
anything but her and your pale son on
the ochre hospital seat), the horsehair
settee, later I…
Earlier light cloud across her neck as she
put out bread for garden birds.
Even here the flies die along with the rest
in the lampshade –
moth, cheese, apple, porch
fold toward nothing, toward the green curtain
he put up facing the street the night she died.

Ears in the machine.
Bite at this
come up with tar.

What's left
is the in-
ability to eat alone
leave a room
completely bare.

The bird is well into the
centre of the wood.
Bright worn hands hold the parcel
and journal of song.

Throaty fire that would
burn even the sceptical skin
of his shoes.
A small perfect bolt alone
with spare change on the bus.

Not just ability
to position the eye
for vision/ but ability
of ear to despatch.

The sun has made a fire of his hair
a certain finality of nothing shames him.
He stands upright against the tree.

Creosote/air/lather
on his metallic smile
that night he walked to the station
and thought
are these spirits or fine oaks.

The bright yellow beak startled
him into grief.
The cold tap dripped all night
continued into midday –
wild with anticipation of new voices.

Some men stand around a car
on the edge of the motorway,
further on a girl crosses the street
in a nylon overall.
He cannot take his coat off but walks
into the university of the tree.
The pilot has caught his breath in a
distant vapour trail.

Man belongs to man.
Dry your eyes with plates
the moon is quite ready.

Between distance. Tears hum on
his evergreen collar   space of winter
trees, the ivy that gags his veined
ankle.
Sleep and almost sleep, the son
wakes, panic flickers on haunches
at the back door.
Wet   sharp   loom.

The last stop on the line.
Clock in with the war damage,
brown rooms.
"Imperfection breathes creativity
grit produces the pearl. We are
responsible only to that filth
that we allow to sleep in our dimension.
Nobody is forever a stranger to another."
He walks across the floor.
Outside the wind is bleak with
human torment,
a blade of grass tickles the sky
bright blue.

He took her hand
the pale skin
fingernails formed accurately
hair shaft caught on lazy eyelash.
                    O
to never be outside of this.
"Come outside,
the air is cool,
possessed by love
with no option."
He kissed her. The green light
of the pub car park behind them.

The afternoon
the sparrow bathing in mud.
He turned, would that she were
touched now restored with glimpse.
Night is a pale shadow to sleep under

his head dark on the pillow. Small.
Silent.
Break the fall with tears and dream.
Outside in the wood, primroses, two women
and a dog, the earth climbs right up
behind the pregnant trees.

After USA

Coming home
all the buttercups are out
lambs adolescent shorn so they
look like young pigs.
It's so hard. It's so green.

What gift is there to buy a child
one who needs so little and wants so much.

I wonder what all this is about
maybe you've never thought of it before.
Perhaps I'll just go home and wait.
If only we could have love without paying for it.
But then there would be action
and the hair
falling across your neck
would be hair falling across
or hair falling
or neck
no hair
just movement somewhere.

Something you can recognise

for Mike Booth

Could it be
      the light coming in through the window
      just damp with condensation from the washing
or is it
      the field as seen through cupped forearms
      explaining the shape of the hill.
it may be
      the line of hair on a man's arm leaning
      bending slightly crooked.
or is it
      the hedge outside seen through tears
      and the little trees all clustered
      together and the river slipping by
      and the sky in pieces bright blocks of blue
      with cloud.

"A soft weeping like rain drumming on dry soil"

I can't settle this.
I can't sleep.
I can't settle this I can't sleep.

What's all this about pricey pain
Grieg's *Holberg Suite*
the sun coming in through the curtains just
for a second or
two then takes off again
as
light
and as airy
as the poet ought to be
as allusive and careless as the poem is.
Winter wheat nowhere near ready.
Walking up the road earlier
sidings full of withered fruit
shed by some lorry or other vehicle
and now new shoots growing right up between the old fruit.

Ownership

Sweeping a veil across
your face or a flannel across the mouth
it's all the same
gift of a few hours
in what would seem like total possession
or a glimpse of
another's passion.
Can I give more than a promise?
Or do we holler at the exhausted
in the dark light cold night
of motorway
and do we not all come home alone
to our own cold reception or return
our faith of human over human.
I would give it all up if only you
would ask me or tell me
but then for you to say
or him to ask
or her to receive or his to give
or him to suggest
or she to give in and walk towards him
to answer
to surrender or his to let go of
or his to break down over or hers to allow
or mine to admit.
I pace between succour and the chilling fright of the gift.

And so much is already ours only we shout for it
like lambs and calves
demanding what we have no need of
surplus
and the hours of labouring in the tight dawn where I cried

at being so at being so
and damned the sky for its light
and if only it had been his to give and mine to have asked for
and theirs to have noticed and hers to be fearful and
to have fought and mine to give
be proud of and yours to have loved and yours to have loved
so happy with and if only we'd have taken more care
of shown the way to
and is it that measured and who is measuring who is looking
and in the dark sheets of her knowing he would never
be hers only the hollering
and mine in the giving
will you look out
will you look out.

Come on
the house is empty
the arms are full but the legs are a
way out.
O take the urgency from my body
He took her hand
she took his number
they walked back again she was certain he was
watching insecure
they took turns at laughing
he demanded
he moved she followed he turned round
she looked at him he looked away she sat up
he sat up they looked down he asked her she
refused blindly saying "it's no good"
he came after her she wasn't there
he wondered about it and she cried
he had tried again but she had already found him
he was pleased she was cross
they walked off together. She stopped trying

she stopped crying.
He asked why she said she hadn't he knew she had.
They ran back quickly she'd changed her mind
he changed his face
he came back they were turning the wrong way
he was hurt
she was pleased he was damaged she didn't want to know
he asked her again she forgot who he was
he wondered too
they remained and she wanted him
he wanted her
she wanted to walk
he ran and he fell
she went to him and cried too
he was pleased he was old
she was very old
they were looking at the same place in the sky
he said come on the house is empty
the arms are full
but the legs
the legs are a way out.

Collecting sheets

from the washing line
take a pull at them
not before
seeing the tiny
sparklets
of frozen moisture
along the top for maybe a couple of inches or so;
the Great North Star up above.
It's vital to be as we are
making no extra demand
as if
there could be anything but the cloudless sky
up and above and the cluster of stars
the quarter moon.

It's very often not who you are but whose you are

for Lee

Watching you
walk upstairs with your tiny daughter
you stop
halfway to kiss her
looking first at her face
before moving off.
    So the hidden agendas we have inherited
bring us back to how and where we are.
From the bridge the workmen on late shift walk back
across the tracks
and we comment on the rail-sidings fill of distanced
flowers and seeds, perhaps from peashooters you say.
Later we speak of the adult fears and the childhood
resilience, the hearts of poets and vital acts of love
and endurance.

Raising You at Night

for Phoebe

Be strong
        be honest and be fair.
Make judgements with difficulty
        and know when others do not.
At night your child's arms and legs
        curl back into foetal pose.
You, my first born who suckled at night
        our tired moon and early milkman
saw us tussling to ease your baby pain;
        the adult ones I cannot cure.
Be strong
        be honest and be fair
see how the new day rises upon us so well.

The Snoad Hill Poems

for Ian

1.

O house, O sloping field, O poplar trees whose tall arms salute.
Bleating
Bleating everything is looking.   The cows call
                                   at night
                                   for their calves
                                   removed after
                                   weaning. Four
                                   days later they
                                   give up
                                   throats sore.

I am at a loss to cleverly describe the lights
from the tiny train in the distance snaking its way
south from London across the Kent land.
"A necklette of tynie golden stones or
a worm of saffron slipping through a lanyard of light!'

2.

                    Walking towards the village
                    the moon as bright as a cat's eye
                    thin film of cloud across the empty
                    autumn fields.
                    I am wondering you see about this
                    thing they call chance...

                    How it was that you and I became this way
                    we hadn't noticed the sun lifting the
                    trees upward... so much power in the trunk.

The way we've chosen to arrange ourselves.
The tired manner of the chin of an
old person standing watching
goes up and down
seen it all before worn out.
Why are we always moving about?

3.
She had the stance of a Snowdrop.
It concerned him that already the wind had
been exposed to her face and that her
lightly chapped skin made an embarrassed glance
appear on her face. Perhaps it was all the crying
that wet her face.
The woman's countenance was bright and her
unusually welcoming mariner was renowned.
"It was always thus" she said to him late one
afternoon as he packed the car "always it
is the woman who waits and says little."
Glancing back as he drove away he caught her
eye in the rear view minor and was reminded
of the first day he had seen her.
The air had been warm during the night and the
next day he had set off to town to buy
an extractor fan. She had been standing across the
road talking to an older man, her hand
on his shoulder, her head in his hands.
He was struck then as now that she was as pale
and thin as a snowdrop and that if she bent
any closer towards the earth she would simply
snap.

4.
And if my light should
suddenly peter out
do not grieve
thinking
I had not time to
admire the upturned leaves.
Just today I brought home
rose bay willow herb
cow parsley and fern
germander speedwell
and this mitre-headed beauty
is bright yellow kidney vetch.
What more can you hope for.

5.
Digging up weeds by the little hedge
the spade hits the store of Bethersden
marble that is the foundation here.
13th century clay threw up *Paludina carnifera*
composed almost totally of freshwater snail
fossilised.
Cut and polished   so striking
Cranbrook and Biddenden pavements show the
pock-marked broken-down snail shells.
Cut and polished   so striking are
the Cathedral and nave steps in Canterbury
and Rochester, the great west tower of
Tenterden church.   In the buildings of
Woodchurch and Headcorn and Hythe the finest
examples are found, the best seen of its 'value'.

Pale and dark brown and blue almost luminous tints
feel alive when touched.

Gentle water-snails skate in the dykes.
"It bears a good polish and is very hard
and durable if dug up in its perpendicular
state but if horizontally found it peels off in flakes."

Ox-drawn sledges dragged these great marble
slabs to surrounding villages and to the lodges
of the masons who worked it.

6.
Our hands crushed
bent back against one another
we turn for warmth and find only dampness rising
from our troubled palms as if
all cypress trees were in troubled prayer.
The tiny branches and new shut buds of our unborn child
lay alert listening to the dark damp womb.
Walking out along Sparrow Hatch Lane the exquisite woodsmoke
no moon but the sharp light from the London train
coming home south.
An alarmed creature in the hedgerow turns round, sees me,
and takes off.

7.
It's this familiar black line from the tops
of the trees making their way up to the woods
from the edge of the field.
Near the small white bridge the cows move off.
Late harvesters come home after dark
tractor and trailer lights blazing as they pass.
Inside me
you my first-born move with such force, pushing organs into your
own shape. Coming to us, as you do, with nothing. I too have

nothing but these arms to offer and this heart from which you take life,
this comfort for always yours.

8.
Waiting
all of us
the Jersey cow and her smooth red body swollen
tight with calf. Long tongue sucking up grass,
conkers hang
some darker than others, always they seem too early.
Acorns tiny in their cups rattle in the air.
Ease. Grace. I am won over and quite ready.

9.
Temperament is related to physique.
Heavy showers on and off all day soaking
into the dry earth. The first rain in three weeks.
Turgid stems turn small flower faces skyward.
"Jesus wants me for a sunbeam" I know he does.
In George's garden a white lily has opened
up and made me think of him a week
before he died saying
"I'm so confused, I'm so old, it doesn't seem
at all right me being like this."

10.
The jetty
just before Christmas
the whole bay out there and the little boats
in the frozen water.
How else can we sharpen our hearts on the first
bleat of morning from our small bed where we lay curled

together in sleep.
Your dark ginger curls on the pillow and the autumn
leaves under the car headlights
are at night the axis for all this living.

11.
The hedge breaks out in bud
giving it that bullion coated tinge
we associate with frost.
Sparrows chip along looking to make nests
and the sheep lay close by too heavy with lamb.
"Why can't we go for walk and come back pleased"
The blackbirds glazed black body on the garden
post waxed against rain the sparklets of water
he shakes off before he sings before he flies.

Notes one two

I

The garden birds listen
                        small heads cocked
on one side   alert for the movement
of worms in the fresh dug soil.

In the street people worry   talk about
ending it all. Pull themselves into new days.

II

Spring is here and I push my thumb against it
holding it back for you.   Tell me
whether once a small bird standing
                        on grass plunges to your belly
sinking heart
with daily catastrophe.
Just to be a voice in the park
where lone golfers
and straggling packs of Brownies gather and are strewn
across the Kent grassland founded on chalk
and no one is disappointed by cloud.

"And show myself and everyone as we are so striving
after everything, so looking."

All this new growth and luck and love
the fledgling inside me flickers and
turns sometimes sleeping.

My heart banging inside its frame.
We walk to make the best of ourselves.
O.K. owl so you've had your say
tonight twit twooing hooting while the
lapwings plummet and dive.
Carry the air and lead us
soon I'll have heard all
your wise intentions.
Primrose you
startle me
so.

Beyond All Other

Beyond all other
fear
that we will be unloved
lost faded in our lives without
the golden mark of youth on our cuff,
there is the knowing that always
we are part.

Beyond all other
hope
love is
being wide open to another, total
vulnerability. An exchange of selves.

Beyond all other
desire
there is the idea of eternity
we listen for its ghosts
finding habit, pattern.

Beyond all other
love
there is this extension of self
moving out against the inertia
that laziness we call work.
Moving out in the face of all fears
courage.
Moving out towards desire
value creates love.
Love then is a form of work
of courage.

"What massive stones. What magnificent buildings."

If You Have to Push It May Not Fit

My hands
have changed recently.
The skin is rather papery
crinkled foil-like
the veins stand out
like small rivers.

Let's face it.
They have been overdoing it lately.
Never at rest
always putting on
fastening
pressing down, into, onto, up to.
Smoothing out,
cleaning round
pushing back, applying this and that.
Making effort.

The light is blinding
I have over-stretched my body
and now it has told me so.
The spirit too willing but pain
dampens its ardour.
The easy tears blotted now by the daffodils
and wood anemone.

The children's arms are like tiny stems
they injure me with such fresh sap.
My soft lips are tethered,
homeless.
The muffled world presses its giant mouth
onto my chest.

I must wait my turn
the blackness boasts a terrible hunger.

We Must Learn Not to Breathe

In praise, Paul Auster

The high-rise flats; our openness.
Long marshland and seascape
quick-growing kale, the
many stones.

Pylons. The lead air.
We have turned to phlegm.
The moon   is as quiet as an owl.

We have broken our promises
made alliance with the rain.
This is where the heart is
inhaling the dark.

"To live in this air we must
learn not to breathe."

The children on the estate clamour
for attention, urgently draw for me,
wanting pen and paper, adult attention.

We have rested
together
leant against those huge stories. They tell me
it is for the heart to suggest problems
and for the intellect to solve them
just for the time being.

Kent

Our mute hands.
December rises over the tops of the trees
        can we miss so much with our arms
high above the night. Consider this:

> The railway threading its polite
> thud lulling cattle deep in barley.

> Our home lit up with love nestling
> into the ink black night. Swallows
> and starlings. Pheasants and owls.

> All chance germination snapped into
> bones, stems, trunks, feather.

A ribbon of sky. I want to talk to you. There are
so many things.

Black square. White edging. Dice. Clip your quick eye.
Ringed ferment clatters
The snow has made a primrose of itself.
Make a note if you can:

> The elderly neighbour walks each day
> further and further from his home
> soon he may not return.

> We play one another off against
> the other and yet there are no winners.

> The stench of mortality shuffling through
> all these mad-made things. Banter. Electricity.

A thin stream of water. I am hoping to cross the bridge before nightfall. Cool the ice.

Frozen river and bleak road-signs tell me that your heart ` is at the cleaners.

This belonging, this us

for Ian and for Phoebe and Beatrice

"Only love gives parents any, authority. Parents who love each other can build something that the children haven't had time to build, and the children can see that and respect it. But when love fades and wears away into nothing the parents are like two petulant children, as petulant and unreasonable without the high spirits of children." — J.W.

Our tiny children's hearts are lanterns
of promise   we are led
and in turn lead by the moss stones   the coral
bark of stripped chestnut wood.
Forgive my hands
              their shakiness. The rivers
dark silt tenders less. Take hold this steady heart.
Forgive my tears
              their wetness. The crumpled
papers damp hand. Remind me of the short seasons
that can cut off a young life.
Forgive my greed
              its youthfulness. The dark trees
at night are only the dark trees of the daytime.
Give up worry and torture.

Life is OK.
It has a lot to recommend it.
By and large.

He lifted up his head.
He lifted up his head all branched made.

Women snap
break the tender days
trapped between their bowed bodies
              guilty hearts.

Children's small fears, open faces
trusted and held. Taunt the women's thirst of love.

Gladly gladly suckle.

"Men Must Live and Create.
Live to the Point of Tears." (Camus)
for Polly Hartcup

I have been touched by the lives of others
brought home
to their beds by the sullen silence
of their wrists.
Experience is a comb
which nature gives us when we are old.

The worn warm ways of the world
weary with repetition
it is the only form of permanence
that we see.
Our learning
does not come from only our sorrows
look how common is our blood.

"Who Takes the Child By the Hand
Takes the Mother By the Heart"

Scabious   paper white
turn inside out making the
everlasting eternal gift one heart inside another
like carrying a baby inside of you
she said
my heart forever with yours like that
as a mother is
knowing where the worry is.
My neighbour here died suddenly
planting willow planting oak
the hurricane killed him
she said
never recovered from the shock
of seeing the devastation
couldn't think where to start
so he planted
just planted too many.
As his wife
knew
some things as a wife
you just know
his heart in mine
like that just petered out.

The Path Between the Yew Trees
With Grass and Damp with Dew

I
"The simplest lessons are those which are taught last."

Often by those we least consider.
Humour.
The sun goes down on our minor
squalls and makes rainbows of our fears.
Illness.
Rest. The sleeping willow does not
ask for water waits for rain.
You won't be as you are now again.

II
"For the first time I have noticed
the lost and the lonely, how, with their
curious apologetic gait, they move through
the world like strangers."

Others stride with determined hatred
some amble honest and humble to salute.
Apology. Accepting triumph
welcoming sleep
watching the dark green trees, the pale
green lawns.
Sitting.
We are sinking beneath the soft stones
of the wearisome. The blue the blue
anchusa, delphinium, purple eyes, green
skirted viola.

III
"I hoped, I think, that she would recognise
in me what I had already discovered in myself."

It is perhaps that understanding which shakes
the tall cypress tree, calls the infant to sleep.
Pretend the sky is only a mouthpiece, the
rain shifting in on the earth.
Lemon trees
    fireflies
the handles of the, drawers are shaped like snails.
A lane with high   overgrown hedges.

Seeing through the trees   to the water in
                      the pasture. The
                      wren sheltering the
                      tiny nest.
Loved and worried for
the children lay asleep adored, cherished, tired
with sun, with the demands of adults.
We sleep under the bright blue painted ceiling of
golden nightingales, sun and moon.
The crickets and frogs sing together
patiently safe in the pocket of the valley.

The quotations are taken with thanks from Peter Ackroyd's
book, *The Last Testament of Oscar Wilde*.

The Shape of Things

for Frances Presley

Having long come to know him and
respect and worry
for the things she saw that mattered
her eyes turned away at the idea
of him
      with another.
The spring in his curl and the way one leg
crossed gamely
      before the other
she vowed never to sleep willingly again
she would
instead be lost in slumber
not asleep
merely dreaming.
Grant O Lord
she said
any careful plans for nakedness
      for rest.
My heart has long been
in formalin
stained puce white.

Run Down

In the dark by the reservoir the lights
       move
       flash on and off.
    My heart is irregular temperate like the
    weather; I hear its dangers. I plant the
    bulbs slowly this year.

Out in the fields even at dark the men
feed animals, shake down hay, level the water.
It is a world we have saved for.

Plums and zinnias in the market place
Old men buy seeds; their hands are like glass,
they touch their caps to me: I am not so old.

Time runs out on us, the person so quickly
vanishes there can be no preparation for the
final disappearance.
I miss my father
my daughters cannot hear his stories.

The strong bindweed in the garden
tiny lilac faces of the Michaelmas daisy
upturned hopeful.
The children lie asleep dreaming of
pleasing me
sometimes I am not shouting.

The Garden

Ripe edges sway into crisp
      understanding of winter
and its small deaths.
      Such solemn grace of things
asleep. Promises gone wrong
      Seeds sweat bulge into spring
and into a blue summer anchusa,
      delphinium, borage, poppy.
Blackbirds' opera of light
      are birds fearful of the future?
They spread and dart
      we watch and sigh.

June 1990

After the Hurricane

Walking out to shut the chickens up
stars stellar worlds
no moon;
so bright
so many.
The chickens shuffle
mutter at my visit huddle back.
In the house the children sleep
by candle light
electricity cables blown clean away.
They are dense solidly asleep –
is no one as tired as me?
The oil lamps blaze
a strange car passes.
It would seem that
children dance to resolve the world.
We tired old ones
collapse on the sides
prepare ourselves for death,
too much knowledge leaves little room
and time for experience.
I will wave my flag and retire.

(1987)

Not What You'd Call a Religious Man

"They gave me the mattress job plenty of times. You know what that is, do you? They get two mattresses, one either side of you so you're sandwiched in between them. A raw meat sandwich. Then the coppers beat hell out of you. It bloody hurts I can tell you but it doesn't leave any marks. Ask anyone that's been inside, they'll tell you." I ask about his family. "Oh my Dad's a looney – brain damage. I tried to murder him when I was 15 years old by beating him over the head with a cricket bat. He was very ill. I got Borstal and then the hospital wing when they couldn't contain me." "Did that help?" I ask with some degree of interest. "No way." "What would have helped then?" "Oh, I don't know really – maybe different parents, maybe not being one of 8 boys and having to fight for everything all the time. I tell you what wouldn't have helped for sure." "What's that?" I ask making careful notes. "All that religious stuff, that gives me the willies. Mind you I always go to church when I'm inside, not that I'm a religious man you understand, but you can do some good deals in the pews for a few smokes. Always worth a few blows the hymns are."

I Said Hold Tight

I travel across the thick fog of the fens to the high walls of the male prison. After a long wait in the visitors' hall where a prisoner is mopping the large floor in an angular, defeated way and the man in charge of the cafeteria has whistled three rounds of Rule Britannia and Silent Night, the man I have come to see arrives. He tells me he was several blocks away and there had been no one to bring him over, says he was playing his guitar, that once he played with the Rolling Stones before he was married, before any of "this lark" was his problem. He says there's a real big shot cocaine dealer on his wing – director of a very large public company – headman, the police don't want much publicity as it might "do damage".

We talk about why I've come – he says, "Well Sherry's not my kid, you know – not mine at all. I thought she was, I saw her being born and I was pleased to have a little girl. Then one day I came home after work and see her sitting on a man's knee, I said hello mate who are you, he said I'm her daddy – I said hold tight I can't hear that."

"Then I left and never saw the other kids until last year. Well, if you're worrying about how I could cope with them I'll tell you straight, none of them will end up in here. I've just been moved from that army-run prison, it was great, cleaned by squaddies, run by officers – they was wary about us at first, then they got interested in talking, especially when they found out that most of us had been in the army at one time or another. Yeah, they talked. I like talking."

"I've never had a driving licence but I've *been driving* since I was 9 years old. My Dad taught me – he was a costermonger. I got my licence taken away before I ever got it and now I'm banned till 1991 – I love cars. It's all I know."

"I know the offences my son's done are wrong and he'll know that by the time I've finished with him. I know he worships me but hold tight – he wants to be a policeman you know. Well can't say as I blame him – you meet a lot of interesting people.

I tell him that the court's unlikely to allow him to care for his son when he comes out of prison.

"Hold tight lady," he says, "I've got a three-bedroomed house when I come out of here – and I'm starting a taxi business – all legit. It will be so legit even the big shot cocaine dealer what's in here will be a fare."

In Revenge of Civil Disorder

*"There is much coldness among men because
we dare not to be as cordial as we really are."*

I

Mottle abuse.
Begin and crown the child
with anything but this.
A false ardour of final steam
its powerless intrusion.
Molotov during field study
measures blunt growth with
the axis that reluctantly
swigs at an excessive tear.

II

Retaliate against the foetus
with heavy discontent.
Street archers move off
suddenly into dusk – their reversed
parables; love in a bitter disease
of mock care.
We are trespassers in our own clothes.

III

No heather there
not soaring to be done
between dances – hyper
nothing.

My embrace is wet from walking
in the river
– shoes run off swearing never
to smile again.

IV

Frantic collision into last week's
observation – you
th and the heath air – it's so close
it cannot be seen.
My clothes are saturated.
I am not worthy of forgery
nor am I the first to arrive.
Better sink with fire
headway up stifle with rem
embr
ance and arrive here to answer
that confidence is not knowledge.

V

Search my flowered mouth
– but disarm, turn to run between it –
final and sweet,
or,
immunity would bleed us
hollow as concrete.
We would be thin enough to leave
without being noticed.

Against the Air

The bright edge of the woodpecker steals
Across the gaunt
Limb of sky
      We are already gripped as she
      Steadies
      Leans and steers into the mossed
      Centre of what is contained, known.

A dark feathering in the undergrowth of woodland
Our tired burdens draw into us
We tread without thought
      Driven by the flustered hope
      Again we are still unprepared
      And yet not asleep
      Or rested, even now.

The northern stars are seen in the south too
Our poems are but small messages of quiet silence
Plain, empty, the air is against us as we try to make sense
      Evidenced by love of
      One to another
      We complete the work in our stride.

November 1999

Along the Landings

*The Landings, as they were known, were several blocks of flats,
part of my patch as a social worker in the early 1980s.*

Along the landings
shrill steam open vents to bathrooms
toilet seats lie open
fox holes
the bitter curve of the road where the toddler lay.
Rubbish chute
lit up at night the noise travels upwards
a belly button pierced
groans in the bedroom   his hand across her face
screams the glass into the vein.

Along the landings
lift shaft urine-soaked cigarette stubs
"I'll get you for this"
torched front doorway boarded menace
the empty siren
lost from the flock the lamb waits while the others suckle
"I'll get you for this"
Washing hangs like a millstone
her neck
he saw her first   blue tattoo
nothing more.

Along the landings
the polished brass door furniture
keep themselves nice
the girl has plaits down her back and across the leather sofa
the moneylenders gather about lights in their cars as they
            make notes, spin, take off.
There are buzzards about lining the trees before making a descent
Graffiti across the new door "wankers"
she sees it as she turns the corner
walks off again not even seeing
give me strength   give me strength.

Along the landings
breakdancing body moves fast
skateboard a sleek pencil movement
the rest couldn't catch him   too fast
Cars rev and line the alley they look out
Steady   a gaze lingers too long
"what you looking at wise boy?"
running he can do it
ducks down   rests while they miss him
Trees break out in bud before you know it the blossom unfurls
palm upwards.

Along the landings
the stairways concrete litter lottery tickets beer mats his
telephone number
part of it all.
no credit on her phone
he never did call
her face against his
over in a flash
her heart pounding worried late
worried late
worried
her mother knew   recognised the look
washed her clothes   never said
tucked her in as usual "see you in the morning"
the pond lays open like a wound where the river meets it halfway
                seagulls cluster and then are gone.

Along the landings
the old lay still sick of it
waiting they listen it is shouting and it bangs about the menace
the upset and upheaval of it all   too late now
too late then.
The white cyclamen blooms all year the warden said so you
          can't beat central heating
the legs were once willing
it hurts
to leave
the chair
"I don't know" the nurse had answered when he questioned her
she had no idea
                no idea at all by the morning he would be gone
made sure of it.
The birds start up at 5 a.m. their brightness startles so.

All along the landings
the others have a better lot   benefits thriving visitors go come
"leave off" she said
"I don't want your fancy words it's not what I need"
Refugee status   fledgling starling falls out of tree lays squeaking
the mother flies   willing it for hours   no bueno no go
pristine clothing aimless drifts loose less use
                                        less watching finding out
seeming solemn carrier bags.
"We can do without you" she said as it slithered from between her
legs
"get you gone you" she said as it was cut and pulsed upon her.
They took her and the infant at her word   never again would he
            have that link
that blood that pulse memory that long that knowledge
that much.

Along the landings
a maze of promises and broken debris fades in
between the babies yelling
adult needs we need adult time we need we need time away
and soon enough they too are children   bleached ideals
white branches silver birched.
willing it different
"my Dad likes drills
and bimbos and doing
his own thing
he would come
only
he's   busy stressed out just now."
Magnetic keylock. Tradesman buzzer press buzzer and wait for en-
trance
she imagined him there waiting for entrance to the flat
the buzzer system dud but instead it was him

dud.

All along the landings
he threw up he threw the hamster at the wall because
he said it shat on him
she ran out down the slope passed the bins the stolen pallets
she wouldn't go back and the Shoesave carrier bag was all she had
leave me out of this said her gran and she ran.

Beaten.

Along the landings
He was all that she wanted
warm
wanting her to be her
for that day
in April the trees were in bud there are so many of them
        bursting out new
like that
it was hard to choose.
Tragic
nothing else to say his car left the road
no one else to blame
nothing.

Along the landings
They shave   too young.
Brazilian.   She wanted to be ready for him.
Instead
being cut
Wide Open
blistered with disappointment
out.
No messing
But it's done on the street in moonlight outside
The Club
kissing and kicking where it hurts
a lesson
learnt.
Keeping things tight
within the family.
It's a blessing
in sharp and deep disguise
Often
too often she would walk to the offie for him
buy him booze
keep him sweet.
Returning the empty cider bottles
paid for the little one's crisps.

Along the landings
Welcome warmth
she tried to make a home
stair-carpet with vomit where he staggered.
"When Daddy shouts my ears want to run away"
she lifted him up
pressing his heart against hers.
"He don't mean it."
"He does, he said he'd kill you, punch your lights out. I love
        your light mum."
She looked away
buckled him up
dropped him.
School reception asked why he was late.
Dentist, she muttered
"Mum" he said;
she walked away.

Along the landings
paint peels
revealing the broken dancers
half-moon chancers, vodka chasers.
He caught her eye as she stood up
saw her plastic see-through bra strap topping
her backless green dress.
The verges strewn with weed and thistle the hedges uncut
broken down not like it was
any more.
Torn through the ripped up message

Along the landings
the price tags fluttered   strewn landscape on the
horizon of the tattooed knuckled stranger
who half jesting
leans over and asks for money as he
held a knife
to his throat a little too close
slipping as he did
and stamped on his feet
although and especially as he saw they were blistered swollen
          veins collapsed.
In her back pocket creased
the visitor's permit to see him on the lifers' wing.
Terminal Alley he calls it.

Along the landings it has been a long morning
"My client would like you to be assured your honour that…"
the voice tails off as he looks over at her
she looks away
it was not
forever
like this
Once they
made
a child
together
just them
one room
a bed
a moment
the child
that now
they divide
tear up   throw away

set apart.

Along the landings
she reads
that the tsunami tragedy claimed a forty percent higher death rate of
women than men. "A common thread runs through the different regions
that explains this. Women were at home on that Sunday morning while
the men were either out in their boats at sea, and therefore escaped the
waves, or were away from the shore doing other chores. Women stayed
behind to help the children and the elderly when the waves struck. In
Tamil Nadu, women were waiting on the shore for the fishing boats to
return so they could sell the catch when it arrived. Stories by survivors
bring out another common factor. Women did not have the strength
to hold onto a child and also hang on to a tree or something else to save
themselves from being battered to death. They could not clamber up
trees with the ease the men could. In all these places, it was evident that
women lost precious minutes as they tried to gather all their children
before attempting to escape the cascading waters."
Precious minutes taken   lost.
What could be more vital than saving your child.
The beginning of it all.
He was never away from her
always in mind
his small hand in hers always like that she never let it go
she hoped that he knew it
some things she only knew
as a mother.

As he saw the wave he ran leaping across nets the wooden railing the
siding stones
Others were screaming he saw them being dragged under and out and
back in again.
Beyond his the trees on the edge of the village were too far, his feet
bled but he scrambled up the tree his feet holding the edges as he had
know been shown what to do.

All along the landings the lights go out.
He cannot find the key to his home.
Still he
hammered.
Empty, silent, the place did not move.
His mother was dead.
She would not be at home for him again.

All along the landings the word is out.
At seventeen the height of creativity burning
mapping the skull
bursting
unsullied
to
start over
stomach
recognize
renew.
Cherish the spark of the
fevered young
who long for, wish and do.
The old are bawdy in their method
garish
they lean
outward for too long,
scared and dim.

Along the landings
he read about the success of the personal adverts
but it didn't cross his mind that she would come.
"They make them like that
heavy and ugly so you don't ask."
He said
explaining his club foot
"Had it since birth. No one asks anymore so I don't say."
"My wife left me, they always do that,
go."
His lips shook
he was
the oldest man in the room
the collar tore at his neck.
Far later
he gave her the poem
saying "at least it'll make interesting scrap paper".
She looked down   avoided his foot.

Along the landings
Found himself looking out for her more than
once and too often.

In Asda their trolleys crossed;
no one asked
hung there
a while.
It was
an unhandled resistance   a difficult moment.

(2004–2005)

225

Faulty Mothering

1991–1996

"We think back through our mothers if we are women."
Virginia Woolf

Faulty Mothering

I

Slip shod
worn through all my empty threats
smarty packets   gold stars
left with maternal comfort   exhaustion
forgiveness.

Her eye saw the back of the Startrite sandal
as he turned the corner towards the pond
Don't play near the water, she said
I'm not, he shouted. Her arms pit high in
suds, legs aching. I only put my foot in
he said displaying the black silt up to his groin.
The baby woke red faced howling then stopped
suddenly. Even children who have experienced bad parenting with
no other relationships do not necessarily abuse all their children…
Rachel ran in.
Is lunch ready, I'm starving.
She picked him up onto the edge of the wooden draining
board and soaked his foot in the sink,
she ran to the baby. Rachel shut up, she said and
ran past her.

II

After she was born
        they let me hold her
her soft head had slipped
from between my legs.
        Such promise.

The septicaemia put me
into the isolation ward.
I never saw her for 12 days
my milk dried
my heart stopped.
It was never the same again.

I lost what we had
         she's a stranger
                  a no-one.
Outside the men were
shovelling grit into the road.
In life there is simply
no time to touch
only brush by in passing.

III

My history as a child
was torn
wanting to please
be tidy
honest faithful
and yet missing
a link a passport to the adult
world
I was muzzled   callipered
orphaned.

IV

I am tired of your trousers and shoes
she said

they are full of you.
When the twins were born
he never said 'I love you' he just said
'great' and stood up when he'd seen their
heads in the tiny plastic cots.
He never brought flowers like the other
fathers, she tried not to be hurt. She
knew he did it on purpose.
At night she would cry herself to sleep
between feeding the babies. One would
wake then the other then the other then
the other. Her breasts felt like sore bricks.
You ought to get some rest he told her.
Her friends made her go out alone but
at feeding time her milk came in and
ran down the sides of her body and formed in droplets round her feet.
When his family came they would love
playing with the twins, bouncing them high
and making them laugh "You are a lucky
girl," his mother said.
At dawn when the children slept she read,
"When people manage to get in touch with their own pain,
they no longer want to take it out on others".

V

There is moment inside of him that he can recall
—a crying out, arms flaying. The sides of the cot
are hard, the mattress wet, he cries out and then stops.

Damp garden clay late blue flowers   seed heads
cut down the new buds breaking through. The nights are drawing in
over our head my arms are bent double with effort. Your socks have
lost their colour in the wash.

Blackened ideas, a dream of soaring
you are there and I have lost my legs. I can never
fail to look out for you. The back of your
jumper never ceases to lift me.

The resolution to be young again to not worry
so often they seem to fade away
her tiny hand, unblemished heart. "Fish do have eyes
don't they Mummy?" she asked.

He turned on his Lotus shoe heel in the kitchen on the
Vinolay and slammed the door
"Where's Daddy going?" asked Michael.
It was the last time he ever mentioned him.

The green edge of winter has opened and into the meadow the yellow
basins of buttercup and vetch tangle around
the gate post.

VI

"I never asked them for much just that they kept the
wood basket topped with kindling. Then I could do
the washing on the boiler see. I had three sons
and a husband that only saw as far as his fishing line.
On the 10th November I went round the house picking
up the dirty washing, went to the Rayburn – no
kindling. They only have to do one thing, I thought,
get kindling, and they can't even do that for me.

I was faced with a mud-ridden kitchen, a mound
of washing, no hot water and no kindling. I
found my purse, put on my coat and left. I walked

up to the village and took a bus, got off and sat
down outside the church, took the bus back again
and waited till after dark and then when I could think
of nothing else to do I went home. The kitchen was
all lit up, he was making the cheese on toast,
they looked up when I came in. Then I saw the washing
still there, the fire still out, the basket empty.
No kindling. 'Where you been Mum?'
'I've been to the pictures,' I said. 'Good film was
it?' he asked."

VII

The steel tempest
is a dreary shadow
I would yet half asleep.
Unnoticed the children
mittened blamed their efforts
on climate, atmosphere, money.
Paper methods.   Tawdry skin.
I will never bounce back
know the child
I am forever clipped.

VIII

We are in air
the Kent fields
cushions of harvest
ribbons of grass wind around
ankles.
His child's idea
Red as her memory

a blizzard of faces
she has found
her mother.
The old birth certificate in its folded wallet.
A sharp pain across her
eye, her back. The gate
was held closed with a dog lead.
You'd better come in,
the woman said
I remember you,
you never stopped crying.
She searched the face before her
the neck the chest,
those breasts were never for me
she knew.
She left after a
promise to meet again.
It was all in pieces again
broken up just like before.

IX

You'd better go, I told him
No use you hanging round here looking
tormented, you go and make your life
with her. He packed his clothes
into a Lo Cost carrier bag.
Can I see Leah again he asked
as he went past your bedroom
down the stairs, No, I shouted,
You've made your choices. I remember
he never looked back once.
I watched him from the upstairs
bedroom window. You woke up and

asked for him.
Daddy will
tuck you up I said. I couldn't think
what else to say.

X

The pansies in the window box are stunning
everybody said so
I don't know where you find the time
the postman said.

In 1970 when her father died she thought she would die
too. No other balance no calm still voice to counteract
her own restless need and shrill accusations.
Twenty five years on she is older
shrill accusatory alive and calm
she has seen the red sky and pale blue trail.

She is worrying that liver they had for tea
will result in a deformity.
His palpitations may be the start of an attack
if we have another hurricane the chimney will
fall in onto the children.
The baby's head isn't growing as fast as it should
the cat's worms will result in someone losing an
eye the plant food she put on the tomatoes contained
the chemical the man on TV warned against
they are travelling on the sinking ferry
she lays her cellulite legs on the British Home Stores
polyester fitted sheet and is borne away and in the morning
is quite refreshed.

XI

At weekends
the men walk around Safeway proud
of their offspring
lay them on their backs like motorcycle parts.
In the week
the women are wrecked
look dazed with tasks
fitting life in between schooltime
jamming toddlers onto the pram tops
their legs are so heavy.

Oval is the woman's shape
her eggs are clear – honest
never scattered, permanent, stationary
internal.
Children knowing this
seek it out know here to go
for rest.

XII

The space between crying and surrender
is a handkerchief away
oblivion makes a lumpy pillow at night
contentment can only be a closing off
a kind of breaking down.

The shimmer of tears lack lustre.
In a nearby garden a young girl a mother
of a baby lay down
her head in my neighbour's syringa, fell asleep
confused and drunk.

They took her baby inside and cleaned his little
head.
I feel sick, she said.

XIII

In the prison he was in solitary;
he was pleased he had explained it
all before.
The psychiatrist who came drew a map
of his family, he even brought a
photograph of the child
his heart was an overblown melon
he ate the seeds, it was best.

When she became pregnant he bought her
a silver star to hang around her neck.
"I want to give you the moon" he said.
She knitted, she was a picture,
they all said it except her mother.
When the baby came she fed her, loved
her, washed her tiny face.
A week later she threw the baby at him
"I can't do it" she said "I'm no use".
He cried, she cried, the baby cried.
The doctor came his mother arrived
the health visitor wrote things down.
"I hate you" she said to the baby.
"Lie down" they told her
The baby grew thin she became fat.
Her mother never came.
I told you I was no use she said.

XIV

The first time I shook her
I knew I would remember it
forever.
Something unchangeable had happened.
She was better in the rain
there was hope and breath.
I drank in long open
shards.
The savage lines in my heart
are forever on my face
great ditches of
poisoned forests.

XV

Or a child's face
          divine
upturned in the half light.

Ask me if I'm six
she says. Well are you?
No, I'm seven!

She moves off
content

Torment   O moon
O princess in mourning.

XVI

I can't please her ever.
I was the disappointment.
The earth is borne about her
Its manners are harsh and
careless.

Once she told me I had ruined
her figure and my pig-like
eyes belonged to my father.

The rain had turned people into
fast moving, shining objects.
Its limp sculptor's
hands confirm the shape of the envy.

XVII

I looked out for her every minute
She didn't come till very late
but when she did it was funny.
Mummy didn't get out of the
car she spoke to her friends
on the CB instead. Her hands
were warm but her legs were bare
were cold. She looked away
when I said her name.

There is a breaking down
inside of her. There is a taste of
rat. It is shorn up
for good
like a dead person.

XVIII

Years later
She cannot recall the things the children said when they were tiny; the
things that made them laugh.
Like so many things, time had robbed it away leaving her naked.
Now the children are adults they say things which hurt her.
Don't look like that, they say when she might cry.
Turning away towards the car park it is full of others,
all in their differing chancy stages.

XIX

And therefore was her labour that much more in washing and wringing

To worry
is to be connected with
The woman's lot is to worry
to be troubled with   concerned, mixed up
Loaded windless the sky takes fear, returns it laundered, ready.
Waiting for fortune to happen upon them
the men take chances wonder at the reeling birds diesel streets.
More work to be done not simply tidied.

XX

The women are gathered, not in extravagant postures but
          huddled weeping, their eyes reddened and dashed.

The white daisies spring up in anticipation they are known.
Women hem garments their hands sick with action
faces wrenched with ideas and sleepless O they are sleepless

footless, heartless hurt.
wrecked reality.
Where are the men standing?
are they alone or in unison rowdy with lofty fear and rage.
Some become tearful expectant
stagger at a loss, tearful,
trounced others swagger on the bridge wide open and forgotten.
We are not simply done for there is more to understand

XXI

You could almost think, sometimes, that their mother wasn't behind
her face anymore

Nowadays the rutted furrowed steps of her brow and
Dark patches swept across like storms, sudden, a strong attack on a
defended place or position.
Bellowed beamless startled by ideas of chaos and catastrophe
There had been so many times like that   endured ridden out
It's what has to be done   a pressing on

For the Time Being

Polaroid

Hand to head
head to hands
we shield
as if to turn inside
away from this into a better
complex
hoping to look
find ourselves
healed restored forgiven.

Unlikely the world of
human systems – body, focus pursuit
will go away
more likely it will run faster
become worse, blur
you might miss the very thing
you're doing this for.

Too busy providing
to enjoy or understand
like taking photographs of memorable things
you miss the point, out of focus
lose your turn too eager to capture.

It's a risky moment

For Evelyn

When the light breaks over the marsh
the sheep huddle together
they know what to do.
There is sometimes a coldness in man
which is borne from the timid fear
about the plight of others.
But look, the air is forgiving and
reparation and hope tug at our sleeve
it will not leave us.
At night across the marsh
the darkness is only the light waiting for its moment,
the lambs suckle quietly without us.

Animals

The vet comes out to see my sick ram lamb that's penned up in the garage.

His long-boned fingers search into the lamb's skull, searching for a cyst or growth. Bending over the body of the sick sheep he places his stethoscope against the ribs and with eyes closed and head bent as if in prayer he stays silent for a full five minutes. What's the verdict? I ask. He tells me that the ram is suffering from a heart murmur but that isn't why he's ill. He opens the animal's mouth and presses the gum hard. The blood returns to the head quite quickly.

Eliminating worms or staggers he suggests it could be an infection of the brain and injects the animal with fluids. Later in my kitchen he talks about life in the surgery.

He says, the farmers round here don't like us younger vets you know, they don't trust anyone that's under 60. I'm no James Herriot and I can't win them round. I tell him that I'm sure he will eventually. I hope so, he says, because I do really love animals and I like to make the quality of their short lives better.

I ask if he is married. Oh no, he says, I'm no good with girls, too awkward really. I just wish we were like animals, none of this courtship performance, just nuzzling down together and having babies.

Wouldn't Mate Again

1.
She is worrying about the limescale in the sink
the area around the taps at the back
stained and dirty.
The bleach shifts it temporarily but then it's back
again in her arms
looking up at her grinning through.
It's like him
she worries about him
whether he's bought cotton socks
for his feet, if he's drinking too much,
whether he thinks of the boy.
The boy thinks of him
calls him dad
wants him home
cries for him in sleep and names the guinea-pig Nick.

2.
Once they went fishing together
enjoyed the day he talks of it continually.
Now and again he's in a mood
walks out like his daddy swaggers
raises his hands like him
but lacks the ability thankfully
says to her, "I'm going, I hate it here,
I want to find Nick," but he returns when she's
not looking for him, finds him curled in his bed
like a baby not like a man.

3.
Next day he didn't mention it, says he's too
busy when Nick calls to say hello.
Went off on his BMX.
Nick bought
Hula Hoops and Aeros that no one ate.
She looked at the sink
worried about the limescale
looked out of the window and hoped the guinea pigs
wouldn't mate again.

Matrimonial

She said:

He never makes decisions, it's always left to me. I ask him, he says, 'you decide'. So I do.

When it goes wrong he says, 'I told you I didn't want to do that, I said it wasn't the right time.'

But I tell him, you never said anything, not one thing.

When it goes right he says, 'I always did say that was a good idea, we should have seen to it before, if you'd listened to me we'd have been a lot better off.' But I say, you didn't say a word, never uttered a monosyllable, not one iota of sound came from your lips. He told me my cooking was grim so then he shops for himself at Iceland and cooks it in the garage.

He said:

She's so bossy, always on about something or another.

She gets upset. I say what's wrong? Always she says 'nothing'. I tell her there must be something but usually she walks away. Later she shouts at me that I don't care about her and why don't I talk to her like other husbands. She hates cooking for me and said to do it myself. I cut the meat up with my angle grinder sometimes.

The children say:

Mummy is always in a bad mood with a cross face. She says she's tired. We draw pictures for her and she always cries and cuddles us then. Daddy's busy outside or at work, he says someone's got to look lively around here.

Once we had a very bad Christmas and daddy pulled down all the decorations and mummy burnt the dinner. Our little brother cried so much I had to take him to our next door neighbour's and blow up a balloon for him. The neighbour gave me a sip of sherry and kissed me, it wasn't very nice but I didn't tell mum, she says she's got enough on her plate.

Mummy looks happier when daddy kisses her but daddy cried when he threw the decorations away. When they didn't love each other anymore daddy said it wasn't us he was leaving but he did. Daddy lived in his car. Mummy said the car didn't need conversation, just maintaining. At the contact centre we saw daddy once and then he asked us if mummy still wanted more than he could give her. I told him she didn't make hot dinners anymore only sandwiches. Daddy cried and so we didn't see him again.

Storm Damage

The clay fields
have sunk, drowned, gone under.
The trees are limbless
amputated struck senseless.

Nature has pruned us.
Brought home our poor circulation and
dull hearts.

Concealed in our differences
our common
identities fraternities
hungers and thirsts.

We hold our palms to the wind
vulnerable and small like children
beside the adults.

Before I go or the gap left after leaving

So, what is needed?
Equipment in preparation for moving away   a logic is needed
but,
in front of that, you need the knowledge of being loved,
known for who you are. *It's belonging* that sets the course.
A ticket and a reason to move away, to branch out or to go, to die *to*
leave and to meet strangers
so then it's a heady divide; driven, determined,
de decretar, interior, heart.

The loss within   collapse   chance *what does not change*
is the will to change
all options but   anchored, we are kept from our worst floun-
dering by correlation, link.
Being in mind.
The sea air is bracing
the pool charms and the plants greenery cuts with a smell   a sim-
ple device   sensory *When the coast was not the coast and sea was a*
shell.

So what to do before leaving
packing away, tiding the unkempt and unravelled.
Cleaning up the spilt

When you went there was so much left behind
I hold it

For Jenny Diski

I.
With the frozen hope that keeping still will do the trick of turning back time

An atlas of your entire arm moves across a clipped face of a baby.
Listen, it was a chancy moment.
On arrival, the cloud was encompassing anyway, spinning some fandango with an aloof mystic you could never get the measure of.
So why try now?
Cut while you can before they notice
your arms being stuck out like that
so needy and wasteful, the heart like a sieve down the drain.
Or is it?
Someone is catching you.
Leave the arms open but don't flail
it makes a mark.

II
I reckon, not to have to do it

All that letting so much   un wheeling   free middle a   free for all
free   muddle.
Permission not to cook.
Taking your own slot.
place divine, no end in sight. Another day a new start no alarm no
terror   need for drawn looks   survival is its own pasture lined
frock.
No catastrophe waiting its turn.
For once   for twice   for ever it is as it is.

III.

For which one side could only comprehend the necessity
The other turns away

You try and there is no answer to it
Better walk on
A strategy for remaining.
Cruelty splits our sides
Battering the memory of a mothers lot.

IV.

A perfectly understandable fidgetiness of creatures cooped up but without
any conceivable foreboding of harm

Hyper vigilant the cost is great   see how the arms flail
The looking out for   being found out
found wanting   perhaps
it's the same pricey pain
The others gawp but what do they know?
More,   *they know more than us* we shout it from the kerbside

V

No need now to go any place at all

Arrival, it is a pact with rest.
Located
Crisis is avoided   no takers
Catastrophe lays in the margin   we leave it be ready to stalk
Calamity rests in our shoulders   the heart heaves quite primed.

Songs for the Faithless

There is a moment in time when
looking at the sky and its emptiness
we wonder about those others
who shrivelled and let go of it before us
before we did
right in front of us
and we gawped
still asked for
succour and yet
we turned
away
prats in our suits
our underclothes stained wet
hidden
not knowing what to do
where to go.
Are they there? Can they see us?
We have hope that they oversee
mediate the worst
are they sorting things out
are we alone
so left
cut
the quick dries.

There is a moment in time when
watching children
we know that there is nothing to fear
nothing to worry for
since
some thing so
right
so designed means that nothing
can be
forever tainted despite our bitter lips so easily twisted
our mouths treacherous, recreant, turned again against
so easily led
noted and seen so weak untrustworthy.
We can sleep easy
surely we could?

There is a moment in time when
chance and luck of life
spots us reeling
opportunity splashing at our own heels so rarely
but we can harvest
we still gape at the even more luckless others
centuries of it
the wrong place
the thousands killed
not us
not yet
still lucky
a charm surely.
It's simply being sensible that does it, nothing more.
Spinning the dice of good health
those reckless nights and wasted days
count for little.

There is a moment in time when
we shout out
seeking that father
a sanction
an end to it.
It's not where you are but where you're headed
your blossomed heart
strung whippet heels
flash clear slow snow.

It's not when you were but when to let go.
The shepherd does not lose sheep
they weather away
dissolve
their tired bones suckle earth.

There is a moment in time when
the trees
the moment gives a licence we mount
spindle legs struggle but
that contact
provides no doubt
it's more than ideas which
sway
the light
waves and duck the dawn
swoon into ashen marble
where the faithless lie
bleeding their chips are sallow
they get fat, a creasing over.

There is a moment in time when
the earth spins ahead
seeing the coast out there rolling ahead of the marsh
the field and the dew
all to play for despite the narrowing time set into frame
pressing on our new boots.
Out there
fox hunts in the shadows
swift his velvet mouth.

Songs for the Careless

Facts must be your friends, I said

Being upright was important
staying in the middle was hardest.
They watched for mistakes
The others seem to know the tune, dancing properly to it as they do.
She cannot get the steps right
better instead to
leave nothing to chance
sit down don't let them see you humming the tune.
The clouds understand everything;
moving in as they do at the wrong moment changing things so quickly.

To see the future so drearily laid out like an allotment garden, with each to his patch of work.

The clay soil is the most unforgiving, it holds such wetness, there is no air.
His furrow was hardest, he trudged every boundary of her, she let nothing
in or out. Once he gave up, but then she had left a small part of herself
behind which he brought out now and then. He turned it over and over
in his palm, the song remained settled into his heart, he did not regret it.
The bulbs are drying out lying quietly expectant, loaded, affluent.
I will take my ways and till them like soil,
raked over they will become changed, forgotten.
Friable soil is best.
In damp conditions the seeds germinate well, send their roots down like
lightning.
Life was easy for them, effortless, there was no hardship to be set against.
A pushover. She depended, leaned and inclined to his leafy torso
but she was an add-on   an extra
an adjunct some things you just knew
she said.

Rats and rabbits die of indecision

The awkwardness of the confident; they are too sure.
Persuaded, explicit they can only dream of bullets.
For them there are no dangers
perils
are for others
there is no risk involved nothing to look out for, avoid, all is welcome.
The careful won't talk, their silence watchful, shrewd
they seek help
gasp too late
already out of earshot.

Go about your business. The spur of necessity will keep you trotting about.

There's no rest, there really is no letting up the sky will swallow you.
What we learn from this then
it's what counts.
Matters.
Is remembered as the day closes down.
Notion, intention
wit
tolerance
all of that
his sleeves hurt
pervasive
the deficient heaviness bruising the snake against his heart.

Leave the washing up and take a look around

Blow the report
they urged her.
She hadn't.
Was it worth it?
She wouldn't know now
is it right to be always that responsible.
What had been lost
could she catch up with the dancing others
where picnics lasted
and time was not measured.
Washing up
onus
responsibility
earning a wage
being there.
These
things
drove her
reckless
wasted
welcomed.
The careless sing and bump into others
the watchful are still waiting, tireless.

Another night lies squandered

He saw her
watched and noticed and spoke of it
sought asked and spoke of it
lay with her and spoke of it

There is blood-flecked urge to go even a step further

Risk is for the secure
the non-compliant
who lean on the uncertainty of others
trading their good looks for
science
others can do the maths she said I do the business.
Along the sea line tide sucks
sucks bringing back returning clean
all laughter coughed up.

Slapdash he is thrown among the muddle. While harassed apprentices jostle the bloody pans.

Haphazard and dissociated the walls have sunk.
Nothing is where it was placed.
Others knew and have gone.
The sky is stripped and the dull trees stand
knowing nothing this time
no birds   blunted the victim of intensity is strewn along the
hedgerow.
The battered slices of self are fried   set apart   moved on
spat.

Is it possible to be a bit braver? Is it possible to skirt round the knowledge of your own ignorance, your half-lit fear of what might be at stake?

At night his courage wet the sheets, he struggled in dream and when wakeful worries rent his mind from his brain he thought about what might be different.
Still the edges became sharper
There was no give   no kindness no knitted warmth no thing to lean upon   no slack.
Risk is a loser's job   there's no certainty in giving bits of yourself away.
People sick up what they don't need.

She slept with sailors and cried when she scrubbed the floor

Knowing what's missing is half the problem she said. If you don't know it's easier,
When he forgot her birthday she swallowed and made a pact with the birds. "You won't see me cry again," she told them. They didn't but saplings were washed away by her sorrow.
The ankle bones of her lovers were as the shells of bantam eggs; their kisses both imagined and lost.
Out there in the sky the birds have the entire world.
Under the planes and across the treetops
there is no such thing as small moments of kindness the enormity spans.

Strut in your scarlet coat. Put perfume behind your ear. Move across the crowded floors of the places where people met, into restaurants, with earnest look, to discuss the mathematics of the spirit, moistened with sweet white wine.

Snowdrops huddle worried to death by
frost and silence.
A man spits in the street its incendiary device
smears the tender lips
of the open.
In the woodland the bark nudges the grass alive

The price of comfort is death and damnation

Effortless and unstudied
they are rash by the waters edge
danger has lapped against their bleary wings
shrugged away discarded.
Being loved never leaves you, like the moon remaining.
The yearning after death affords no quiet repose or rest
which can be forgotten or tied away.

Songs for the Harmless

The danger is that our action maybe driven, not just by thought, but by powerful subconscious indecisions.

Was he her lightship, his albatross, a saviour or a drain.
Was he a star to steer by or a mirage, a bud or a weed.
His fathers words in his head,
she never wanted you from the start, wanted your seed thrown out
of her, she's rubbish, crap, shite, deal with it boy.
In the street a mother is pushing her toddler who is holding a bottle
to her face, the mother is talking at a friend, the child sobs throws
the bottle to the ground.
Mayhem, chaos, chipped teeth, rape and rage, rape and rage,
buggery and stench. Salt and wound, wound and vinegar.
His mother's words and her chipped face in his head, he controlled
me, I was 15 years old, same as you now.
The muddle consumes everything
the sheets, the toys, the indecision.

His life and his death is among me all the time, it's in everything
I do and who I am

Across the playing fields the swings and slide hold time.
Sunken
areas where the children have passed by spent time landed on
            the swings
scuffing their feet, back and forth, back and forth. The same
            action wearing away
sunken.
Now they're adult
mature
don't come here anymore, lay low
only shoot a glance across the play area
now and again
he holds her up against the wall just there
skirt above her pants
he's an adult
trying it on.

Knives are out.
It's tricky.

A dread that without his mothers eye on him, he too, would blur and break up into pieces.

It was behind him
alright
the noise
someone creeping up
shouldn't do that to me
not from behind me
not a man.
Vomit in his face
the blade dissolved slid easily no effort
slid O so soft like a child's bottom along a bedroom floor.
The blade slipped into him without sound not like before
not like he remembered it
the gagging
the pain until he'd finished with him
leaving him there like rubbish.

Waving from the deck, your perspective is changed

As he runs he can see her face change
when she knows it's him and
not his brother.
Running now the blood is in his shoes again like before
but it's not his blood today.
In the park the swings are frozen the metal chains catch at his hair.

The Meaning of Things

Dedicated to my parents,
Daphne Pauline Randell
12.2.1927–20.9.2005

Henry William Randell
8.5.1919–12.2.1979

I

Day's work

Face yes

Turning to me he says
that Father Christmas had not known what they had wanted
so he hadn't come that day but still
it had been the best day of his life.
The boy looks at me for a long time studying me;
he says he knows why I have come today.
"It's about the baby;
he's cute" he says.
The boy's long white thin arms are like glass
His face his face his face is totally opened to me.
Is the baby dead now, he asks.
I tell him so.

On the street yes

The dark bodies muddle across the road
The men move together laughing in doorways watching the girls
their legs studded with mud
they walk as if
there is some uncertainty ahead.
The men start calling out, *Hello slutty,* at the girls
who turn
raising ringed hands to their beehives.
Giggling they shout back at the men,
Hello tiny dicks.
There is a scuffle and one of the girls is now on the ground
with a man above her;
the friends are squealing and laughing.
The dark bodies are tangled against the sodium lights.
One boy walks away across his back his tee shirt says
Screw Perfection.

Day Centre

In the damp condemned Methodist church hall
I visit Susan.
Her varicose legs in bobby socks
fold under the broken chair
as we speak of her children
now 6 and 9 she has not seen for
two years.
Susan's
16-year-old boyfriend cuddles her
calls her Mum.
Above us on the wall there is Jesus
in a faded print
"suffer the little children".
We wait outside together
passing the font, the hymn books are
under dust sheets. The nurse calls them
back for their 'medication' time.
Susan grabs my arm,
"You will tell them won't you
that I'm marrying Pete." She
nuzzles his neck.
"Only I want the boys to
make me a card."

Air

I was there

Just by it

When it happened. He said to look away and he shouted but I didn't. It sort of compels you doesn't it when someone says don't look. I wasn't the same after that.

It probably took only seconds and I could hear mum's voice in my head that tea was on the table. Odd isn't it, the things that go through your mind. I remember the edge of his trouser leg that's all I could see. The noise reminded me of air going out of balloon like the day when Sonia had the party and dad couldn't tie the ends up and she laughed a lot. Only she didn't laugh when it happened. She was still, very still and dead quiet. Dead dead quiet and very still. I shan't forget how still she was. Years later I've thought of that.

When the police asked me what I saw I told about his trouser leg and me being on the top bunk all the time and him knowing that.

Hard to Place

'Hard to Place' was written while working for 'Children need Families', a project of the Children's Society which places children with special needs into adoptive families.

I

His mother, a petrol pump attendant, was said
by those who knew her to be far less than bright.
She had not wanted the child but had wanted his
father. She grew very fat with the pregnancy
but told no one of the forthcoming child inside
her. On the forecourt of the garage she went
into labour while delivering three gallons of
four star. They stifled screams with the
rag that wiped the dip stick and mopped her waters
with the sponge that cleaned the windscreens.

Now eight years later he's a tiny child and the
doctors write notes about his tiny head
circumference and his stammer. He has moved foster homes
eight times in the last three years. He is a
difficult boy. The woman from the children's home writes
on his review form that he's a nice enough child
but that he often uses situations to his own
advantage. His gait is odd, she comments, and
he frequently limps to attract the attention of
adults.

II

It must have been an odd thing from the start.
The way they had met, the differing backgrounds
from where they both came. He was from a strong
Jewish family, his father had been murdered by the
Nazis, his mother was said to be beautiful but no

one could recollect what became of her. It is
known that he was proud of his Jewish heritage and
that he played the violin. He was nineteen years old
when he met the girl who later became his wife.
She was a farmer's daughter who developed an addiction
to heroin; later she became a prostitute. There is
a photograph of her on the file wearing a tiny black mini
skirt and holding one of her sons in her arms; her face is
tear stained. A few days later she
killed herself.

The two sons have no living memory of her, they have,
throughout their lives met their father on three
occasions but the interviews were brief and his
whereabouts are unknown.

The boys don't form relationships very easily and
they tend to test adults out to see how far they
will go before they snap. They rarely smile and
say they want to live in a family where someone can
teach them to play the violin.

III
After her brother had been killed by swallowing
bleach she came into care. Her mother had
asked that she be taken away before she harmed
her. The last she saw of her mother was never
to be forgotten, she has no recollection of her
father at all but it is believed he works on a
fairground. She frequently has terrible nightmares
that wake the whole home. The staff say she
encourages the boys to come into her room. She has
absconded on two occasions when the Fair has been
in town.

Her mother is now in prison and she had written
to her but received no reply.

The staff at the home would like her to live
in a family to be taught some discipline since
everyone believes she is promiscuous and could
be in moral danger. She is nine years old and
calls her dolly 'Mummy'.

IV
It is noted that at the age of four years
he possesses a very full and foul vocabulary.
His toenails were broken and bleeding caused
by his walking with his toes curled under. He
is a very anxious and tense little boy. It
is rare for him to show affection but he is
keen to please. His birth occurred an
hour after his father had kicked his mother
and subsequently he was three months premature.
She is now an agoraphobic, quiet, sullen with
bleached hair; she has the appearance of a
clown. It would seem that she cannot read and
did not attend school from the age of twelve.
The boy's father has toes missing from his left
foot due to an accident at work; he has a sister
who is blind. He was a baker who became a miner.
It is fair to say that neither parent wishes
to have care of the child but both will fight
through the courts.

His foster parents say that he is most unsettled
and appears to be worried. He has pulled out
handfuls of his hair but he is an attractive
boy who will respond to constancy.

V
The first meeting the couple had with the child
they hoped they would learn to love was brief
and during their stay they were told how wearing
he could be and how he pestered for new activities
every few minutes. At this meeting he kissed and
cuddled them both and as they said goodbye he
refused to watch their car draw away.

At the second meeting they took him out alone to
a café and he told the waitress that she was
beautiful. They took him to the seaside and he
jumped into the ocean fully clothed.

When they took him home for a weekend he sat up
all night and picked the stuffing from his mattress.
The next day he was taken to the Dreamland amusement arcade
and rode on the dodgems; he ate ten Bounty bars and
was not sick. Later in the afternoon he pulled the
chandelier from the ceiling and threw the standard
lamp across the room, he kicked all the chairs and
dented the washing machine. He told the couple
that he loved them and could not face life alone in
a children's home. Their efforts to control him
failed, their efforts to love him collapsed.
At the next visit they told him he was
too much for them. They were distressed and disappointed.
"Who will take me to Dreamland now?" he said just
before he was driven away.

VI
"Sometimes he holds on to me so tightly at
night I fear his heart will burst."
The infant is three years old and suffers
from Down's Syndrome. He is a strong happy

boy whose eyes can barely focus. He is
partially sighted.

At the hospital after the delivery was over
his mother was heard to continually shout
"Don't let me take that monster home, don't
make me, don't make me." His cries were
quickly stifled from the other mothers but
they knew. His father, a large stocky
friendly man, an ironmonger's assistant, wanted
to keep the infant but later conceded to
his wife's rejection.

"Sometimes I feel the harder he holds on
to me it means the stronger he loves. No,
I rarely think about his natural parents,
only once perhaps when he was dangerously
ill and they thought his little heart would
give out—then I thought, "They don't know
about all this and the fight that's in him.
We are delighted to have adopted him, he's
our own angel."

VII
Late one January night when the whole house
was sleeping the young mother put her careful
plans into action and slipped away from her
family and its life. The three tiny children
remained asleep until 7.00 a.m. and their father
until 9.00 a.m. It has long been agreed that the
woman has returned to Ireland and all efforts
to trace her through the newspapers, police and
Salvation Army have now been terminated.

When the children realised their mother had gone
they tried to ring her on their toy telephones
and sent her letters through the Mr Men post office.
They cried themselves to sleep most nights and
became greedy for food constantly.

When their father realised his wife had gone he
spent the family allowance at the bookies and
told the welfare that something would have to
be done. He signed them into care and jumped
beneath the Northern Line train on the way home.
It is true to say that the children, who are
6, 4 and 2 years, are a handful and tend to be
clingy. Only last week the eldest boy was found
asking a policeman to please find his mummy.

VIII
Weighing only three pounds at birth there was
much concern expressed by all who knew the
circumstances. Both the child's parents had learning
difficulties and the mother had not known of her
pregnancy until the morning she woke earlier
than usual feeling rather wet between the legs
and pains in her stomach.
She was delighted to discover herself to be a mother
and those who knew her endeavoured to
help her as much as was possible. She was unaware
that babies defecated and was once found pushing
tissues into the child's mouth to stop him
vomiting.

At the court hearing to secure the infant's safety
the parents agreed they could not care for their
offspring and preferred their childless life which
was mainly nocturnal. After dark they cycled

miles together searching amongst tips for clothing and other things
that interested them.

The child has always been of a slight build and he
finds feeding difficult. He has been asking about
his parents and if he could meet them soon.

IX
It has all been rather too much one way and
another. The fact that her boyfriend had
been taken away in a police car that morning,
her phone being cut off, the flat reeked of shit and damp
then the child was fretful.

She collected together her purse, pushchair
and raincoat and set off for the shopping
precinct. Once inside she felt better but
the child moaned for sweets and the piped
music mixed with the lights and her lack of
food made her dizzy. Sitting down
next to an elderly couple who were rearranging
their shopping, she inquired whether they
would keep an eye on the child while she
found a toilet. Two hours later the couple
continued with their attempt to extract information
from the wailing child. Eventually the precinct
security guard took the child away and a police
woman was called. The sobbing of the infant
drowned even the piped music.

Now, four years later, the little girl has a new
family who worry about her insecurity and dreadful
fear of open spaces.

X

"All I know about me Dad is that he
murdered my little sister when she
was eighteen months old and I was five.
I know that he was from Glasgow and only
had one eye. My Mum came to see me just
after I came into the home but she was
very ill and they took her to a hospital
for diffy people where she still is.
I think being in the home with all the
other children was better than being
with my parents. I miss my little sister
though. I hope if you do find me a home
it won't be with diffy people, I've had
enough of them." She laughs and shakes her
head of yellow and green streaked hair.
At thirteen years she possesses the
body of a woman and the warmth and humour
of a friend. "I don't remember much about
him doing her in really, only that one
moment she was laughing because she'd
pulled his newspaper to bits and the next
she wasn't."

Punch Your Lights Out

Across the tarmac
sick and torn up
adverts from Pinocchio Pizzas flap in the roadway.
Running heart attack   Racing stroke   Retching tumour
He didn't mean to watch
she didn't see him staring
did she
might she
did her eye turned in like that make it
possible?
Vomit on his shoe
"I'll punch your lights out" he heard that.

In class they told him
"concentrate, concentrate for God's sake for one minute will you."

We're lucky really

She said
The large child freed himself from her lap forcing himself on
                                                    to the floor
It could be worse
I've seen them
She said
The boy's head lolled from side to side as he lifted himself up.
"Bastards, you're all bastards" he screamed
into her face lifting his heavy arm towards her shoulder.
Slowly she stroked his head
wiped the wetness from his face
handed him a Cheesy Wotsit.
Some boys can't even speak
she said.
We're lucky like that.

II

Poems insist

to be written.

*Those kinds of poem which take place between people are ones I'm
particularly drawn to.
Silences are places where poetry starts and stops, where taboo subjects
wait to be touched on. If there's something that isn't able to be said,
poetry might try to make it sayable, or find a way of pointing to what
remains to be intuited.*

Hard to say this   but
I feel you're on the edge of something.
A skylark bursts out from the field
swoops low, then, halfway up drops down.
Black reeds, Glyceria maxima line the dank dyke but
lit with sun and light wind they perform dark green sweet-grass song
and dance. St Rumwold's church leans over, heard it before. The steady
shoulders of the chalk Lymne hill, "*that chalk cliff in whose rift we lie.*"
Topped with its clean hair style of trees, their grade four point cut.
I remember being like you as this age.
What can I tell you that you would hear?
Don't waste this time I might say, buck up.

*Peter Robinson, *Through Frosted Glass: An Interview with Peter Robinson* by
Ian Sansom, *Talk About Poetry* (Shearsman Books, 2006).

Against the Air

The bright edge of the woodpecker steals
Across the gaunt
Limb of sky
    We are already gripped as she
    Steadies
    Leans and steers into the mossed
    Centre of what is contained, known.

A dark feathering in the undergrowth of woodland
Our tired burdens draw us
We tread without thought
    Driven by the flustered hope
    Again we are still unprepared
    And yet not asleep
    Or rested, even now.

The Northern stars are seen in the South too
Our poems are but small messages of quiet silence
Plain, empty, the air is against us as we try to make sense
    Evidenced by love of
    One to another
    The bridge edge of the woodpecker.

November 1999

Advise Yourself

At the clouds of starlings
a sudden bequest as
the round, broad, elongated, flock shifts
funnelling and then thickening, thinning, spiralling, banking on the
edge, veering into and against the wind across the marsh they fly
united.

Advise yourself
about the loyalty of birds how the starlings turn the sky black with
their closeness
wheeling, turning, sinking, downward
young wings mix with the old.
This swooning aerial dance
as they locate a communal night-time shelter
reed beds and cliffs find them safety, warmth and confidence
peregrine falcons
struggle to target in the
hypnotising flocks.

Advise yourself as
starling flocks poised to tip
instantly and completely transformed, like metals magnetised or liq-
uid turning to gas. Each starling in a flock is connected to the other.
A starling turns when its neighbour turns operating in proteins and
neurons hinting at universal principles as yet to be understood.

Advise yourself
quickly for there is safety in numbers.
The bees cluster and suck
driven by success and protection

glorious honey sold on roadsides by children
whose clear blue eyes scald into their devout weathered features.

Advise yourself
for there is only so much to see
by glimpsing
as we dash from our own shadow's.
Rest from competition as the sparks of the night bend from our taut
    bodies.

Field

Bursting flight instant
out of
bushy cover
rattled calling
the pheasant gives his warning
into air
skimming
veering into
wet ditches but for sudden quiet
forestalling
a new
intrusion
into shrubby wetlands.

An Old Person Says Goodbye

There is now a glazed artificiality about her
Sickness is the loneliest place on earth she says
The fear is there's no telling when it might strike
No insurance policy to guard against it
No special diet to be certain

up above
the shooting star
a gift a sudden thought flashes across
it's over
gone but
It's been good, nothing to regret she says

The cow turns   to her calf
Moans for its survival
its safety
That's all

Bulletins from Corrèze—1989

At the circus in Excideuil the woman who sold us our ticket was also
the woman who balanced a wooden post on her gold slippered
foot; she later put the snakes around her neck while holding
their heads away from her face; she didn't smile.
After, when the Ringmaster, wearing a brown everyday suit and
Monoprix brown plastic casual shoes and carrying a whip, said,
"Le spectacle est terminé," the woman began packing her gold
slipper into a tiny space on the trailer next to her tumble drier
and the snake basket.

Phoebe has learnt to skip; she asks me to watch her.
I marvel at her beauty.
She picks cowslips and dandelions and dock leaves and sings, sings
"Mr Bluebird's on my back".

My Janet Reger top is a disappointment. Its brief life has fallen short
of the advertiser's claims. The £17 has been wasted. Firstly it
fell out of my suitcase and caught in the boot of the car before
departure, leaving heavy oil stains from the boot lock. "It fell
out," he said, "I didn't see it." I washed it when we got to France;
it caught in the washing machine door and was torn so now it
has oil stains and a tear.

At Chourgnac-d'Ans
We walked in silence while the girls collected cowslips, competing for
the longest. The dogs barked at us making sure we'd gone out of
sight before stopping, pleased to see a stranger to finally see off.

Beatrice eats goat's cheese from the packet; she leans on her sister.
"You're making my germs sore," said Naomi, "get off, I want to sleep."
We watch her two-year-old frame struggle and kick.
Later she says,
"I feel better now, sit down," and we see her watch us from the corner
of her eyes.

Commune Rurale—Saint-Agnan, France, July 1991

for Beatrice

In the stone church we go to the corner, we light a candle
"for a soul", I tell you.
You are six years old and remark on the light from the glass as it falls
        onto the wooden statue as it holds an infant Christ
An old woman bathes her head in the holy water.
We turn and head towards the door.
There is light across an effortless sky
Blue
Pink
We hold its
long shadows
In moments we chance to love
you dance.

Courage Was Cast About Her Like a Dress

Whose form we lean upon
This oiled hope is loosened between our eyes
A man waved, raised his hand
Was that all?
On the parapet at Château Puyguilhem red orange ochre fields
A man leans, pauses
Spends time by the gate with a friend
Was that all?

Easter 2014, Romney Marsh

On such a day the skylark
heard above the tractor before seen
up that high.
Who could not be charged
by his ecstatic salute to life
upwards and yet further up he shows how to sing while flying
while
plummeting
vertically effortlessly hovering before parachuting back.
On such a day you had also heard this
known perhaps that despite their aerial activities,
skylarks nest on the ground not in trees which may catch the wind.

For Barry at 68 — July 18th 2014

Arriving that first day, face forward
occipital posterior as they say,
meeting head on   the gall
grit   while
others were having their say. Plenty of it seems. Swallowed it whole and
as a child
         like a man
but you a child
took it on the chin
into your heart lipped with fear.
Marred
Spleen smudged with angered borrowed scenarios,
Shelley moulded your wrists into poems.
Cradled in visions of hate and care,
And each one who waked as his brother slept,
Sweet songs that spoke with ruptured frenulum
shock tactics which became real
Commotion   ordeal   thrill and gladness
It shook you up
as a child,
proper bruised you
making that cankered
tender wound, harden
getting even
as a child   assaulted
scar tissues that wreaked upon others, left you
draped over a sick bowl.
Meantime
buried distress in red boots
The days are bright and filled with pain
Enclose me in your gentle rain
clenched by Tyneside steel air.

In Allendale our forearms drenched your entire step in my
floured hands.

Still, I see you worrying the stars like a terrier,
the May mornings lost beneath the cowslips' shadow
carry you high these days.

Forest Poems

Stirring

Then there is the frog with his single
Thin note
Defending his territories
Until the crickets chime into the middle of things
Leading the cockerels with dogs in their unison towards the
                                        call to prayer
Calling
The bright wanton light wakes
Swabbing the soil.

Wedding

First there is the drumming, a gun shot and then the sound
                                of the Zurna is close
Statice
Car horns
There is trust in planting anything, troughs, trees and promises
tortoise glide effortlessly into bright thickets.

Cairns

A marker on the track side
Bee man at work, stream nearby, burial place, water, a warning
something to be recalled, not lost, reclaimed later.
Waymark, trail blazer
No simple stone piled on to another but deliberate passed on,
cautionary.
The cut branch, hatched tree, an old net, each bulletin
that others went before.

In Time

For Naomi 9 August 2008

The sky drives us forward
as the edge of sun tilts us headlong
across the scented bay, pine forest air.
Crossing, our paths, take off as the sun climbs
hearts chasing   ants scupper
tortoises lay   stone still
bees cluster   frantic driven
in tune
as ideas are forged
our feet pound the ground
we move at the very edge of things
in time.
The earth urges us headlong
as the moon watches out for our
sleeping frames.

On the Birth of Ada

Seagulls swoon
wheel into the light
as your head crowns into a first morning
The castle on its volcanic seat glimpses
the fine pink edges of you as the first summer morning
flower blinks into the fresh open
beauty of your face
lit
with love for there is
such abundant sky

Parents

I smell the lilacs for you
Because you couldn't
And as I did
your voice
was
just a thrush
lighting up into spring
a new blue
a glimpse and then gone
like you
just gone
like that
and yet often here
within the white
within the purple here
here with me
just
knowing and being among the
intention of you

Peeling Quail's Eggs: At 60

These tiny gifts: stolen clutches
prying hidden
fingers age and swell
shells crack   fracture
under pressure.
My own steel grey hair now
a nest of neither wise nor foolish.
The quail's eggs with their slightest, hearts of finesse, wait their turn.
Three children now grown; I watch them.
"Therefore a hen, even when she has left her eggs, always has the
          attitude of listening with a bent ear."
When we become older
Hesitancy drags around our ears
Caution flaps and scars intent
Doubt drums on our shoes
and
yet even though we know more than the nonchalant youth
we find it
tricky to show what we already know
unable to
toss caution to the breeze and benefit bravado as easily.
The quails know something new
make the most of it and give up their eggs for pleasure

Suppose the Unpredictable Wave Was God

We have been hoist by our own petard
that caught us out after all.
Was that just our own fear upon which so much is based,
especially love?

To feel safe the falcon faces the wind
On the whole our backs are turned.

Catkin powder
dense, cylindrical, often drooping this cluster of unisexual apetalous
          flowers
willows, birches, and oaks
they stain her dress.
O brighter star with keen eye
the day so much wants to see itself in you.

The body is still the measure of all things

and we are caught between bright mornings and heavy soil.
The vulnerable change us
we steal their goodness which stunts,
our vitriol clashes against poisoned need.
Our separate torched wisdom shrivels before the defenceless
                    and exposed.
The unprotected are not weak and their strengths lifts our hearts.
We hang back ashamed by our inadequate limbs
and abandoned best.

The Flower Has Spent its Energy and Has Gone to Seed

Beans

Like skin of
old long dead persons
burnt bodies
scorched frames
those too tired to live any longer.
The hard nut brown content implies secure
assured
A universe in hand a
believable steady prospect.

Poppies

Random
impatient
to be gone
to spread
a colour
impetuously
never missing a chance to lend few kind colours
sudden and disinhibited enmeshed and ready.

Tomatoes

Hidden the yellow specks slip
break out when left alone
leaving their withdrawn secret
fruit to the end.

Candytuft

Humorous winged and ready for dispersal
their shuttlecock faces
turn to the light
letting go emblazoned
cavalier.

Nicotiana

Understated, the miniscule
modest dance of almost spores
Shaken but firm in the idea and inkling of chance and opportunity
of future five pointed florets
the seeds leave suddenly
startling the ground.

Aquilegia

Percussive and persuasive with swaying bucket shapes they tip
conclusive and driven
their ambition rides
on helter skelter arbitrary cloudless skies.

Cabbage

Round and plenty
A promise of more they slip between and under
Leaving us in no doubt of their intent.

Lettuce

Eye like they blink and wide awake
Their suddenness shakes us revealing a
Frowning knotted self which folds open hearted upwards.

Nasturtium

Resolute gritted soul with fleshy promise
Seducer your wrinkled nose
rolls readily steadfast with
its thickset ample voice.

Pumpkin

Confident its opportunity remains buoyant
Potential rattles its parched
desiccated home
insulated by bulky prospects.

And Therefore Was Her Labour
That Much More in Washing and Wringing

To worry
is to be connected with
The woman's lot is to worry
to be troubled with   concerned, mixed up
Loaded windless the sky takes fear, returns it laundered ready.
Waiting for fortune to happen upon them
the men take chances wonder at the reeling birds diesel streets.
We are not simply *done for*
there is more to understand. The women are gathered, *"not in*
　　　　extravagant postures but huddled weeping, their eyes
　　　　reddened and dashed with tears."
The white daisies spring up in anticipation
they are known.
Women hem garments their hands sick with action
faces wrenched with ideas and sleepless O they are sleepless
footless, heartless hurt.
Women sweat at night
finished with swooning they know what to fear and what
　　　　　　　　　　　　cannot be avoided.
Wrecked on reality some stumble on stones, heave the giant
　　　　　gems and play, toying with the needy boys.
Where are the men standing?
are they alone or in unison rowdy with lofty fear and rage?
Some become tearful expectant
stagger at a loss, tearful,
trounced others swagger on the bridge wide open and forgotten.

The Light That Is

for Phoebe

Sometimes the light is so
it reaches to the bottom of the sea.
This is a sign.
hope and what we might yet get to know.
He had ruined part of this, his whole life, by worrying.
Should they have fallen
one by one like dead trees heaped up
it would stifle or smother
possibilities, a child even.

There is a fleeting second
when you
see your children no longer being yours but another's.
Lit by prospect
they dance
as you stand by
spare and quite blinded
with their awful radiance.

The Meaning of Things

1

By the canal
Down feathers wait to be used
to line nests
or lay just lay.
The simplest of all feathers
the down touches
the heart, the whiteness the most tender
natal covering.

The sheep
eye up watching then resume grass while
hooves press Marsh down-edged dykes.

Nestlings develop their down layer within hours of hatching
body down lies under the contour feathers, the very edge
of who they are, what dependence we see.

Yolk yellow
the gorse is tucked into the armpit of the hill below the
languid cattle   necks stretched towards.

2

Look how the trees are thrust up against the window
like young girls taken against their will
bruised, their lips shake against a swollen tongue, they are
                    not to be the same again.
A sense of wool between the teeth
The stone pine, *Pinus pinea*,
O so we see you Umbrella Pine gawping across the city as
hopeful tourists gobble buildings as their own.
No wonder poor Keats died in the middle of the Spanish Steps with
the cold in his bones and thoroughly disappointed like that what with
the others barging past not seeing the binds of his chest or the caution
of his heart. Ignoring his worries that he
"*may never live to trace
their shadows, with the magic hand of chance.*"

3

The Meaning of Things
Slips through our fingers
In winter the trees pledge a future
The clustered flower buds of
wild cherry bluntly pointed
Rowan grey with a hint of purple with dense white hairs
Elder spiked and arranged in pairs
Beech long thin spindled solitary.

The meaning of things
barely glimpsed
The birds in winter hunker down
save energy although many still sing.

4

The Meaning of
Things
a blessing in
disguise an effective
camouflage
of optimism rains on
our new shoes.
The sheep follow
watchful for a smart change in direction.

A blessing in disguise
no masquerade for this erect evergreen with its leafy stems.
Shy bowl-shaped flowers are borne in loose clusters here now
                    in the ice packed soil
where I summon your steadying hand on my back, there at all
                    times. Helleborus niger
St Agnes Rose Christ's herb
spread perhaps the final supper stamens silk against worn
lips.

A blessing in disguise

A sense of wool between the
teeth.
Over time, the disgust is unfastened from its original fettered
horror. So, to the forest at night. Frog cricket dog cockerel of
which we are part our sleep noise joining
before the light hits the tree.

5.

The Meaning of Things
wrapped into Evensong
could it change something inside a person
an idea of
being borne aloft before the heart stops. Dead.
Mandolin wind
perhaps only the striking limbs of the fallen girl Pearl
is all that speaks
tongue tied as she was
trees line the path   their rotted
roots letting go behind the scenes.
Those who have left us here press their seal;   it's where
we are
"and above this vast open countryside rose a hot sun that
soon thrust the mist back into the ground".

6.

The meaning of things can be

The emergence of something like personality comes from the falls and
tantrums and the striving.

But don't forget the wave of chance.
A light drizzle of sun
lighting.
Buzzards circle
and their mewing across the field stays all day.
Their preoccupation with food shapes the field
small birds steer clear   rabbits flit   pheasants rattle off into
blackberry hedgerow.

We can only be loved by anyone as far as we are willing to
have our own hearts broken.

What Would This Day Want from Us

what with the heady
stretches of the south downs beyond the field
its flawless stippled prospect.
The heart's movement towards a chance that it might stop
a reminder to see the bolt blue iris
backed by Conker red beech hedge. All things in time
all things in time he said.

What would this day want from us
while silted fields lean into the canal
as Romney sheep clutter the ridge. Their whiteness herring-
                         boned loose across sky largesse
as white Egrets pepper the field
their snowy whiteness plumed stark
touches the lime green field.

For LH at Brighton Station

Both eyes closed
we hold that

just a
flash
of you walking towards the beach away from us. *The blur of
sky this white grey morning*
it quickens the spirit
and maybe only you knew the inevitability.
But it brings us here
now together as
poets
holding
holding
ourselves fast against the inevitability.

Harry's red shirt and bright eye slips into the crowd
touches his hat in greeting
I tip my umbrella
we find different trains, joint purpose.

20th August 2015

From the Window

These are the days he had called his life
some were harder than others   he dragged his feet
spanning a gulf between what others seemed to enjoy, available
on offer, a special chance each week leaving him less to play
                                                with but more
short bursts of envy and regret
outside the tips of trees opened outward and up
nothing should ever be feared again
this he knew.
Honesty and renewal
this is the life he had called his days
he was having his turn
even love usually rests on dread
this he knew.

After Dusk

Time after time someone slips away.
Just leaving the table and are gone.
No word
there was no plan that they would do this, vanish and not return,
        become extinct.
Too often we lose those we love
and those who we did not love enough
How easily the body lets go of itself, glad of the sleep.
The meal left unfinished
for the others to tidy away.
Instead we set a new place, round off the edges, make it fitting.

November, the earth is cold and sodden, the trees push through soil,
its long slow hard shadows, brave leaves, some gone, still a few bright
golden somehow hanging on.
It no longer matters that the chair is in the sunshine or that the long
shadows fall across the grass too early.
There was too much to do before sunset and somehow the last beam
went unnoticed.

To Be Loved Is to Be Noticed

Seasons creep into our features.
We grow accustomed to hiding
slipping as we do over the long autumn wand
held by the eucalyptus with its red tender red blood veins.
We remark on its likeness to the wrists of children.
Spilt onto the world from our mothers' hearts,
the first taste of longing begins.

To Love Is to Notice

Plants are sociable it's known,
their acoustic signals generate
from cell to cell
allowing rapid
communication, chatting between nearby plants.
Did you hear them?
We skirt their long gowns they gossip between themselves
spilling their seeds secretly behind their hands.

Note Love

Presumably, many birds die in flight   their bodies drop
from the sky.
Still the magpies prolong their fight over the Liquidambar tree
marking it as their territory.
late November and the sky is folding
collapsing into rapid dusk.
Are the dead birds
devoured or
buried or
perish rotting
decaying
rapidly before we wake.

To Notice Is to Love

How the sun runs into the room
when children are born they guide their parents towards hope
as she passed by
the faintest smell of mimosa mixed with cedar
it quite caught his arm.

Try to See This Then

The darkness is only the light waiting
the lambs suckle unaided
bent heads of flowers
open in time
without comfort.

Try to see this then
what is remembered as the day closes down
acts of warmth
joining.

Try to see this then
at night across forest
the cockerels call out
sound leaping on the backs of the dog howling across the tracks
bees suckle, their anger bleeds into mistakes
swallows swooping lower leave too soon
the tortoises glide effortlessly into bright thickets.

News—One
Gulf Crisis

18.08.90

The Foreign Secretary's tie
is slightly askew.
Sir Douglas Hurd tells us
"the military situation is prepared and ready.
I am investigating all avenues."
In Baghdad Sandy Gall looks old,
looks ill with hair too short,
tells us that people are fleeing with their
roof racks bulging, looking for homes.
King Hussein raises his papers in the air
the people praying in the mosques kick
off their plastic shoes, kneel down on
rope mats.
The American soldiers salute the USA and
hold up pictures of Uncles Ben's rice and
Big Macs. Their tanned bodies lean against
the metal tanks.
President Bush rocks comfortlessly side to side
in his golfing buggy – tells us about sanctions
and strategies. He mutters
and waves reassuringly.
The plastic shoes in the temple shuffle.

It's Easier Now

1

What is left of my father's harvest
has lapped into the soil to bear fruit.
The birds have that look about them
I saw them thirst and suckle.
Tethered against the moss stones the tiny
violets shy away from fame.
Without the energy to form a shadow he moves
through us into laughter. The light breeze
against my foot, minute ideas chase the tip
of the afternoon. Nightingale heart.

2

Dream air. Flap away you quiet hours.
The heart is but a token of the body.
Stubbled visions and the hair runs wild
with blazing ink.
Walking like this O floss O talcum:
a bright stream of sunlight lights up your hair
but I can't say how this holds me here. Hold on
to that piece of your target. The dry weather
has made the nettles lose their sting.

3

What are the poets doing tonight?
Rounded mouths fill with petals
my arm is lost. It's only paper
on which they write. Despair
maroons. Walk on grass. Sleep on stilts
and eat water.
In the dust skulls wake up.
Look we don't love like the flowers
we haven't got it in us to be that
open.
Of exit and idea it's a wanton
access across your shoulders.

4

I try hard.
The geese in the moonlight. A bloated stiff
dead chicken drowned in sheep dip, white daisies
under my lips, my gums have cracked with effort.
All swimmers must take the plunge. It's too easy
to be still let me light up the mud.
My face is lines. A map is retrospect.
Revisions response issues we see we feel we read
we turn over a new leaf and
find no index.

Uncollected Poems

Laid Down by a Corner

"As to Myself about whom you are so kindly Interested, I live by Miracle. I am Painting small Pictures from the Bible. For as to Engraving, in which art I cannot reproach myself with any neglect yet, I am laid down by in a corner as if I did not Exist"

> Extract from a letter to George Cumberland from William Blake, August 26 1799

1.
not only the loss
someone pushes a wheelbarrow
touched by blank earth
The child
frightened in blue slippers
16 years old today
(a lip throbs)
and the ambulance driver holds her arm
maimed by a tree.

2
Where the trees take up &
and make tremble stop.
Candles for
the near dead. Pristine
availability for the adolescent
who sits plaiting fingers.
The ox labels the sky and *'the
awful waiting where they lead you.'*
When home is a handkerchief
clothes hang limply between legs.

3
From the window where
plants did not wither

but involved the lungs
as two birds fall out with a mating frenzy
it's too late to
leave. So you're left to trust
the recorded messages in your head
where
pigs
cry
golden bacon juice.

4.
The heart well before
it season.
leave some in rain,
staggered into a violet circle
gently allowed into a dream line; a waft
of the keys.
How failure bursts on his lip
words change hands
the earth
permits forgiveness to court
a race against sound.

5
The pin falls
           draws three
perfect circles. Stops.
(A draft of their spirits
skirting inside her curtained
smile.)
he comes out of the arch, holds
his roseate senses to the warm
attic sky; engineers the apple
to seal an open bud.

6.
Opaque eyelight.
It's much
than
falling toward.
It's too far
forward.

Return them.

7
A body tidies the geraniums.
Leaf fauna of a child's nape
– his immediate likeness to the tree –
sleet across mud tracks; the
sea line changes   swirls into
beatific humour.

8
     A
Sudden grief
   soars
between dawns.

9
Moving
kissed wood.
Arthurian spells of her
empty holy grailing.
Corrugated roofing to the head
it rolls to and fro, sultry
– the eye of the man
in a circular window –

10
Spiels that set him
dancing into daylight
pining for grasses as hair.
Divine beetles rise up.
Clinging
saintliness to the narrow
window, a marketplace from whence he came.

March 8th 1860

Dear Sir,
I am in a madhouse and quite forget your Name or who you are. You must
excuse me for I have nothing to communicate or tell you and why I am
shut up. I don't know. I have nothing to say so I conclude.

Yours respectfully
John Clare

Laid Down by a Corner was written while working at Mabledon Psychiatric
Hospital, Darenth, Kent between October 1971 and May 1972

Clover

(upon finding a four leafed with JHP) July 1972

1

News of a near death.
St Augustine in a panic
of lavender pawing
the silk town
a chromatic land musing.

II

Cirrus of our moon
spelt high in
the cows purse. Clover.
Fodder promotes a higher
terrain of something more
useful than a white four leafed
message.

III

The children suck
at light
their tilting growth
beats against each stem.

IV

Tre
foil in a lip of cobalt study.
The ewe in a valley of Hazel.

V

Clover is the night cushion.
The cluster held by Pans
irresistible heart line.
Lemon is no aid to the tongue.
The tree stands besides its leaf.

VI

Does the thrush equate
a dying plant or
the miniature need to be found in
warmer dew.
Hounded by a ridge
the pilot drops into a
terrifying baize.
Clover now kicked into a certain redness.

VII

Manna of leguminous leaflets.
Foliage trental lobed in
ornamentation of tracery pulse.
In spate of.

VIII

Mountains sketched on the arm
of his Arthurian face.
We take the clover
for
granted
no better
than
the
cow.

IX

Knowing   we kiss not
the palm of a sister.
O eyes
raise this plant.

X

Clover beneath his islands
The wind has sold us
terribly.
Clover
in plenty
in place of
touch.

Rousing the Sleepers
for B

Weeping for the street has me
thus
in tortured prowl against
night that grips me (see I do not travel
easily).
Turn to see you watch me leave
from the window.
I could not last another day.
A couple walk the High Street.
He ignores
her unwieldy womb, stilettoed heart.
Traffic lights butt against
a generational pouch of trauma
you spit, stagger, drunk on rage.

Now
you are quiet in the rooms
facing the graveyard whose stones flash
their new teeth
showy under a wolf moon.
Many bleed your delicate lip dry
their tough northern banter rips at an already chapped wound.
Here by the river things
cramp into ice.
We have burst
the winter sun.
If I come back the leaves will mute us,
heave us towards assembling a light
as poems cuff the edge of the day;
tears predict the morning.

July 1973

The Other Absolute

For E.M. 1977

"Time is the other absolute.
Time is critical to mapping
the heavens; we do not know in the
first place how far away stars are only at what moment
they pass across our line of sight.
So the mariner's world called for the perfection of two sets
of instruments, clocks and telescopes.
The poet called
for intuition and song."
This hints at greater ideas,
experienced horror, love, loss, belief, suffering and recovery.
Childless in ribbons he stood
but many were fathered
and as trees pulled from the earth's
water store so he too provided and spoke.
He always spoke.

There is a moment in time
when all knowledge is forgotten
and only our primal hearts are sure.
Opportunity is the other absolute
we feel its great weight and tardily
we study its desire.

Open letter

My dear
I would be, as it were, caught into action of non-action.

Drawn as I am to the pavements of this town, the low ploughed hills of Kent and, missing you, as I do, I walk into rooms and study the plants again, span the length of raw days with my palm and a sob comes *simply because it is the coldest thing we know.*

So you leave and the climate is holding. I long for silence and thin air. I am as stoic and agile as can be for this time of year.

Briefly encountered, who sees him as to feel him, it is in the dying apparent sunlight that we prospect for and only after dark streetlights grow old ghosts on my sleeve.

My dear, the swans are asleep, like foam, you say, protected with muddy brown undersides from the Thames which I cannot leave. You tell me, I cried for no reason at all, and that we see nothing until we truly understand it.

Scotch pine on my desk how the cone so finely formed who could guess it blisters at the stem despite your warrior kiss.

Autumn could find me out running my hand along the cut edge of stone. The purr of your teeth along my lip, tender it haunts and I fall in as youth sketches the horizon. Alone in cloud for so long now I have spoken of touch without fertility I have used up the sepia of afternoon, my hands are quite numb, wounded water rains teeth within another's mouth.

Taut against ribbons of attempt how we battle against circumstance, meet the daily goal of human tears that demand much more than this.

My dear, the sky is now open to leafy green vineyards. The fields are blue with young stubble, the trivial rain it's sparkle on grass.

Laurus nobilis, I would give you this, to mark things, velvet magnolia tree, the afternoon so promising of touch.

It's that simple, the things we admire in others; of us in our better moments a composition of stance.

You are here again, the tired afternoon formed on your arm. How easily I can love you when nothing takes you away.

Arms linked in sleep, anxious wakers that we are, rooks on the marsh make their nests high in trees about the tiny above the tiny grey churchyard the evening moves on. Swans flay themselves at telegraph wires; *loving you is the one thing I'll never regret,* you say.

Flint, these round chalk hills are an early mud bath for sparrows. Today, alongside me, you are small, quiet. An unruly sun as we walk along the damp stone yard with the tight buds of hawthorn over our heads. But I am below the surface again, swung by obligation. Church bells prompt lives firm within this peculiar electricity we call hope; the larger breath of all things. When stars cease to be light they take all that is around them and absorb without giving.

We must remain worthy of fire like the poet growing older.

My dear, the rose with its double centred light, the wagtails on the bowling green at Wookey, a late afternoon. *She was looking for reasons to unlove him, the air so solitary she could only liken it to the Hepworth in the park and the way he'd suddenly told her of the rabbit, its head gouged out by some unknown event, perhaps a fox.*

There are pink stones by the water's edge. Here children run along pavements, their bright hearts too often lost while parents swear momentarily about them in sleep.

From the kitchen I watch late couples lean against the fence then take up again, as does the thrush that lighted on the lawn and off again. I see the years are getting shorter, certainly they press for some fine line within me but I have seen the evergreen replace itself, yet still I am drawn to the low hills of Kent, the pristine orchards that find me knee deep in leaf so close by.

1977

With Glee

For Maggie O'Sullivan

The Lady is in Pink
we can hear her sing
resting through
the back woods as if
expert
at misremembering her heart
shaking it into the air
like she does
like she did
with the muddy doormat
trodden too many times.
If I were a bird I would be
a starling she said, one of the common
bunch who peck away hoping for
some main chance but the lady
is in Pink we can hear her
humming with more than a little anxiety
as she spreads the thoughts of death and separation
over the kitchen, wiping them clean with a surfeit of candour.
Once again not quite ready for the new year, a fresh start
but
she is singing now
quite clearly singing from her Pink open mouth.

1980

Anything more than what we are

For Billy Childish 1981

This growing up
into and out of
things
finding the grit under our nails
to be a giveaway
of where you've been
no marker yet for where you're headed.
Trees rest
before they break out
into your hand.

You see Billy,
the old men shuffle like they do
along the wards of the hospital
their urine-soaked trousers
too far from their feet
the gap showing too much
white flesh
a white ankle
now drained of action.
They shuffle because the dancing
stopped just like that.

Mid

I don't get around much anymore he said
I just don't get around.

Five English Spring Poems

for Lee Harwood, 29th March 1984

1. At first the skies are so clear
    you would be forgiven thinking
    "summer oh summer."
    Bird dart make bids
    picking up all manner of downy silks
    to line sweet beds. Pushing through
    breaking voluptuous phallic buds.
    Surprise!   O Lupus you have
                     Stolen the purse
                     From the rabbit's
                     Quick ear.
    Dark these woods at night clamour with
    hooting pheasants, fox wails, waiting
    soft muscle to tear open.
    Look it is here, inside
    the poem
    all of this,
    all of this,
    the cat sniffs at the blade of grass
    then
    walks on.
    Navy blue evening skies sink down behind the
    tall English oak trees.

2. In the barn
    young lambs
    orphaned by morning
    bleat out.
    Looking out, smelling for milk, bleat out
    nuzzling against rock, bleat out
    while others suckle freely never leaving nor left.
    Watercress streams under sparkling bridges.
    Nothing relieves the ache of being left.

3. Thin wrists of primrose
   startle the mist.
   Trumpet daffodils battered by 48 hours of rain.
   All the geese huddle and grumble they just hiss at the wind.

4. Metallic black starling
   Sturnes Vulgaris) The glossy purple glints
   dip in and out
   brown tail feathers
   body of white wing feathers
   roosting in the old English oak again.
   Untidy nests, grass, wool, moss, wood shavings from our door.

   > Listening for worms
   > The sharp little heads
   > Tilt forward
   > Then sideways again.

5. The wheat is three inches high.
   St Luke's little summer has come and gone
   it is wrought of a sunlight far too light to come from just sun
   alone.
   Can it be that which the woods are tangling with,
   along with the Ivy?
   Or is it the necklet of tiny stars above us as the wood smoke
   curls up in tongues.
   The heart is a repetitious dancer
   whose feet trip and blunder
   despite all this practise.
   Yet still we sit together while sweet wallflowers are budding in
   the garden
   all of it so young and alone.

Recall

I wonder about the dark houses
my memory of them
his way of bending slightly backwards
as he spoke
arms out
almost as if singing.
Strange to think of it now
so long ago
so small a thing to carry around
the memory of him
like that.

1987

Communion 1988

For Phoebe

The damp cobbled path of
High Halden Church
our hearts being bells, lifted up
sung with the ancient stone-cold feet and ideas
'Jesus Good Above All Other'
we cuddle close in the pews
warm melted jellies in the pocket
moulded into the car keys.

France, 1989

i
At the hospital, Hôtel Dieu, Hautefort
the small strips of faded cloth – patterned in parts,
flowers, dots, carefully sewn, hemmed in hope, mark
the lives of mothers without choice,
in despair.

Outside
you skip, say that your tooth has fallen out,
we wrap it carefully.

ii
In the Church of Badefois d'Ans
the priest lines the village children on
slim fine wooden benches, wears his beret
and Monoprix shoes. Tells them,
Jésus avec l'amour dans son cœur,
his small feet crossed at the ankles.

Outside
you ask why
I didn't stop the seesaw from hurting you.

Hôtel Dieu had a vocation to "care for poor people". The hotel / hospital / church has a small wooden "tower", a cupboard with a revolving door to make it possible for poor parents to abandon their children into the care of the religious order under the cover of anonymity. The alternative was to leave the babies to perish on the mountains.

Between 1790 and 1847 the revolving door was used 1,947 times. Parents were asked to affix a little cloth ribbon to the infant's clothes so that, if they had second thoughts within the first 24 hours after the abandonment, they could identify and reclaim their child and bring another part of the fabric with them. These coloured strips were also attached to the baby's entry in the town's records. There is no evidence of how many of the babies were reunited with their families. It is also not known how many arrived too late to reclaim their babies or lost the tiny piece of fabric.

For David Annwn and Lesley Newland

On their marriage 16th March 1994

She is sitting on the veranda
at first seemingly gazing out.
On reflection she could be sleeping
or reading a journal. One simply cannot be sure.
A green dress
surrounds her, like Ireland it is
her jewel.

Love is a bonnet of chaos.
A chariot of storm.
A bracelet of wisdom he once
said to her.
She had only been trying to please him.
She stirs from her position, sits up, faces him.
"I'm quite here for you" she mouthed
love is a fickle enemy,
you can never count on its order

He touched his sleeve and
her heart jumped to see his slender hands
"I am but a minstrel to the garden of your flame," he stated.
"All love is forever hope and danger,
easy rife and lasting."

Birthday

Fifty three
years
treading
pavement
path, steep.
Listening, waiting.
Hearing, watching,
thinking, speaking,
eating, digesting, putting paid to the waste.
Knowing what the waste might be where the waist isn't anymore.

Saying, regretting, retrieving,
hoping and finding,
digging and not seeing

music, flowers, dogs,
steam, damp, sunshine blue,
poetry, line, measure.

touching, being sure, illness,
being worried, reading.
Being driven, wanting to stop, to end it there.

Mothering, being a child.

Swallowing, yawning, laying down, repetition, feeding, being awake,
sleeping, shopping, clearing, weeding, planting, harvest, style.

Meeting others, cooking, farewells, deaths, men, learning.
Reparation.
Sighs, celebration, reckoning, reasoning, shouting.
Resolutions, new starts, tablets, dye, innovations, reports, hairstyles,
    dreams, pillows.

"And I shall never see her again"

for mum

Warm cushion to the world
a making sense.

Worn to my shape
never again
so loved
like that

without such a place to be lost from.

20.9.2005

Couples – bus

You've got that look on you   what look
The one that says I don't approve but I'm not saying anything   I don't know what you mean.
I saw you look sideways at Melissa's shorts with the pockets hanging out of it and the neckline on her top and then how you inhaled loudly when I said how nice she looked.   You can make up your own mind about how your stepdaughter looks but I don't have an opinion, not any more I don't, not after the last time, it's not worth it
But you do, you have a strong view about it and that why you have a face like thunder and a pinched mouth like an envelope for the last 20 minutes   I am keeping quiet that's all I'm doing. I am neutral on everything, everything
I'll have another bevvy before I turn in when we get home   Suit yourself but I'm not looking after you when your liver packs up Perhaps Melissa will be at you beck and call just like she is with that married man so called boyfriend of hers.
That's below the belt, it really is.   Melissa's belt has nothing below it, does it.

Dave tells me

Dave tells me, it's like a funeral every time I take the sheep in the lorry. I take them there alone, by myself, don't want anyone else with me. I can't think about anything other than their faces and how I have looked after them, brought them on, up half the night, early morning, all weathers, revived them, bottle fed them, had their warm faces nuzzling my hand at night.

Doesn't seem right does it. I drive them down the ramp and into the holding pen and that's it, slaughter, gone. I don't eat lamb myself, can't do it anymore – know them too well. What's the answer then Elaine he asks me, I can't go vegan I like a bit of bacon now and then. It's what being a farmer is. Doesn't mean I have to like it all I suppose. What's the answer then Elaine?" He jumps into the truck, his hand on the steering wheel amongst the twine and antibiotics.

For Andrew and Beatrice

16 June 2018

See how the sheep with their steady
sure   silent   step
protect their young, watch us moving among them
as the Romney Marsh reeds shelter corn bunting,
linnet, yellowhammer, tree sparrow, starling and swift.
Fairfield Church, often water-bound,
always field bound, vigilant,
watches over us here assembled in promise
as we are bring the strength of love towards its tender place.
We watch as two become constant against the ever changing sky.
Our hearts look up as skylarks greet your steps together.
They, knowing more
radiate their song, soaring evermore in tune.

December Anemones

for Polly

You bring them wrapped in goodness
as we stand sentry
to the new generation
while they determine,
light upon their own days of unease and bliss.
The sunlight does not yet fade us
nor will fear and shame pull us
downward but rising from regret with striving
to make maternal darn and repair.
The garden saw us look out from our vantage point
across the water
valuing all that we know.
Indigo, red, plum, bright violet, you brought them
anemones, symbols of protection wrapped in good.

9.12.2018

Dear Roy

You were right

Sound jams against ideas; results in a poem.

Here the Kent streams snake against the gorse, your furze bush, yolk golden as dykes across the marsh slip past silk reeds, the blackened heron doing the tour.

The *I Ching* today tells me, 'Thunder and Wind the image of duration, thus the superior man stands firm and does not change direction'. Our cheeks burn at the thought.

Your face

its stark gentle wisdom against the clay, piano, the jazz piano. Like Mose, we don't get around much anymore

but seem to be none the worse for that.

For RF
March 2021

Five Poems (after Rilke)

The Housemaid

At the pond's edge she'll surround the trees
like a cloud or a duck with tired small cardboard baggage
she may face the pool and name it Laughter.

So she will wait with the birds
and let the tongues waggle and rejoice spilling goodness
over her splendid heart.

We tenderly sip from her idea. Eat,
such passion, watch with no inside knowledge the courting couples
immersed in their forgiveness.

The Owner

Remembering giant visions which have
gone, now lost in some tribal game we aim
our shots ever hopeful that this passion
this
triumph maybe The One.
We cannot, though, mark out the days long enough
to see ourselves through it so we protect
our children, mother, parents but we angle far more
knowing we
ourselves are the mark.
In an old diary he read the words,' stop clamouring.'

The Stockman

See how small
trees old village dwellings nestle into the hillside
the sheep worry the grass and the grass worries the earth.
Is that how I worry you?
Nature is so tidy watch her strip her sleazy summer leaves into cool
bleak honed forests.
the rooftops of houses have seen it all before heard the mutterings
beneath in the rooms,
it's all to be forgiven, renewed one way or another.

The Wife

Disown my impatience against others. I will part
from such arenas with a shrug. These arrogant ceremonies
spill from me. I swallow bile.

Now the lane trees
scattered across the horizon. Shall we be as forever lost?
The days are marked by pretence. I promise myself too often.

Tired, we blackbirds make our nests
feathering the prospects for new hopes.
All things rest sooner or later.

The Banker

Envy
I'll take you up and learn to love
your child like play
crawl from enchanted gardens before you are
plucked weed like from the succulent plots

of young hearts.
Why, when this little life we hold onto so tightly is shifted do we turn
to see all at once there never ever will be a time
it will always be frantic, greedy with longing.

Five Songs

1

The sunlight already pouring into the room when they woke had seemed to question the reality of what had taken place in the darkness. And their nightclothes had all the warm, safe sleepiness of childhood on them.

Mariners use red markers to keep vessels safe from the edges of things.

Rocks bleat like hazards as sound flounders upon a wreck. Searching a safe harbour, keeping distance from entrapment, while leaning towards a gulf; tidal attraction is inevitable.

When she looked at him again he was quite changed although his aloof necktie ensured a certain kept score. Only the once when the night fell upon them did they succumb to the tide; its drift left a dent.

II

The street shrank on itself on the hungry city claimed them. He felt brave, foolhardy, slightly unreal, hunched forward into the breeze. An odd sensation of being outside himself, frightened and admiring at the same time.

A murky pond, deep but the verge appeared as clear water. We will go in he said and taking him by the hand they moved forward, their feet finding the silt.

The lapping water laid a veneer of purpose over his resolve. Desire pricked at an ankle, it was invisible but evident as the liquid sound of warbling skylarks rang almost against the very air.

From the corner of his eye he saw
just briefly
or perhaps not,

the mark of his lip.

III

The day was wool-grey and wet. Their feet went cold and damp-feeling back into their boots. The air was clear, sharp as medicine going all the way down. There was a stream at the bottom of the garden, the water noisy and purposeful, splashing past oily rocks.

So very dark, a corner without space.

Everything taken internally shifts faster. A mottled landscape of glide and tears, a life without purpose, dragging a useless idea into silt.

The world has been too busy being. Blast the hopes, open the window. The air is only the air. Stop, just taste the rain.

IV

At these moments, it came back to him, as it did with particular smells and sounds (the stale sunshine stored in the fabric of a deckchair, the shushing of a fountain in a park, the nibble of a paper knife): the warm fleeting feeling of last summer's friendship.

Making sense of ideas and all that has been before, trodden down, raked over, left behind.

Waiting on the kerb of a season the mark is in the very air, a collective understanding of all that wonder.

A balm of what we can hold to, who we can conjure. To be invisible, not thought about on her own account. Breaking the waves before the others notice.

V

Outside, the evening was vastly calm, the encompassing of all London more intimation than sound. A tentative shiver of happiness ran over him. The street, patterned with deep shadow, had the smooth, still look of a stretch of river flowing under darkness, it's reason made mysterious

Chancing into the day perhaps nothing is unknown, no lesson already understood.

The Hawthorn breaks out   nudging the air into summer. Expectation smarts the current.

Often are we but attempts to field hope with chance. Buzzards mewl across a brilliant sky.

A mystery of belief, alive to being alive

that's the nub.

The quotations are from *The New Life* by Tom Crewe,
used with thanks and in praise of.

For Carl Rakosi

"I need to laugh out in triumph because of this marvellous precarious immortal human being, in spite of the weight of death."

The infant
                          milk
and other creature comfort
                          comforts
from the breast.
                          Love
understanding, solace, grace
                          memory
A mothers continued reason
                          nurture
Impulses, bread a
                          Leaning.
Into warm lambs
                          suckle
skip away
                          can
it be so easy
To let go.
                          yet
Contain   to turn
                          the
unthinkable into love.
                          Mothers
first gift this
                          quenching
this quenching thirst
of an imaginative life

For Constance

6.2.2020

You
come
lit luminous, ripe from a maternal galaxy;
we can only marvel.
Bright in prospect as lambs, catkin dredged,
salute your every step.
Relaying the news of your new life,
Francis holds my hand, tells me,
I have a sister now Grandma.
Pathways of crocus beset with primrose;
early the daffodil touches our sleeve as we
slip into the new lightness of this
your first spring morning.
Early sun worries the earth in every sheltered place
while snowdrops incite this brightness
that paves your way.
Fieldfare and skylark further your dazzling skies
all known now to be yours.

Mask – Hackney Downs. March 2000

On Common Land for common people where pit of stomach
meshes spit   heady bird song,
Dandelion, cuckoo pint, and elm
breathes through missing ventilators,
the basement flats, the high risers,
the scalding steam of the argument smarts a lip.
So,
I threw the mask out of the car, it meant nothing;
it had not stopped anyone dying. Watching it flap across,
riding a stiff breeze,
across common land used by common people
weathering unifying fear.

April 2020

For George and Naomi upon their wedding

3rd September 2022

The Marsh, its still certainty holds
the golden tipped Chestnut,
careful pink Valerian,
a true-blue catch of Vipers Bugloss,
Thrift and
Shepherds Purse.
Skylarks dip beside yearling lambs
who nuzzle blackberry thicket, ivy, hawthorn.
Tender, the marsh willow has a silken silver grip,
it secures this, your promise, today.
A church, set in farmland knows well
these tempos and other rhythms, witnessing
beyond seasons
and across the valued pulses, the heartscapes of many.
Loyalty, love, trust and hope pilot these your united strides
as we salute the happy beacon that is yours.

With Grace

for GS

Just A Man
dazzled by light
his glossed plumage emits from a quiet home.
A heron startles against the scarlet flax,
that brace of skylarks lifts the lid as the nested poppy seeds
rupture
along the cliff edge where we hang
limp until poised again as memory chants us back
into the warm domestic relief.

Just A Man but Such A Man
dazzled by light
above a scree of gorse, yolk yellow
racing the slower heart. The buzzard clips
the ear of a soldier at dawn its mewing offspring.
A hedgerow
simply a hedgerow calls us back
for its tender jubilant chimes suggest
to only lay down among them, to be dazzled
that's all, just lay.

October 2022

Forest – Degirmenyani, Turkey, 2022

Scalped mountains, threadbare now.
Charred sap sucked by flame
100-foot pines collapsed in ash,
tortoises, boar, stray dogs, we hear their fear baked hearts.
Villagers stay put, pray for a shift in the wind.
Bald mountains now face the open light across new worn edges
Run down now the earth is rutted, marred by trucks.
TIn between, the gentle fur of new growth.

He frightened away the best of our health

Limping, the tall days branch into spasm; his bleached face torn into the scarlet letters of his heart, the beseeching way of him sidles up by the Bank Street café. Snatches of sleep, the foundry shudders.

His arm across her face, he saw it twice. Swiped at her eyelid he did and then heaved himself into the wicker chair, newspaper across him, her, invisible to him.

Across the tarmac the same bruising sewn lines of faces weathered with gristle the slap of a November winter in the town between the broken sky and run of pain.

He couldn't ask for his mother to stay but together they sank into the milky dream that was the best of what they had.

Helicopter parent

It's like a hummingbird she said
Hovering
Pausing, waiting while it searches
oscillations and harmonics
searching nectar
searching
people to suck
from the sea
spilling them back on dry land after all that.
Enlarged corneas enable nocturnal vision
to spot a speck a tiny vessel barely topping the waves.
Border Control sometimes turn
a blind eye, but not the
hummers who flare their tails,
point their bills at intruders on their territory.

Across the garden and the Kent marsh three times every day,
the last at 8 p.m. they fly.
Wings beat above the yew hedging.
Calm weather, flat seas mean a gamble towards
just that one slit of a chance whatever the stakes.
Worth it. Dice with death on a January sea.
A folded prayer safe in the pocket,
hold the child against you, no matter what

The parent bird keeps looking.
But, with a chance of the light,
some slip through,
some vanish into the sea.

Night feeds Last Supper

At day one
bleating
everything
a struggle
but her ewe head, turned, is not towards your sound.
The box warm
the mixed milk
drip by drip   slow revival
your head held by one finger.
At night the Marsh set out below to dark hoots and scurries.
You nuzzle in close now. Moth, fox, bat and badger
spot us here in late spring
wind, dim drizzle, mire, mud.

The "voice of all black animals crying to drink,
cries of all birth arise, simple as we,
found in the leaves." *

Barn owls hunt
swoop
quartering the field, hover and dive.
Calling to defend while owlets rattle and hiss.
Nightingale gives pure dots of melody
patrolling territory, mate-seeking.
Pre-fledged chicks wheeze under hedgerow,
frog and toad chime underfoot toward the water.
Companions at our vigil
you have always waited for me
raise a head to the torch light.
Your weakness known from the off
that which prompted the rejection.
Now twelve years on your legs give way in age,
I feed you still, one last supper.

Again I watch your struggle.
Bleating, everything is bleating,
the noise is everywhere.

*Muriel Rukeyser, 'Night Feeding' from
The Collected Poems of Muriel Rukeyser

On finding your copy of *The Observer's Book of Geology 1960*
for BM

Falling
open at Fool's Gold
the stone that would create sparks when struck against.
Struck against, railed against but
it's still tender, sore,
The heart in flames again seeing
Seeing your name on the frontispiece
with all that hope in the margins
knowing now
how it would unravel, pan out.
Still the margins carry the weight.
How static the margins against which we shuffle.

Outside the gates at visiting time

Women hold the damp cloth
mop the spills of men
inside.
Outside
toddlers trip in the mud on
tree roots cut away to
accommodate the perimeter fence and those
inside.
Outside
pregnant girls carry bags
fripperies
encumbrances, their hair scraped
eyes taut
things forgiven against those
inside.
Outside
mothers stand in line, first to arrive as
younger brothers swagger.
Where are the fathers? Not all
inside.
May have
walked on.
Might have
moved on.
May not
have replied
been traced.

Sunday night poem, for Naomi, aged 15

Your eyes are so blue
and they follow
the small creatures who need you,
that nest and feed quietly and sleep soundly as stones.
All this,
always within your grasp,
well within your stride.

Adolescence, how we cast aside the stale air of wisdom
and know the taste of fresh simple breath.

So instead,
make music
make believe
make trust
make amends.

I follow you
for it is I who am now behind.
Yet still I aim to be ahead
to pilot
as I
stand ready
when you
will go about
forging your own caution.
I bask in your steady warmth.

Upon Sitting for FA 2 — Summer 2021

From the chair
you are
in the artist's Italian cleaner's dress.
Paint ridden, idea stained and
standing back
you step into my face
you catch an eye, a crease, a mark made by
a loss, a change, a kiss, a suddenness.
From the chair
the woman opposite pins washing in
her triangular garden.
Women's work

*"it is in the nature of women to be fond of carrying weights, you may see
them in omnibuses and carriages, always preferring to hold their baskets or
their babies on their knees, to settling them down on the seats or by their
sides...... she prefers to load her hands with a bag or other weighty objects"*

From the chair
I am
uncovered
hand movement captured
by yours
depicted stark against the white.

Upon Sitting for FC 1 – Summer 2021

What we now think is
that carpentry would add to a spec
but Weybridge could well have been dull as a town centre.
Some hair and eyes with a certain fretwork skill
would now sustain our loins
but
are we permitted ungirded thighs
unless tempered by our careful needlework along a crotch.
We manage
easily,
a number of things;
the loss of mouths,
the widening of a nostril or two,
increased leg material.
Your bone structure remains enviable.
What we now think
is that the goal is a connection,
an appreciation of heart and children.
We see the
men look up
not quite in focus

agape.

July 2021

Untitled

For Bea and Andrew, the cabin at Ljussjön

Swedish white blanched
stems of birch
their thin arms
raised by
supple winds
bend in mellow light
watch
the early frosted lake
the cabin's glow.
Papered silver bark
waits
for warm light
before
flushing its
spring growth
as bluetits suckle
the silver bounty.

December 2021

The transformative power of the minute

Unsteady
these days but one
tiny shift in
pace/direction
changes arrival/destination
prospect/outcome.
She cries easily
at many things
departures arrivals
mothers with children
fathers without children
the rise of the hills above the edge of the sea
the weight of the buds.
One drop of pure chance
and the landscape is changed
the skid of the tyre, a heartbeat missed
the horizon quite altered.

Diary

For Simon Smith

Tuesday

Things that mattered.
    The lace winged insect staring at my face.
    Swallows dipping staying, leaving just when you've noticed.
    When the wide Turkish woman with wider trousers sold me the oranges from the road side at midnight she hugged me like lost child.

Wednesday

At the shop they paint my toenails, tell me it's free as they like to do something for old people once a day. Last year they asked if I wanted my moustache removed. Time for a change.
    The man picks up his wife on his scooter, her large legs tapering to tight black sandals heave across the seat, then she hoists the child and collects the mirror from a shop as they pass by. They scooter off towards town, shooting the lights.
    I change into my swimming costume in the toilet. Take off my shoes, step into something wet and slimy. It's worse than I thought, it's brown. I then drop my shorts on the floor, wet through. Leave hurriedly.
    I am obsessed by chips. I need them   Too many grains and organic moments to counteract with chips.

Thursday

The nature of bodies and birds and things.
    Give back what winter took she said and disappeared into the rushes.
    Mosquitoes feast on my right arm and left leg and the top of my head so thoughtless, do they know the implications.
    Restless all night am sure you got into the bed but it couldn't be, you're 500 miles away and didn't say you were coming.
    Frank Zappa sounds as good as he did years ago.

Friday

Joni Mitchell playing Canada.

I think often of your pocket with The prelude always there, we had such hope but didn't count on the impact of many things, childhood, history, us as we were.

The donkeys at home! But here the cicadas, wood pigeon, neighbours calling across the forest, the underbelly of blue swallows as they; chirp and swoop.

A car gets stuck on the mud bridge at midday cutting others off from leaving the shore. Several men give up; it's too hot, too hard.

I am reading James Kirkup. Recalling his letters to me from Japan that I miss. Always such fine fine paper.

> *Remember, no men are strange, no countries foreign*
> *Beneath all uniforms, a single body breathes*
> *Like ours: the land our brothers walk upon*
> *Is earth like this, in which we all shall lie.*
> *They, too, aware of sun and air and water,*
> *Are fed by peaceful harvests.*

My neighbours call me in for a chai, we look at one another, they take off my shoes, suggesting I feel their soft grass. There is a lot of nodding and the same Turkish words I know. I leave with arm full of tomatoes, cucumber and Erics, Plums.

The forest is being sprayed with chemicals against mosquitos tonight from a loud van. I'm not complaining.

Saturday

Full moon escapes and pours out onto the forest floor, puddles of gold, tortoises languidly drink speed on.

Sunday

Don't take anything for granted it can surprise you.

Birds can close one eye and switch off one brain, and leave the other eye with the corresponding brain fully awake and alert. In fact, they can turn this on and off depending upon the circumstances.

Monday

We are here.

Irrfan Khan – actor recently diagnosed with an inoperable tumour. *"All I could do was to realise my strength and play my game better. A realisation that the cork doesn't need to control the current. That we are being gently rocked in the cradle of nature."*

Few places have no aerial bird song.

In any event they never try to get their song right.

Low slung   late birds flit swoop as they dash in front, first home in the nest.

Rocked in the cradle of the cosmos we insist upon choice.

Fight not to see it close up.

Tuesday

My second unborn grandchild is growing until ready to emerge – what else could be better news for the world.

The UK braces itself for the hottest day on record. The legacy rail tracks are melting. 50 years ago we put a man on the moon.

Wednesday

Found your Observer's Geology book dated 1966. Your name in the front, a neat hand searching for gold. You were 17 years old and granite coursed your veins.

Thursday

It's August but the leaves are changing to red photo receptors measure red light and cryptochrome measures blue light. Trees detect changes in day length of as little as half an hour. O dear.

Friday

Intent, it's all about intent.

Watching you sing

for Beatrice

I cannot look I can only listen
for if glances exchange
faltering
becomes easy
an emotional mother is a liability nobody deserves.
In the air, that sweetness
the lightest heart upon the air.
Such gifts are these.
A child's forgiveness is the sword of hope
we cling
nourished.
The cathedral stands with its wall far too measured
for uncertainty
clarity and
rest
the morning is quite new.

Round the Corner

for Basil King

Painting you said was
to explain
something.
The Lightning War, Blitz, the East End of London, running
hiding from what you heard,
a name change, keeping it close
in the family.
A making sense of.

Painting and I see you
at the canvas
is to
belong
be with the others, close, around your corner
in the heart of.
To mark out what you know
now
after all this time
just how it feels,
what you see.

Painting
colouring it in
keeping it safe, around the corner
not to be overlooked or
set aside.
A London Blitz burnt on your shoe
is still so locally yours.

Neighbours

My Turkish neighbour is shouting at his wife again, "Yok Esma"; this is very loud. I speculate the row is because she has a cleaning obsession which he has mentioned to me before, "Esma, she clean, clean, clean all day, too much, she ill". Esma cries back at him something unintelligible and then she comes into the garden wringing her hands before going, returning inside through the screen door. Her small covered head I know is now concealing some bald patches. More, very loud shouting ensues from inside; it goes on for twenty minutes without a break. Esma's mewling sounds don't appear to placate him. Coffee is brought out to the small table and they sit in silence. Now and again, she tends the aubergine plants.

I often ask Esma if she is okay and she smiles and tells me that she is "taman". I know that she is not. Things quieten down in the house and he goes out in the van but then yards and yards of washing comes out on the line, brilliant white, 15 of his vests and pants, then she beats the rugs and I see that her little hands are quite raw. He returns and there is more shouting. Later they go together down to the market where I see her buying cleaning fluids and he is carrying a bottle of raki.

PROSE

I

Gut Reaction (1987)

Him on foam and me on fibreglass

"You see the thing was that at the time he was on foam and I was on fibreglass so I had to keep bumping into him didn't I? Even after I'd run over him that Sunday I'd go to work at the factory and there he'd be on foam and I'd be right next to him on fibreglass. Actually that Sunday had started off quite well all things considered. He offered to take our old table over to Sheila's in the back of the car and I drove. I felt good, in reasonable spirits I'd say. I wasn't especially cross with him or anything, no more than usual seeing how he was always an aggravating bugger at the best of times. But anyway, I offered to drive and he agreed; he always agreed about everything. Well, on the way over we started talking about Sheila – she's my daughter by my first marriage and he began making comments about how pretty she was. I didn't say a thing. When we got there with the tools, he opened the back of the car, took the table out and stood there in the middle of the drive looking at me in that way of his, you know, sort of sly, as though he hated me and I looked at him, and he looked back at me. I thought to myself, 'I really wish you were dead, that you just didn't exist anymore.' Before I knew where I was I'd run over him, twice in fact. But he wasn't hurt, hardly at all. I was surprised – but then he always had a hard head. When you think about it, it's awful. I had four children by him and still I'd felt nothing, but for the fact that I wished he didn't exist.

"Of course, now he is living with Sheila, his own stepdaughter, it's disgusting.

"But as I say it's worse at work because I see him. What with him on foam and me on fibreglass."

To always look after it

A Monday. I go and see Richard at the children's home. I'm told that over the weekend Richard committed another offence with some of his friends and that he will be interviewed again by the police today. Richard took some beer from the backyard of a shop with a girl a year older than himself. At sixteen she had already served her time in a girls'

Borstal. Between them they climbed over the fence, took six cans of drink and a bottle of sherry. They came home after drinking the beer with red faces and pockets bulging. It is the girl's eighteenth offence and Richard's third.

I wait for Richard to return from school so I can talk with him about the events. Eventually he shows up. I watch him get off the school bus outside the children's home. He is laughing, his brand new outsized school blazer is stiff and boxlike. He looks up at the window and seeing me he makes a face and laughs. I ask him about his weekend. He tells me that the day before the offences occurred he went home to see his parents. In the morning his mother took him to the park, handed him her wedding ring and said for him to always look after it, as she had taken many sleeping pills that morning, and that she was going to die. He ran and found a policeman and within an hour his mother was hospitalised again and Richard was taken back to the children's home.

"Tell me, Richard, about the shop you broke into and the beer and sherry."

"What beer?" he says. I tell him he knows what beer. "Oh, that beer – anyway I was sick."

For me to clear up

I am called out as an emergency to visit the family home of a woman in her late fifties who tried to take her own life last week by swallowing every pill she could find in the house. The house is a council property with no garden. It overlooks a bald, brown playing area where unwanted dogs meet up, fight, make their mess, make other dogs and frighten the children. Inside, the home is tidy and very clean. The woman cries as soon as I ask how she is. "My husband is dead," she says. "He was crawling around on all fours at night with the pain of it. I'm glad he's out of that. He used to try and reach the bathroom, he didn't want to make a mess for me to clear up, you see." Yes, I did see. I could see from her anxious wringing hands and her lined brow and her thin, shapeless body. "He died so suddenly and then within a few months our daughter, Frances, told me she was pregnant, sixteen years old. The baby was born eight months later, little Sam, beautiful baby. I brought him here, she went to work. I found it hard to manage on a widow's benefit but I got free coal from the pit and mates of Stan's visited regularly and gave me a few bob now and then. I loved little Sammy. She just upped and went you see, taking Sammy with her. No warning. He was my life, my grandson." I watch her constantly wringing hands and her feet moving around in the oversized slippers. "When Frances met this lad they were going to get married. I was pleased for her, he seemed a nice boy. She wanted a white wedding and a reception from here. I agreed to do all the catering for them and so for weeks I prepared food for the big day. Bearing in mind I'd just recovered from her dad dying I did well to work so hard. I paid for it all out of my cleaning job. It was all laid out on the front room tables; I borrowed glasses and chairs and cutlery from half the people up the street. I came down from bed at 7.00 a.m. to find Frances and Sammy already up and dressed and her looking sheepish holding a note. "What's happening here?" I said.

"I didn't think I'd see you, mum," she said, "I was going to leave this note." She handed it to me and then went out the back door with Sammy. Before I realised what was happening a taxi had taken them off. I read the note, it said that she was sorry, very sorry about it, her and Joe were already married, they'd done it last week in a Registry Office with strangers as witnesses. The big white wedding was off, he couldn't go through with it. The reception was off too. She'd decided to go to London to live with his parents and Sammy. She said she didn't know when she'd be round again. I haven't seen them since. I had all the food laid out, can you imagine it? I couldn't take it all in what with her dad dying like that and all of it. That's why I took all those pills. I am alone."

Outside on the bald playing field the dogs yap and chase. The woman sitting inside by the fire roaring away all the free coal-board fuel, next to her photo of herself and her husband, a wartime shot with him upright and handsome, his arms round her and both of them laughing.

As much as it takes

A short man, Mick, aged thirty nine, is "balding too fast for comfort" he tells me. His large deep-set eyes poke out of a ruby red face that bulges over the dark moustache that he grew last year "in an attempt to make my face seem more interesting". He has a rash over one cheek and ulcers in his mouth which all add to the general feelings of complaint and disfigurement of which he speaks. He talks with one eye on the clock every so often and the other on his wrist-watch. I ask if he is in a hurry. "I've got no plans, there's no rush, no-one at home waiting for me. That's just it, you see; when I was at work I used to race home to see the kids before they went to bed, try and play with them as much as possible. They do love me those kids you know. I brought them up when they were babies. Sandra had that postnatal depression or whatever it's called; she couldn't or wouldn't do a thing for months. When those kids screamed in the night it was me that got up and saw to them, still would now if I had the chance. I'll give as much as it takes to get those kids back again. No-one's going to tell me that my own kid don't want to see me. I can understand Sharon saying what she did and anyway I know that Sandra's been poisoning her with stories about me but Lenny, I just will not accept that my little Lenny doesn't want to see his daddy again. Lenny is only seven for god's sake and Sandra sits there telling me that he even refuses to speak to me on the phone. It's nearly a year since I've seen them now. I have tried, really tried. OK, so I have been working out in Saudi for nine months but it was only to raise a home and money for those kids. You don't seem to understand that Sandra's not a real mother, she can't look after those kids properly, she can't even look after herself, look at the state of her. I admit that Sharon is different, she's always been a quiet kid. My nerves were bad when we had her as a baby, I was worried about debts. But Lenny, my little Lenny he must want to go drag racing with his daddy again, he must. I'm going to give as much as it takes to see those kids again. Whatever's gone on with Sandra and me is water under the bridge now, why she can't see that I don't know. We did have some rows I admit. There was a lot of shouting but it wasn't only me they saw fighting. Sandra can land a blow or two I can tell you, she's a strong girl. Once she slashed my arm with a razor." He lifts his shirt sleeve to show me the scar which stretches from above the elbow to his wrist. "OK, so I forgot Lenny's birthday once or twice but I was busy, I've had worries. I love that kid. I think about him all the time. I never go past a shop without wondering if Lenny would like this or that. Lenny is a daddy's boy, always has been always will be. He'll come round in the end. Whatever it takes I'm going to make that kid see sense. I am his dad after all. Nothing can change that, can it?"

"No," I say, "Nothing can change that."

Gerry

I'm talking to Rita in the hospital. She has put on weight and her new skirt rides up over her knees as we sit on the plastic comfy chairs in the Dayroom. Rita has always liked to look nice and today she shows me her new jumper and skirt recently bought from a catalogue. Round her neck Rita wears a tiny gold heart that she tells everyone her husband has bought for her, but Rita and I both know that she herself bought it last year, as her husband Gerry has been in prison now for six.

"Some of the things that my Gerry used to get me to do for him before he went inside, really when I think about it I could scream, no wonder I've had this breakdown. I remember the night he took me out on a job with him because his mate Brian wouldn't come. I had to stand outside in a yard and hold a ladder while he climbed up really high and got into the top attic windows so he could drop down into the stairwell and then into the shop without starting the burglar alarm off. I will say this for Gerry, he was very good at it, that as well. We got through thousands of pounds together before he got caught. But I was telling you. Gerry told me to wear something dark for this job so I couldn't be seen easily, so I wore my plunge neckline black dress with the slit up the side, black tights and my black boots. So I'm standing there in the freezing cold like this holding the ladder while Gerry gets up there. Once he's up top I'm supposed to wait half an hour while he gets the gear together and comes down before we shoot off. Anyway I'm standing there at the ladder bloody freezing to death when this bloke walks up to me and says 'Hello, Gorgeous, where are you going?' What could I say, I couldn't tell him, could I? So I wink at him and he gets in the back of the car. He gave me £5. Well, by the time he's finished and trying to make another date with me for next week. Gerry's up the ladder shouting 'Rita, Rita, where are you?' and I go off running across the yard. We got away alright but when we get home he says to me 'You alright, gal?' I tell him that I'm fine. 'Only you look a bit flushed I'd say'. It's just the night air, I tell him. If he found out he'd kick the bloke's head in. He was like that was Gerry."

You can't odds what your eyes have seen

"We come round the back that afternoon and made a cut through the cul-de-sac when Darren pipes up, 'Here, that's Dad's lorry'. I was amazed but then you can't odds what your eyes have seen can you? I told him it was just parked there because Dad's mate had borrowed it but inside I was afraid. I knew something was up. Anyway we passed by on the other side with my yanking Darren not to gape like that and got him home as smart as possible.

"When his dad got home late I asked him if he's had a good day. 'Tiring pet,' he said, 'Tiring.' I said nothing.

"A few days later I picked Darren up from school and on the way home he pipes up again. 'I saw dad today with a bird and she hasn't arf got big tits.' I kept on walking and into the front room where he sat snoring. 'Hello love,' I said, kissing him on the cheek. He just carried on snoring, must have been worn out. I went upstairs and wrapped all his dirty washing into a big towel and put it all into a plastic Tesco bag. I took it downstairs and woke him up with a shake. 'Trevor,' I called, 'Sweet Trevor, you know your mate what's round the corner, the one that wears the skirt, well this is a present from me to her.' Then I whacked him hard across the head with the bundle and told him to go. He went.

"But our Darren's so rebellious now. I reckon he might be better off without me. He's that mouthy. He's always on about his dad, how we've never seen him since that day. He often asks me whether it was his fault, if he hadn't seen the lorry that day, you see he thinks I wouldn't have found out and his dad would be here still.

"I always tell him 'You can't odds what your eyes have seen, chuck' and then I give him a cuddle but he shrugs it off. He doesn't arf look like his dad."

Making progress

"I would have written sooner, the letter said, but he seemed to be making such good progress. He was eating very well to the last – everything mashed up finely as he liked it. His sleeping wasn't as sound as usual, but then with him being unwell we had to strap him down that much firmer to make sure he wasn't going to fall out.

"Always a smile though, everyday he smiled at us – our golden boy we called him.

"I'm sorry to break this news to you in a letter but we tried to get you on the phone and the social worker called round several times and was told you were in Spain on holiday. I know it's a few years since you saw him but he really came on well in the last two years especially. The illness wasn't very serious at first, the doctor gave him some antibiotics and drained his tubes. You know how often these children need such special care.

"We all thought he'd rally round as he was doing so well and playing his little card games on his own as usual. The doctor said he didn't suffer at all at the end, just slipped away into a deep sleep. Matron has his belongings here for you to collect when you want to, there's not much just his toys and a few clothes and his photos of you and the family at home.

"Yes, I'm sorry to break this news to you in a letter and as I say, I would have written sooner to say he was ill, but he was making such good progress…"

That sort of man

"Fourteen months ago he had stroke and died. Just like that. No warning. They wore him out one way and another. All that work to do and they never thought he might want a day off. I'd never been on holiday myself and neither had he, well it isn't easy with stock work. You just can't leave animals and they never offered to help out. One morning he said to me 'Dot, they're trying to kill me before I retire, trying to get the last drop out of me before I go.' Of course when he did drop dead they didn't like it when I said that he'd been worked too hard, they didn't like that at all, said it was his fault if he didn't speak up a bit. Two years ago he was up every night with the lambing, making money for them. I never see a sheep now without wondering about him and if he'd delivered that ewe. Then it doesn't do to go on thinking about it, dwelling on it. I just feel half dead myself, you see. You can't be married for thirty-odd years and not feel it can you? But then he didn't suffer at the end, he wasn't that sort of man to drag anything on, not even death. I can't believe that I'll spend the rest of my life without seeing him. I always imagine he'll walk back in through the door like he always did saying 'Cup of tea, Dot, will do well'. I look outside and think he's only round the back, he'll be in soon, but then it hits me and I think – he's not at the farm, he's dead."

We walk through the cottage hallway into the other room and on the hall stand are all his old coats waiting for him. He was a huge man and the coats are as big as blankets. Sheep's wool and string hang from the pockets.

"I can't start life again although people tell me I must. My friends take me to the Zodiac Club; we do laugh, I'll say that. I've never drunk before but it seems all the women do now. We never went out, you see. I worked at the house cleaning and he was the stockman, that's how we met. Never regret a single day of it: … but they shouldn't have over-worked him, they should have helped him slow up. Lambing, lambing, lambing, calving, calving, calving – all for the money in their pockets. Now I have to leave here as I'm no use to them. I have to find another home. A man from the council came and offered me a flat but I can't live in a flat in town, I'm too used to fields and the lane here. I keep on at the boy to get a farm job like his father but he wants a factory job. Well you can't blame him really, can you, having seen what it did to his dad in the end.

"Well I must say though, my husband loved it here. Watching the rain come down from his little hut out on the marsh. He loved that little hut. I can't bring myself to go out there. But I will, before we go. I must. We were going to go on holiday together when he retired. My daughter's asked me to go to Butlin's. I'm going. My first ever holiday. I suppose if he'd come with us then he would only have spent half his time wondering what the animals were doing and worry and all. He was that sort of man, you see."

Family

"When my brother Carl was six we were evicted from Castle Street. I remember it distinctly because it was his birthday and the woman next door had made him a cake that he was clutching when the bailiffs came and he was flung by my mother across my small shoulders to stop him crying. Instead he yelled louder and was promptly very sick as he had also, that very morning, sunk his teeth into my father's tobacco and swallowed enough for a good smoke. In fact my father was more intent on shouting to my brother, 'That'll bloody teach you to go poking!', than he was talking to the bailiff when they marched through our hall. We went that day to live with my Uncle Ernest who ran a grocery shop the other side of town. It was a fine greengrocery and my Uncle's pride and joy. His wife, my Aunt Cissie, was none too pleased at the prospect of us four invading her neat and tidy home but Uncle Ernest had said 'You can't see your own brother and his kids out on the street can you?' and that was that, we were in; at least for four months. That was the limit according to Aunt Cissie. My father said it would be just a for a few weeks until work was found and all that was needed was a place for the wife and kids to lay their heads as my brother and I would be at school and he and my mother would be out at work.

"The only thing my parents did well was argue. They fought over everything it was possible to discuss or not discuss. Nothing was too slight to argue about. Never was there a day I can recall when my mother wasn't in tears or silent. My father was constantly smoking and his nicotine-stained fingers were a constant source of mystery to me. Over the four months exactly that we lived with Aunt Cissie and Uncle Ernest not a day went by without Aunt Cissie reminding us of how much longer we had left to stay. 'Two months and sixteen days and mind you don't steal any apples or grapes from the shop, and clean that sink.' By contrast Uncle Ernest was quite a wag. Carl and I adored him and could never control our giggles when we saw him mimic Aunt Cissie from behind crates of fruit that were always piled up in the shop.

"At six years old Carl would run through the shop yelling and clutched at everything in his passage in order to place it straight away in his mouth before anyone could see. Often it was a potato and sometimes the bright yellow moon-like grapefruits would catch his eye and in it would go. Sooner or later chunks of all sorts met up with the bits of tobacco, hair-grips, coal and paper that lurked inside him. My mother always said it was because she'd breast-fed him for too long. My father said it was because he was loopy.

"My mother's nerves became terribly bad after the eviction and she spent most of her time on her work-free days tidying up after us or keeping us quiet and unpicking the sleeve of her home-knitted cardigan. Eventually she had only one sleeve intact and an enormous ball of olive-green wool. My mother worked in the laundry a mile or so away and the continual steam in which she worked made her hair fall in minute ringlets around her head as though it were on fire.

"Looking back, I suppose my mother was a very attractive woman and, given all the continual rush and stress of her whole life, it is amazing how she looked as good as she did. My father was a very stocky man who was balding fast. He was always quite well turned out in spite of our financial setup and he usually wore a three-piece suit which, although it had seen better days, he always had cleaned and pressed by my mother at the laundry every other week.

"Eventually my father found work. It was in a bookbindery in the centre of town. He was no craftsman himself but he processed the accounts and new orders which in those days were plentiful. He had so many changes of job throughout my short lifetime, which by now was ten years, and considering how difficult work was to come by it was a small miracle that he was rarely unemployed. However all this hard work never seemed to get us anywhere and we were always in dreadful debt. He drank heavily and although I never saw him unconscious he was either very merry or extremely nasty. He virtually chain-smoked, much to my mother's horror and spent at least a quarter of his waking life in the betting shop; hence our eviction from Castle Street and the arrival of the bailiff.

"Uncle Ernest and my father had been raised in the north part of London that is now fashionable. They were two of eight brothers, only three of whom now survived, the others having died in childhood and the last one alongside of my grandmother, who being undernourished and doubtless exhausted, shuffled off this mortal coil at the delivery and prospect of her eighth child. Father and Uncle were then raised partially in an orphanage from the ages of six and seven respectively. Their father was killed in the First World War, no one knew where exactly but it was suspected to be in southern France. They therefore had scant memory of their parents and I frequently asked them both for stories of their childhood, which I found fascinating and rather daunting. Neither could understand my interest in the past or them as children, bearing in mind that they were always telling me off for being one myself.

"Carl and I enjoyed living in the greengrocers for it was a brand new experience and playground for us. We found sources of entertainment in the earth the potatoes arrived in and gazed at the exotic pictures on the sides of the boxes in which the imported fruit was packed. There were lemons from Cyprus, oranges from Spain, bananas from the Canaries and swedes from Devon. These magnificent dusky red objects were never quite the same for me after I stood next to Uncle Ernest as he unpacked a particularly ripe-smelling box to discover the carcase of a dead sheep inside. The beetroots would be boiled in the yard in an old zinc bath and the pink dye ran all over the lawn, much to Carl's delight. Uncle Ernest hosed the area down once a week and somehow or another Carl would end up with his clothes soaked and face beetroot red.

"Aunt Cissie and my mother got on together in a passing sort of a way. They each sympathised with the other for being married to a Clark, which was my family name. They had in fact done some of their courting together when they were young, having met the brothers at the same place on the same day. This, I understand, was during my Aunt Cissie's period of employment in a florist's shop in the centre of Pimlico, and my father and uncle had gone together into the West End in search of a job. They had stopped at the florist's shop to enquire directions to a local factory. Indeed it was my father who invited out Aunt Cissie and to make up a foursome she suggested she bring with her a neighbour's best friend's daughter who was staying at the time and needed 'a bit of a shake up'. The courtship, it seems, progressed quickly from there but halfway through they changed partners and my father ended up proposing to my mother in a matter of six weeks. A year later Ernest had married Cissie and by that time I was born and I am therefore present in all their wedding photographs as a tiny baby wrapped in a shawl in mother's arms. The florist's shop was owned by Aunt Cissie's parents. They also owned two greengrocery businesses which were in South London. They presented these to the couple on their marriage. They were a childless couple, a factor that had caused Cissie great periods of sadness throughout their married life and one that she now got over by claiming that she loathed small children due to the amount of mess and chaos that accompanied them. Ernest and Cissie were a devoted couple in their own way, so very different from my parents' constant battling. Cissie shouted a lot and nagged openly but she was tender in her off-guard moments and certainly Uncle Ernest praised his wife's management abilities and had deep respect for her, despite his often tormenting jokes, practical and otherwise. Having us come to live with them over this period obviously brought their lives into a different focus and little Carl benefitted from all the extra attention he received from his uncle, which he never or rarely received from my father. My mother, being as harassed as she was, had little time ever to talk to us boys and I found myself arranging my own care and devices much of the time. Largely it meant keeping out of my father's way, unless of course he'd had a win at the bookies, in which case he would pick me up on his knee and say 'Come here little one, take that frown off your face, here's a bob or two for some sweets.' So I would learn to take advantage of these times and seek pleasure with my father when I could."

When he kicked her

Mrs W comes into the office to see me. Three years ago she placed her two children into care because she "couldn't love them or stand their constant arguing". Mrs W visits the children every month; they are usually pleased to see her but recently their interest in her has begun to wane. Mrs W is crying as she sits down and she doesn't stop. She has one eye, the other having been removed by her own father's boot when he kicked her as a small child. Mrs W is married to a man half her age and size who injures her too, but she rarely leaves him for longer than a day or two. "I'm upset because my mum called me a slut. This bloke, see, he bought me a cup of tea in the transport café when I was running from Bob the night he assaulted me. Everything is my fault, the children in care, it's all my fault." Before I can stop her she runs from the room. The hem of her skirt has come undone in the front and as she rushed down the corridor fumbling in her bag for a cigarette she hits her elbow in the door frame. Outside in the car park there is a man waiting for her – he stands huddled against the tree, the strong wind taking all the hair from his face making him look quite pinched.

Love from Karen

I go and visit Karen; she's nine years old. Her mother is an alcoholic, her father is unknown. Brother Francis is in care some miles away; she sees him every week. Karen is also in care and lives with foster parents. Her mother does not wish to visit her as she claims it will upset her and admits that "in any case I feel guilty as hell and can't deal with it". Karen is waiting for me when I arrive. She is sitting tense and alone on the settee. I sit next to her. Usually she snuggles up to me but today she appears rigid and frightened. "You tell your social worker what you've done" begins the foster mother. "All of it?" she asks. "All of it." The child stares up and bites her lip. "Promise nothing terrible will happen if I tell you?" she asks. I tell her that I promise. "You see I was in a sweet shop and I stole some of these chews and a bar of honeycomb and chocolate for my brother. I did it with Mrs Simmonds' daughter; we got caught and the man from the sweet shop came here after us and now I think I have to leave here because I'm leading everyone astray." As she tells me this she climbs onto my lap and throws her small arms around my neck. "Also I put up two fingers at the teacher in class today and now I have to sit at the back of the class and I can't hear anything," she sobs. "Also I can't use knives and forks properly because we don't have them at home, only spoons, and I keep dropping them." I talk with the foster mother and before I leave Karen runs upstairs and brings down several small items. "This is for you, so you won't forget to visit me again." It is a small photograph of herself taken at school. There is also a child's picture book which she tells me to give to her mother if I see her. "Your mum will like that, I'm sure," I say as I leave. "Make sure she reads it all," adds Karen. In the car I thumb through the book and inside two letters drop out. They read:

– Dear Mummy, please will you visit me ever? I have been a very good girl. Perhaps I shan't ever see you again. I have bought you some soap. Tomorrow is firework day. I love you Mummy. Come soon. Love from Karen.

I will say that

Joan talks about her marriage. "But I don't know really what happened. I went back and he started on saying how it was all my fault and that he'd had chances too and now he is going to do what I did, you know go off with someone else. But I'm never going back to him again and all those bills, they aren't mine I'm not paying them. He says he will strangle me; he will you know, he'll kill me. He doesn't want me now anyway. I don't know what will happen from one day to the next. He told me that he'd let me know when I could phone him and we'd talk. Not that I'm going to be in when he rings. He put those plants in the garden last weekend and told me to go to the doctor about my rash; he can be a good man at times, I will say that. Down at the pub he told them a pack of lies about me, said I'd been carrying on and then I asked him who that woman was that rang up. No. I'm never going back to him but then he doesn't want me anyway. Oh I don't know, I'm just so confused, you've got to help me, you must."

Antenatal ward

In the Day Room the girls talk together all day, flip through old maga-
zines and baby catalogues and use the mobile telephone. The room is
thick with smoke; they are all at various stages of pregnancy.

"I've been here for three months now, low oestrogen level, see, I lost
the other baby at 6 months, that was a boy – I called him Dean after his
dad. I get really bored here, I just sit smoking and watching telly. They
keep telling me about smoking but I got nothing else to do and I get
worried."

She shifts her enormous frame from the low plastic chair, moves
some stray bleached locks from across her face to behind her ear which
has two single emerald stone earrings on the lobe. There is another hole
punched but there is no earring in it. "My bleeding back aches, I know
that much," she says. "Men, what do they know about all this. My old
man don't want me home; he's knocking off the girl next door. I reckon
she's a single mother cause I've never seen the same man go in there and
they all come out laughing. He's always fancied her anyway. He comes
in here to see me once a week and brings me the bills and he stinks of
booze."

"They're going to induce me tomorrow. I'm so scared. They use a
pessary and the pains come on really quick. I saw a girl yesterday on
this ward doubled up and her waters broke a few minutes after the
pessary went in. I hope they phone my husband in time, sometimes it
happens so quickly and he might miss it. He's looking forward to this
baby, says he's going to call it Kevin whether it's a boy or not, after Kevin
Keegan, the footballer. I'm wondering if the baby is all right because
they keep monitoring it and sometimes it feels funny. Yesterday they
had a power cut in here and I was on the monitor and the sound of
the baby's breathing stopped. I thought he was dead, it gave me a right
shock."

"I got a friend who had a baby and she said that having it was that
painful she almost died of a heart attack. Mind you she had a 9lb baby
and 15 stitches. Her husband was there and he fainted – he had to be
admitted onto the men's ward. Fat lot of good he was. My mate met
someone who'd had a baby without any arms or legs and they wouldn't
let her see the baby afterwards, my mate said it was because she drank

a lot of vodka when she was first pregnant to try and get rid of it. I'm looking forward to having my baby, I hope it's a girl." "What you had?" she turns round to ask me. I tell her. "Oh good, there's too many men about I'd say."

Labour ward

I am lying on my bed in the small room with my newly born daughter beside me. In the corridor outside the ward, orderlies are stacking away piles of fresh clean linen into the cupboard. They are talking and laughing so loudly. "I couldn't watch them with another couple, I'd get too excited and have to ask them to go home. As it is, my husband and I can't wait for the children to go to bed. That's why we're buying another video for the bedroom, then we can watch it with no one barging in. Really gets my husband going I can tell you, me too. The other night we had a real crude one called *The Cat, The Man and The Curtain*. I never did figure out where the curtain fitted in but anyway she was holding this thing and the cat walks in and then I got called away by the children squabbling upstairs and so I missed it but when I came back they were cutting it up and eating it…"

"My old man and I sit there of a night waiting for the children to go to bed so we can get started watching it, we look at one another laughing. Saturday afternoon, like today, he'll go down to the Video Club and get some more. Hope he brings back the one of the big black man – he's like a bloody monkey!"

"Especially abroad you've got to forgive a lot, haven't you? Our manager at the hotel was German, I know that's why the food was as bad. We had veal with tuna fish and tomato sauce in Spain, it was green and red. I like veal but not with fish, don't smell right somehow. My husband touched the waitress up at our table. I told him off but we got two helpings of chips. You don't realise how much weight you've put on until you put your skirt on to come home. I drank that much beer. I remember the night just before we came home we had fried kippers and a salad made from olives and brazil nuts and we had some purple Spanish liqueur. Me and Brian was throwing up all night."

"If she thinks I'm doing it she'll have a surprise. I'm sick of her leaving the side room for the day staff. That's the third time she's left that note on the door. I tell you I'm pissing well cheesed off here, I am. She comes down here hoity-toity, Miss Marks and Spencers 1979, she thinks she can boss us all up. Well, I'm going to see Mr York today and tell him he can stuff his job up his arse or he can tell her to stuff her arse out the door."

Postnatal

By the beds of all the women is a tiny plastic cot on wheels. Delighted parents and relatives peer inside or cuddle the baby. The new mothers are excited, bleary, tearful and tired. In the nursery where the staff teach you how to bath the baby and feed it we all gather by request, eager to learn how to cope with this new life.

"I haven't slept now for four days. I don't think I'll ever sleep again. I've had that many stitches I think the doctor must have been to embroidery classes. I can't sit down or stand up and I'm feeling faint all the time. I wish I had some energy to pick up the baby. Feel so dreadful." She begins to cry and we hand her a piece of green kitchen roll to dry her eyes on. "I've only seen my husband once since he was born and then I don't think he was very pleased; he can't cook for himself, you see, and his mother has gone on holiday." Her baby screams from its plastic cot and waves its minute arms in protest. "I can't breast-feed it, I can't. I don't care what they say, I'm bottle-feeding it. Why does it always cry like this? I don't think it likes me. Look at his little face all crumpled up like that, isn't he sweet?" She picks up the baby and holds him; he is quite wet with her tears.

"I don't know what I'm going to call her. I hadn't thought about any girls' names. I just wanted a boy really. Still she's a lovely baby alright but it's a pity she ain't a boy. I can't really call her Steve, can I? That's after her dad. He was called Steve." I ask whether he is still called Steve. "Oh yeah, I expect so. I haven't seen him for about 2 months. Someone told me he'd gone to Folkestone to live with his dad so I don't know if I'll see him again."

"I knew there was something wrong with the baby when I was carrying her. They told me when I had the scan. They said so. She's a Mongol baby. They can't make me take it home, you know. My husband wants to keep it but I can't, I just can't. They can't make me take it home, you know. I haven't seen her since she was born. I had an anaesthetic anyway when she was born but I did see her the next day and she was ugly and all squinty eyed and squashed looking. They've given me tranquillisers. I want to go home. My husband's going round home with my mum today and they're going to take all the baby's clothes away. She's in the Special Care Unit now. They keep asking me if I want to go and see her. They can't make me take her home, can they?"

A right laugh he is

Warren calls in to see me. He is eight years old and the youngest of three sons. His older brother Wayne is eleven, and bald from shaving his head with an electric razor last week. The oldest, Frank, is known in and outside of the family as Wank. Wank, or should I say Frank, is due to go to Detention Centre for the second time this year. He thoughtlessly stole the front double gate from the home of a local magistrate and sold it later the same night to a local farmer around the corner for twenty pounds. Warren tells me all his news. He has had a good Christmas. Loads of toys and also saw his father just before the New Year. Quite an event, since he hadn't actually seen him in four years and therefore had only vague and slight recollections of him built upon things overheard. "We have a new man living with us now though," he says as he walks towards the window and kicks at the wall. "He's called Ripper, a right laugh he is." "Why is he called Ripper?" I ask. "Oh I dunno. I suppose it is because he rips my mum's clothes off." Warren sits down on a chair; his feet don't touch the floor so he swings them continually. Now and again they hit the rung, hard, but he seems not to feel it. "Ripper looks after us. It's good really. My mum tells him not to have any rubbish from us lot but you know what Wank's like, he always spoils things. Mum says for him to smack Wank in the mouth if he won't do as he's asked. The other night he kicked him up the stairs when he wouldn't go to bed." "What did Frank say to that?" I ask. "Oh nothing really, he just sort of stayed in bed and when he got up in the morning all the pillow was red with blood from where Ripper has kicked him."

Seven pieces from the sauna

I

"Life without men is such a relief," she said. "Their strong hands and hair curling across warm shoulders. You can do without it," she said. "All that dressing up and the looking and the waiting and the hopes. What a relief," she said, "to be without hope."

II

"Luck. I was born lucky. Totally devoid of it," she said. She laughed. "At the nurseries today a coachload of young bronzed Dutchmen came to look around the tomato house and all the girls came out and flirted. A whole coachload of men and who do I get – the female teacher comes and talks to me. Luck, I was born without luck, totally devoid of it." She laughs.

III

"Oh the effort to be healthy," she said as she sweated away her huge limbs on the wooden slats. "Ten years I've worked on that Hoffman Press. For ten years that metal bar has struck into my side. Look, look," she said and showed me the dent and mark where the machine had injured her. "That's why my legs are so huge," she said. "You can't stand for ten years and not expect a result can, you?"

IV

"I told the Judge, I did, when I came to the Court. I don't want no maintenance from him. He can keep his money and his smell. But you can't reason with men can you and he made me take £4 for the girl but of course he never paid so we had to go back to Court and I told the Judge then, I said, 'his money stinks worse than what he does and I don't want it and he don't want to give it.' 'You're a special sort of woman,' the Judge said, and it made me feel all sort of glowing and happy just to see an important man like that say those things to me."

V

"They measure your legs and then they wrap you up in these bandages, tight as you can stand, then they cover it with cold stuff like unset jelly and then they leave you. We didn't half laugh, me mate and I. Then they take it off and measure you again and let you hold the tape measure so as there can be no cheating and you can see what you've lost. It's great. I lost three inches off my hips and two off my thighs. I don't know where the fat goes, they say it distributes it. All I know is that mine was all back by the end of the week."

VI

"He was conceived because I got an electric shock. I was plugging in the washing machine, I had wet hands and the next thing I knew I was on the floor on the other side of the room with my arm and hand all black and the nails gone and the arm jerking up and down. I was in a right state I can tell you. I rang me mum and we went to the hospital. I was in for two nights. Well I never took the pill those two nights did I and when I got home we conceived him. I didn't give it any thought. But he died at eighteen months old. Hole in the heart. I'm not being horrible or nothing but it was best really, seeing how the marriage was all wrong. I took him to the hospital almost every day at one time but he still died. Bill left the day after he died. He never even came to the funeral. He used to smoke Players and the morning of the funeral he put a note through the door written on the back on an old Players packet saying: 'Can't come. I am working.'

"Just that on the Players packet. Not even Dear Sandra or Love Bill. I didn't cry about him dying for three months. I had Theresa to look after see and I was all alone, so alone and then one day I lost my purse which was the end of the world for me as I had no money at all. I ran into my neighbour and she put her arms around me and said 'Never mind love it's only a purse with a few bob in it.' I cried and cried and cried. No-one had touched me you see for such a long time and I suddenly let it all go. I never have cried in front of my mum. I like her, I feel sorry for her actually but she can't accept me when I'm weak. I always have to be strong for her otherwise she'll just say again, 'you should never have let Bill leave you like that, you have to work at marriage, you know'."

VII

"Do you live in town?" the woman with short dark hair wearing only her locket asks me. "No, no," I tell her, "I live out across the marsh." She shifts uneasily on the warm slate. "How about you, you local?" I ask. "Yes we live over Stanhope Estate. You know it?" I tell her I know it. "I can't stay in here as long as I'd like to today as my old man will be waiting outside. He's changed his shift this week as he reckons I'm up to something while he's at work, thought he'd catch me out today he did by changing shift without mentioning it first. Slimy bugger he is. I've got nothing to hide, more's the pity I'd say. I work at the fish restaurant in town. I used to think it was a right hovel till I went to work there meself. Often my old man would say to me on a Friday night, 'Take you out to the fish restaurant, save you cooking,' and I'd say 'Last of the big spenders, no jolly fear, I might catch me death what with it being fish as well. But it's not that bad, in fact I'm seeing if I can work longer hours just in case I need to." "Need to?" I ask. "I might be leaving my old man soon you see and I'm going to want the money. The solicitor says I've got more than enough grounds, so I'm thinking about it. We've been that unhappy for years now and it's only a matter of time. He's had so many girlfriends, they still phone him up and I answer and I say to them – 'Lover boy's at St Moritz I'm afraid,' then I hang up. He's not at all exciting to look at, so I can't understand it. Most people wouldn't want to look once at him, let alone twice, but there's no accounting for taste is there? Take me for example, and I wish someone would. I used to think he was great at one time, five years ago. Now? Now I just think he's a barrel of shit." She shifts her hot red body on the wooden slats. "Cor, my bum's hot," she says. "What about you, you married? Don't answer that, I can guess – you look too well to be married. Well, it's all over now and that's for sure. One night we had just finished dinner at home, lovely dinner I'd cooked – pork chops, carrots, roast potatoes, peas. I can see it now. But anyway I'd had a very curious day with him not talking and me keeping out of sight just talking to the cat but anyway I still made dinner, lovely dinner and he ate it and read the paper, fell asleep. Sometimes I was relieved when he fell asleep because at least I didn't have to try and avoid him, did I? But I was buggered if I was going to wash up and clear away after all the trouble I'd taken. So he fell asleep and I read me book and the next day they were still there and the next and the next too.

"They just sat there for a week and a half going mouldy. They went bright green in the end. They became a sort of monument if you know what I mean, a monument to our marriage. It all represented his lack of feeling for us and my dislike of him. Being pork of course it solidified and caked up and went a very strange kind of white and purple mixed in with the green.

"Eventually I threw it all out, plates, cutlery and all. 'I don't know why you did that,' he said as I closed the dustbin lid on it all. 'Don't you,' I said, 'Don't you even trouble your head wondering about it then.' I was that upset. So you see it'd been a right loveless match from day one and I'm only too glad of this job at the fish restaurant so I can save up me money and buzz off." She moves her large limbs and makes to go. She fumbles at her neck touching the locket. "Cor, that's got bloody hot sitting here." "Who gave it to you? It's pretty," I say. "Oh he did of course. He's always generous with his money and his bloody moods."

No life in to him

I visit Grace. "Sit down, sit down," she says. "I've just been thinking, I've just been thinking about all those terrible days when the baby died and now I see his ghost all the time, you've got to make it go away."

Grace has been discharged from the mental hospital for just two days now and she sits sewing a grubby white dress which she tells me is to be her wedding dress when she marries another patient she met in hospital six months ago. He is still an in-patient and likely to remain so for some time. Her first marriage ended in divorce and her ex hasn't been seen in the eight years since. Years ago Grace had lived in an old caravan with the children outside of a small Kent village; they were not gypsies or travellers but they were the talk of the town. Grace has told me her story many times before and I sit on the moquette chair that's stuck together with dirt and impacted grease of years and Justin the Alsatian dog sniffs in my pocket.

"He hadn't been ill and was screaming so loud and Jim was shouting too and the two little ones were out shopping and Ben and Francis were working out the back chopping logs. So I picked him up and put him outside in the pram to give us all a bit of peace. Finally he stopped screaming and I went back into the caravan to peel the potatoes and start the tea. It was April and it didn't seem all that cold really. Anyway I called the boys in so they could have their tea before the little ones came back and then Jim and I had our tea. They came running in saying 'Mum, Mum, the baby's all blue and stiff, look, look!' I ran out and Jim ran out but we could get no life into him, he was dead. The doctor said the cold killed him but I just think he stopped living. He wasn't ever happy."

Grace then sobs for a long time and paces the room with the huge dog following her every movement. "And now I see him all the time, I sleep downstairs now as I'm too afraid to go upstairs but he comes up to where I lay on the sofa tugging at my nightdress calling 'Mummy, Mummy, let me in, I'm cold'."

Tommy

Tommy is a chatty and open child. He has four sisters who call him "champ".

He has a photograph of his father but he doesn't look at it very often.

When he was born, his father left the family. "I don't like boys," he told his daughters and wife. "I don't like Tommy."

Two weeks later he set up home three blocks away with a woman who had two boys.

Tommy never knew his father but once he saw him collecting the boys from the school gate. Arm in arm they were.

When he was six years old his father bought him a five-foot teddy and Tommy calls it "Big Dad".

It's very soft and warm and Tommy keeps his clothes on it at night.

Lee

"Yes, I did shout out 'Shut up, you little cunt' to the baby but I didn't hit him."

"She was running down the stairs with the baby and his head was shaking side to side – it must have been the shaking what caused the injury."

"She shouldn't have sold my radio then I wouldn't have been so angry but that kid cried all of the time anyway."

"The neighbours heard it, banged on the walls at us. She never had any patience with the kid. She threw her boots at him when he cried at night."

He stubs his roll-up onto the bare floor.

"So what if I did shout out, 'Shut up, you little cunt,' at the baby? He deserved it crying all the time, he should have learnt by now; he's six months old."

Wendy

The child was tiny for her age, short, thin, odd.

A lack of love since birth, constant separations from a mother who once blinded her sister in a rage.

The child disliked food and lacked any ability to show enthusiasm.

Those who know call it emotional dwarfism.

Constantly wary and on guard, she hears the conversation of adults three rooms away. An unpopular child with controlling manner and sinister gaze. The five-year-old greets me slowly. She draws minute figures for me and tells of her dreams in which a "huge witch will come and take me away from here gobbling me up as she flies".

Mark

He was locked into a room with his four brothers and two sisters for three days before the police broke in.

Finding his mother collapsed and hysterical in the kitchen, demented from the pressures of her solitary and luckless life, the policewoman removed the potato peeler from her limp white hands before escorting her into the ambulance. The children were hungry but not unhappy. The baby had slept for twenty hours after crying for fifteen. One of the older ones had painted the walls with excreta.

Mark can remember some of it but hasn't seen his mother since the day she closed the door. He is curious about his brothers and misses his baby sister.

Mark is waiting for a new family to adopt him. He writes stories about a hunch-backed boy who lived in a cave and he always asks me if I will love him forever.

He left us

Dawn is a difficult girl; her mother is afraid of her tempers. They remind her of her own. Her father left them three years ago for a woman half his age with a car, energy and no demands.

I am asked to talk some sense into Dawn. I ask her what music she likes. "I don't know," she says. I ask if she has a boyfriend. "I don't know," she says. "People at school are worried about you, your mum is concerned that you are so depressed," I say. "I don't care," she says. In the corner her mother sits and weeps and I suggest she leaves us alone.

She does. "Your mother is depressed and tired," I say. "I hate her," she replies. "She's so miserable and weak and let my dad go off with that woman. I hate him too, he left us, he left me." Dawn's large angular body is laying on the settee, her acned face is streaked with her old make-up. "Was it all her fault?" I ask. "I don't know," she says. Her mother comes back into the room and the two women look at one another for a second before looking away again.

Odd but deeper

Robert says, "See I just woke up some time last month and asked one of the staff what the time was and my throat felt all sort of odd, not sore exactly but strained. I thought it was probably all that glue sniffing that I'd done but then when I shouted at me mate across the football pitch it seemed to make a queer sound and not come out really." We walk together through the grounds of the children's home where Robert lives now and he shows me some new bulbs appearing through the soil around the base of the trees. "That reminds me," he says, "I must have been here nearly a year now because the flowers were all out the day you brought me here. Anyway, as I was saying, I shouted across the football pitch and nothing came out but then eventually it did and it sounded odd but deeper. For a few days I hardly spoke to anyone because they rib you something rotten here. Then me mum phoned me up and she said. 'Who's that?' and I said, 'It's me, Robert,' and she said, 'Get off, it ain't'. I said 'It is, it is me.' Then she said, 'Your voice has broken,' and I said, 'Yes, I know.'" We walk back to the house and I tell Robert how he is taller than me now and he laughs and says, "That's not very hard, is it?"

Too slow you see

"She was one of the last ones out when it came to it. The last one out of the dug-out. She was too slow, you see, and in any case they didn't care that much where she was at any given time. I always did though.

She'll always be my baby, my June."

She hugs the fifty-year-old Down's Syndrome woman to her breast. "When she was five they didn't believe in them going to school, they wanted me to send her away. 'You'll get tired of it,' they said. I said I wouldn't and I didn't and I haven't, much as they know or care. I will always remember her being the last one out of the dug-out after the bomb fell. Her little face bewildered and lost. It made her afraid of being alone for life."

June looks up. Tells me she wants to make me a calendar. She makes them all year round for the year just past.

In sickness and in health

Mrs James is tired and worn after the weekend. Her husband tried to commit suicide again and she is left to calm the children down. Mr James went out on Sunday night to a local quiet spot, drilled a hole through the floor of their maroon Cortina, placed a hose through the floor to the exhaust pipe, put the other end under a woollen blanket then sat underneath it and breathed in deeply. He was there for some hours; his jacket had caught over the hole and he had eventually woken quite dazed and driven home. Mrs James had been searching for him, so had the neighbours and the police. She brought the blanket and green plastic hose pipe to show me. They were burnt black and stank of carbon monoxide. Mrs James leant against me and she cried. "Tell me," she said, "Tell me why I love him, all the terrible things he's done to me over the years, the injuries, the bruising. I've seen the police doctor before when he's clouted me so hard. But he's always been the same, never know when he will change, for years he's been moody. One day you think your life is in order, you relax and then, snap, off he goes again. I'm just terrified of him now, a permanent state of fear. The children just avoid him. The other night I came home from work, cooked the tea, cleared up, did the washing, sat down, asked what was on TV. Well, he went berserk, threw his book at me, shouted that I was a lazy cow. How do you have respect for a man like that? Now of course he's had this breakdown and I have to chase all over for him and hide his pills and put up with it. He's so pathetic really I could cry for him if I wasn't so afraid of him. In sickness and in health, my God in sickness…" We stare at the blanket and the green hose lying on the floor.

Chances

Billy is serving a life sentence in a Kent prison. He is twenty-two years old. At eighteen he and two other men went into an off-licence with two sawn-off shotguns and demanded the takings. The manager declined and they shot him at point blank range in the chest. Dead. They ran outside and into the police van.

At the Assizes the judge summed up by saying that Billy had been given every chance in the past to be an honest citizen but that he clearly had now shown that he was unable to be trusted. In view of the cold-blooded murder of the manager of the Ruislip off-licence, Billy would go to prison for life. He tells me about it. "I was numb, man, totally numb. I knew I'd go down for a long time but I didn't think it would be forever. I was just lost when I was eighteen. I'm more lost now. They say I might get out in another twelve years if I'm good. I used to work in the tyre factory but I was black and I had no woman. I wanted money. Fast. I suppose I was given every opportunity. I came into care when I was seven years old. My mum disappeared, you see, and they put me in one of those homes where some nice women cared for me. My sister was in care too but I never saw her, she was three miles away in another home. I went to a good school, we had a uniform. I was good at school but I could have done better. I had a grey blazer with a badge. At fifteen I was still in care and I had this social worker who let me meet my sister. She'd grown a bit in those eight years, she looked like a whippet without legs. I liked the social worker, he was a good bloke, gave me fags – you got any? Well anyway I then started taking things from a shop and then I didn't go to school and I kicked a bloke's head in at the home. After that it all seemed to happen. I got caught stealing again and then I went to Detention Centre for six months. I got really fit that six months. Muscles like barrels. I had met some good mates. I came out and I used to fold up my blankets and do hospital corners. The home couldn't believe it. Anyway then I had to leave the home as they was closing down so I went into a hostel. I started work at the tyre factory and then out of the blue, after ten years, my mum came to see me. She arrived on my doorstep at the hostel with a new geezer who tried to push me around. One night he got really heavy so I showed him. I broke his jaw. Anyway I did go and live with my mum again and then I met this girl, really nice girl she was, we got on well, but then one night we had a fight and I split her lip. She'd been good to me, she had. Yes, well then I met these blokes in a pub one night and finally we got together this plan for the off-licence. We worked it out, took over six months. We didn't intend to kill anyone, you know. It just happened. Johnny got these shooters from his brother. I had never used one before."

"The judge was right though; I did have opportunities in my life, didn't I? I suppose I just didn't take them.

"I work in the kitchens now here. I start at 6 a.m. and finish at 7 p.m. It kills the time. I earn good money and can buy me records. It scares me shitless to think of going out of here. It's all I think about, getting out and what I'll do. But it does terrify me. I don't think I'll cope. I just want a good woman to settle down with. Still I try not to think about it. When you've got a life sentence, tomorrow's a long way off.

"Funny really, talking about all this, my old lady came to see me yesterday and she said it was all my dad's fault for kicking her around because then she wouldn't have gone off and left us. But I don't know. I reckon it was the best thing she ever did."

Right at the peak season

Deal is flooded, several feet underwater in parts. Homes ruined, people uprooted from their homes. A tragedy. A declared disaster area. A handicapped woman living close to the sea wall has been pinned into her home by shale, drifting wood and rubble. The army and police force her door open and let me in. Luckily the house has escaped much water damage but there is no gas or electricity and for thirty hours she has sat cold and terrified. I ask her if she would like to move out for a while but she refuses, telling me how, until seven years ago, she had worked as a lavatory attendant on the front here at Deal. "For years watching the women come and go, and some of the things I've seen, my dear." She begins to cry. "I'm sorry it's just being trapped here for so long and being unable to move, and the dark and no heat." We are told that gas and electricity will be restored shortly and until then she speaks to me of her working life on the front and her fun and laughter with the man from 'the Gents' and how he died on the job one summer morning right at the peak of the season.

Up town for a bit

Julia has come into the office to see me. She comes in every week on a Wednesday at 2.30 by order of the court. She is supposed to come after school but we both know that she hasn't been for a month but, at sixteen years old, with a diagnosed mental age of twelve, and three weeks before leaving day there doesn't seem much point. Julia's parents are divorcing, her sister is due in court for stabbing an animal to death and there are important things on her mind other than school.

She stands in the doorway, a large girl wearing a padded jacket underneath her padded anorak. It makes her seem enormous. Julia has shaved her head in the week, which makes her face seem even larger and her spots bigger. "Do you like me hair?" she asks. "I'm going to get a job shelf-filling at the precinct and I thought this seemed genic." I ask if she would like to sit down. "No, I can't stop, Brian's outside waiting and we're going up town for a bit." I ask how her mum and dad are getting on. "Oh them, they're like a couple of tomcats. Anyway I got to go now. I'm glad you like me hair."

Julia slams the door after her and I watch her disappear across the carpark alone. There is no Brian and there is no shelf-filling job. Just an oversized young woman with her shaved head and a sadness.

It's this house

Mrs White is a large woman. I sit on her PVC sofa while we talk about her child who, at eighteen months old, she claims, is maladjusted and violent, like his older brother. Mrs White tells me that the child doesn't respond to discipline of any kind and throws his toys at her. He had cried solidly almost for two whole months after he was born; nothing would pacify him. His birth had been difficult and it was some time before Mrs White was able to cuddle him. She had been told that he might die as he seemed unable to digest his food, although there were no discovered medical reasons. Mrs White has her theories. The child was one of a twin, the other being born dead, the body had begun to decompose; she was sure it was a punishment. An Indian doctor had told her at the ante-natal clinic that the twins were well and thriving and that in his opinion all twins were in communication *in utero*. Mrs White was certain the baby was in mourning for his twin and that the trauma of it made him cry non-stop. Mr White sits in the corner of the room quietly while we talk; he watches half smiling. He begins to speak and so does Mrs White. He interjects loudly, "Be quiet, woman. You stupid cow." He glares at her. "Let me speak, you ignorant bitch." I look at him waiting for his words. "Bloody child cries all the time, it's violent too, you should do something about it, you people, you should do your jobs better, call yourself social workers!" Before I can ask him what he feels should be done he gets up and storms out of the room and we hear him mumbling as he walks up the stairs. "Bloody bitch, bloody bitch." Mrs White and I remain on the PVC sofa; she is in tears. "It's this house," she says, "It's this house…"

PROSE

II

Prose from
The Meaning of Things

Court in Progress

The girl is physically large; her face is blotchy with the crying, mascara running. She glances across the court at her mother who will not look at her.

"Will you tell the court – did you notice anything strange about Kim on the Friday evening?"

"No, she was fine, she got down from the sofa herself."

"Did she eat her food?'

"No, she was picky."

"Did she sleep that night?"

"No, she was whining as usual."

"Who put her to bed?"

"Brian, he always put her to bed."

"Did anything different happen that night?'

"Yes, it was a different whingeing, high-pitched."

"What did Brian do about that?"

"He told her that if she didn't stop he'd hit her until she shone like a beacon."

"He said that? What did you do about it? It was your baby daughter he was talking to."

"He always said that to her, he wouldn't hurt her, only slap her, but she was always whingeing. He usually made her stop. She loved him."

"But Kim is thirteen months old and she had very serious injuries which the Consultant confirmed were inflicted that Friday night. What have you got to say about that?"

"I don't know. She was OK on the Sunday morning but she didn't wake us up as usual by throwing her toys at me; that was when I wondered if she was all right."

"She was far from all right, she had an arm fractured in four places. Did you look at her arms?"

"Yes, they were swollen and bruised."

"Did that worry you?"

"No, she always bruised easily. Debbie's children had fallen on her in the week."

"Is it true that you dragged Kim across the floor on Friday night?"

"No. I dragged her across the stairs."

"Why?"

"I panicked."

"What about?"

"She wouldn't listen to me."

"But she's only a baby, did you not understand that?"

"She has to learn. I was frustrated by her."

"Are you concerned about her now?"

"Yes."

"Why haven't you visited her in hospital?"

"I didn't have the money. I didn't know I could go. The social workers didn't tell me I could visit her. I thought she'd been taken for good."

"What do you want to happen now?"

"I want Kim back. I didn't mean to hurt her. I love her but she won't do as I tell her. I want the social workers to show me how to be a good mother."

The girl's mother stands up and shouts before anyone can stop her.

"You can't have her back, You're not fit to be a mother. I should have finished you off at birth, you've never been any good. You won't listen to me. You've never listened to me." She sobs.

The clerk tells her to sit down; the social worker goes to her, comforts her. The girl in the witness box starts to shout out.

"I never was good enough for you. You never gave me anything."

The chairman of the bench says "The court will adjourn for 30 minutes."

The three magistrates stand, turn and walk away.

The clerk follows, pressing the red button on her desk that lights up the sign on the door "Court in Progress."

In the Village

1.

Nora tells me she has a fungicidal foot. Not a suicidal foot I'm glad to hear. It's all swollen up and when she saw the doctor he said it was through wearing vinyl shoes, there being no escape for the sweat. Nora said he told her to wear leather shoes or no shoes. As she tells me this I notice she's wearing a brown pair of vinyl shoes. "Why don't you wear leather shoes?" I ask. "Oh well," she says, "these look like leather don't they, with imitation grain, the doctor will never notice the difference." I tell her that her fungicidal foot won't get better in that case. She says, "It will because the shoes look just as good as leather ones."

2.

Just behind the factory set back in the field they say a German man lives on his own; he's been there since 1947. He was there before the factory and they say he's a Nazi war criminal; it was he who saw the end to thousands of lives. "Of course you can't prove it," the plumber said, "and there's not much anyone can do about it." They say he never goes out but when he does buy potatoes at the village shop they give him green ones.

3.

I ring up to order my Christmas meat.

"I'm just finishing the ironing," says the butcher's wife, "but I'll take down the order. George has broken his shoulder," she says. "Terrible – he can't move until the 23rd."

"He was in the abattoir, had gone down the steps. His feet went one way and his body went the other. He was unconscious on the floor for some hours even though the other man was down there too. He had the grinding machine on, couldn't hear him moan."

"When he got home he took the bandages off and started work again for the Christmas meat – he collapsed with pain. Now he's strapped up again but he's undone it twice. He can't believe that a butcher like him can be laid up at Christmas, trussed up like a turkey for three weeks with no guarantee of freedom."

I enquire about capons.

"Oh no, they have withdrawn them," she says, "they used to put pellets in their heads to turn them off female birds, save their energy for the table, but now they've discovered the hormones react in a funny way."

"Tell George we hope he's soon better," I say.

"Thanks," she says, "he's under my feet all day, fussing with his arm in the air. I wish he could have a pellet, I can tell you."

Luxury Goods

His father was a broad man, wide but tall as well. A large man. Solid. Ran his life by the book. A VAT inspector. His death was sudden, unexpected but not dramatic. He simply died while everyone else slept.

"When Bobby and I went to the undertakers with Dad's measurements we saw to it that the coffin was a good oak. None of your sapele or teak." "Will it make it a luxury good?" Mother asked. "If it's classed as a luxury item we'll have to pay VAT on it; Dad told me that."

Bobby and I told her not to worry but the undertaker told us that "dying is considered an essential item. It was classed," he told us confidentially, "along with women's sanitary attire." He shuffled uneasily, his face glowing, "although you can't get away without death or bleeding it is classified, nonetheless, as a luxury good."

We had a headstone and entered the name in the Book of Remembrance.

We paid VAT on both.

"What would Dad have said about it?" cried Mum. "He tried hard to avoid paying VAT himself. Always said that anything that was a luxury good was avoidable. VAT is strictly for the stupid, Barbara. He would have been so cross. Strictly for the stupid." "And for stiffs and bleeding women," Bobby added.

Queuing

Queuing in front of me at the Sainsbury's checkout the slim dark-haired woman wears overalls. Nylon beige with gingham inset. She has a shopping trolley with chrome handles. The aisles are so cramped we can barely get our shopping through them.

"Good of Mr Sainsbury to give us so much room, given the money we spend in his shop," the woman in the queue shouts out. "The girl at the till shouts back, "Started at 6 a.m. finishing at. 6.00 p.m., haven't I? They're going to knock this store down and move into one of the big superstore spaces out of town. It suits me here you see, I can just about walk it. That's why I do my shopping in bits so I can carry it meself. I work for next to nothing for being on my feet all day."

Another cashier, young schoolgirl, acned face, label on her breast saying *Frankie* rings her bell, puts up her hand holding a packet of fish fingers. "85p," says the other girl. "I reckon I know everything in this store, I've been here a year. It's not been an easy year. I'm on my own you see. Two children at home, both waiting for me to get home now, they get worried if I'm not back. I'm their only security now. 14 and 10 they are. It's a lonely life. I have to run after work to get back to them, run with me shopping." The girl at the next isle rings her bell again raising a tin of pilchards above her head. "42p," shouts the other woman. "Sometimes I'm cashing these things in my sleep." Finally it's her turn and she piles up her groceries on the desk showing her staff pass as she pays. "Good luck, love," says the younger woman. "I'm no need to worry about me. I'm quite content now he's gone, set up home with a manageress from Richards Shops, didn't he; she's welcome to him and his snoring. Anyway she had a face like a cream cake." The girl starts on the next shopper's trolley, holds up a packet of biscuits as she rings the bell. "24p, love," says the woman as she leaves pushing her shopping trolley in front out. The price on the side says 56p. She winks and says, "Getting my own back on Mr Sainsbury, I am."

Sharply Across the Top of the Head

The mother's case was simple. She wanted the child returned to her. In the evidence she claimed that life was now better. She had changed, now happily married to a man who didn't beat her; secure housing. What she didn't say was that she loved the child.

The Local Authority evidence said that adoption was in the best interests of the child seeing how the relationship between the mother and her child had always been poor. They claimed that even now the mother's life was in turmoil and that the man whom she had married had a record for injuring children and women.

In cross-examination the mother's barrister asked the social worker whether the child had been happy since coming into care. In truth the social worker said that the child had cried easily and constantly and suffered from a quick temper; she also shook with fear if she wet her knickers.

In cross-examination of the mother the Local Authority barrister inquired why the child should shake if she wet her knickers. The mother said she could not think why it would be so since if ever the child did wet her knickers she would simply tap her hand with a stick.

The barrister went on to say that witnesses could be called who would say that they had seen the mother holding the child out of the sixth-storey flat in which she lived by her ankles and that also scalds had been found on the soles of the child's feet. People who knew about it said the mother did it to teach the child a lesson. When asked about it the mother broke down.

In her evidence the mother said that her relationships were now stable and happy but later agreed that her new husband had recently left when she asked him to mend the hoover. He had now returned. She agreed that he was a good man and that although he had accidentally injured children in the past he had now changed and would be a good father.

When asked if he had ever injured her, she said that he had hit her but only once, sharply across the top of her head with a cricket bat because she had lied to him. The mother added, "I hadn't lied, but I often look as though I am lying, I can't help that, can I?"

That's How

We are standing by the baby-food counter looking at the tins and jars, the rusks and bibs. A mother, shopping, has a pushchair with a sleeping tiny baby and a walking toddler who has grabbed armfuls of tins and is spreading them on the floor, an older boy racing round too who has taken one of the baby bikes from the display unit and is careering between the Saturday shoppers' legs. The tiny baby stirs and starts to cry. "Oh Jesus," the mother says. "There's nine months between each of these; you want to try that." The walking toddler has now taken off all the bibs from the shelves to add to her pile and is making for the plastic pants. They slide easily in a devastating pile before her. "How old is the baby?" I ask. "He's two months now, was two months prem. He's been such a worry; I never thought he'd make it. He's had one thing after the other, chest infections, collapsed lungs. I had a Caesarean and couldn't move for two days. He was on special care and they wanted me to feed him, I couldn't. I didn't want to. I felt too tired out. I thought I'd recover first and then go and see him but the nurses wanted me to go straight away. I didn't feel ready for him for another two months. But there he was so I did my best, but I kept on crying every time I saw him. I didn't have one card sent to me. No one even knew I'd had a baby. My husband is a lorry driver; he's gone for four days when he does the Scottish trips. This time he was in Italy and had gone for ten days. My other two were with my neighbour. I was that low. Then, when I checked his pockets when he got home I found he had been staying in the red light district with a whore. He told me I was wrong but I'm not daft." The older boy rams his mother legs with the car. "Bloody hell, just finish me off, why don't you?" she screams.

Without Blinking

Mrs C gives evidence. She is barely 20, she wears a blue nylon suit and high heels, very short hair, dark. She speaks easily and loudly.
   "How long have you been married, Mrs C?"
   "5 years."

"A happy 5 years?"

"On and off."

"What have the difficulties been about?"

"We had personal problems and rows, he wouldn't understand that it was difficult to keep the place tidy with four of us in one room."

"For some of the period after living in one room you were hospitalised and very ill. Did Mr C understand your problems with health?"

"Yes, he understood."

"How long were you having disagreements about the standard of housework?"

"About 4 years."

"So you were always arguing about it?"

"Yes."

"What personal problems did you have?"

"They are personal."

"Your sex life?"

"Yes. That and the housework and being in one room, the four of us, him, the child, me and his mother."

Which We Weren't

"Talking about death," said the accountant, "which we weren't, I remember, when I lived in Hythe as a child, the old thick waxed gas capes. This old dear who lived on the front used to wear hers all the time; there was no need, they were terrible things. Hot and heavy and sticky. When her husband died she put him under the bed and told no one. But people knew; they suspected he'd gone. He'd never been very strong and when they didn't see him they wondered. Several people tried to get in the house but she'd never let them in, just came to the door in her cape shouting for them to go away and to leave her and her husband alone. She said she was all right, didn't need a doctor, that he'd never looked better in his life.

"People left it for a while, a few weeks actually, then she had to go out one day and when they saw she had gone they took the front door off its hinges and put their gas capes over their mouths and went in.

Under the bed they found him dead as a dodo.

"A number of the men were sick. I was watching from the beach side of the road. When the old girl came back she ran into the house screaming from all the windows. 'Someone's stolen my husband. Help, help.'"

I said that it must have been frightening for him as a child.

"No," he said, "I always found it quite amusing, quite amusing."

"These figures of yours don't add up here," said the accountant.

"Talking of humour," I said, "which we weren't."

Achilles Heel

In the harbour there was a boat, a yacht more accurately, which had been named Grandson. She wondered, was this yacht instead of a grandson, or perhaps because of a grandson or for a grandson. It was maybe none of those and, in truth, she would never know and what did it matter, people had lives and ideas that no one knew about, for sure.

Truth was, she felt that usually she knew too much about people's lives, the details, the ups and mostly the downs. What he had said, what she had done and when the police had been called and when they left and what the children saw. Always it was about the children. Problem was that the children didn't get a look-in half the time, there was no room for thinking about how they might feel, stuck trying to make sense of it and where they stood in the muddle of it all. It wasn't about the children, it was about how the adults might use them to muster up support for their own cause.

She found herself saying the Bob Dylan words, "She just punched my eyelids and smoked my cigarette." Or was it the other way round, punching the cigarette and smoking the eyelids, she would find out.

But, here she was on holiday and already she had been thinking of what something meant. Grandson......, maybe one day she would have one of those herself. But for now she could stretch out, pause between the responsibility of her own children and supporting the next generation. Sitting on the lounger at the small beach in what was called "A Beach Club Resort" she read the newspaper and did some of the quick crossword. What could 8 Across be? – Orange cushion. Plato's life, an egg joke perhaps… Such clues required an education far different to her own.

A Brazilian family a few yards away sat, or rather splayed across the seats, their enormous frames bulging from the loungers and seats. They were eating chips and the adults were smoking. After a few minutes they ordered more chips from the passing waiter. The smaller of the two boys in the family cried out as his mother wrenched an electronic game from his hands and he started to wail. The mother was firm and held on to the gadget, the father remained motionless, smoking. Across and to her right, two men laughed and combed one another's hair, a young couple lay sleeping rolled up in each other's arms. She noted the man was, however, eyeing a young woman's bottom at the next table as she walked by in her thong. The resting woman was strong in her lover's arms, innocent that his thoughts were far from being upon her.

An hour later she walked down the main street and sat at the Demetrious Fountain Café. No fountain, also no Demetrious but a café of a kind, and as she approached a seat in the sunshine a large man with even taller companion approached. The taller man had his arm resting along his companion's shoulder. After a formal greeting the pair sat down and she watched them. She was almost instantly aware that the larger man was disabled and his friend was caring for him. The pair ordered drinks and food before her and she watched as the smaller, older man took charge. He was, she now noted, much older and that his companion was perhaps his son or younger brother. Over the next hour she struck up a conversation with the older man; he told her that he lived locally and that his brother was visiting him, this time for five months, usually he came for three, this time longer to give his mother some respite. She was old and tiring, herself. His brother, he explained, had been injured in his brain at a young age in a bike accident and was very damaged. He could function well mentally but needed constant guidance, especially in walking and talking, but his arm was dead and unless he could rest it he could not walk. He was fine, but the guidance was key, he explained. She noted that during the meal the younger man barely spoke but laughed and appeared happy and was prepared to be helped. As the pair left the café she saw that the taller man leant very heavily upon his brother, that his arm, his huge arm, his very dead arm, weighing maybe 5 stone or more, leaned upon his brother and that together they walked home from the café like yoked oxen, steady, slow, very slow, the older man clearly burdened. The younger, knowing this, walking slowly.

Easter Holiday London Trip

On the Circle Line in the Easter holidays a young family boards the train at Oxford Circus. The children are aged about 2½ and 5. The little boy sits next to me with his father at his other side. He is sitting on his knees and his hand is between his legs. His sister and mother sit opposite. "I want to go to the toilet, I want to do a wee wee," the little boy says. "You definitely want to go now, son?" his daddy asks, "why didn't you tell me before we got on the train? We will have to get off now." "No, I don't want to go now," the boy says. His sister pipes up, "why does he always cause so much trouble when we go out?" "He's not," the mother says. "Yes, he is, he is," she added, "anyway I want something to eat." A few minutes pass and we are now at Euston Square. "I've got to do a wee wee now, now," the little boy says. "We have to get off and go," the father says. The boy shakes his head fiercely and repeats that he no longer wants to go.

The mother has given her daughter the remains of a McDonald's which she starts to eat hungrily. A few seconds later her mouth puffs up while she makes vomiting sounds. "Are you going to be sick?" asks her mother. "No," she says, "I'm fine." The little boy is now clutching his genitals again and is jumping up and down. The father is holding a drink carton and says, "We are all going to have to get off and you are going to have to go in this cup." "I won't go in the cup," the boy says, "I don't want to go any more, I will be all right, I will be all right." The mother says, "We will be getting off soon." The girl has started to choke; the mother offers her the drink. "I don't want that," she says, "he might go to the toilet in it." "But he hasn't," the mother says. The child continues to make gagging sounds and the little boy jumps up and down.

I get off.

What She Said

What she said, when I asked why she hadn't seen the children, was that she had meant to but hadn't, she had wanted to but then as it had been so long that she thought it best to stay away. Then she cried a bit and I asked her if she wanted a tissue. "I want my f…..g kids," she said. I told her she needed to show the court that she was responsible now and could care for them properly. She looked out of the window. "Why don't you take someone else's kids away?" Then she spat. As she walked away she turned back and shouted, "Anyway, you can have them, see if I care." I watched her angry back walk into the heavy doors.

When she came back she said that it wasn't me she was angry with. She told me that she had been twelve years old when her mum left her; she had never seen her since and hadn't wanted to see her anyway. "I can't be it, I can't love them enough."

She walks away pressing digits on her mobile phone as she walks out of the building. I watch her as she passes the hoardings on the roadside advertising milk.

In Her Caravan

She has his photograph, it's a blurred picture of a tiny baby propped up by the Tampax box. She tells me she has no regrets.

He had to go, what with her health and all that.

Signs the paper readily to make him someone else's to love and restore back into focus.

"My Dad, yes

will show you all up, taking the Mickey out of him isn't a good idea if you want to live a long time, lady," he says as his pierced face, red and swollen, leans into mine. The gold ring is bent and he catches my eye.

"Costs you to look, want to kiss my arse?"

As he walks away down the path the dog on the leash barks, gets too close for comfort; it's eating a Happy Meal.

Danny

Won't speak to me, runs round the room and then shakes the dolls by the throat, stares at me for a while and then writes on his left hand with biro "left". Throws sand for a while and then says he wants to sleep, drawing up the cover over his head; then he shouts out, "She left me."

Susan

Tells me that this baby will be her fourth and that it is a boy again, that his father treats her like she was a film star. "Then he tells me I'm an old slag," she laughs.

"I got an infection in my privacy from him," Susan says and starts to cry. While she fumbles in her pocket for a tissue her phone falls to the floor. "I was on the phone to the doctor about this pain but he hung up on me."

Susan wipes her face on her sleeve. "When I went to hospital, no one visited me, not that I wanted anyone to hold my hand but you never know, do you, it might be OK if they did."

When He Asked Her

She had been standing by the photocopying machine when he'd asked her. "Would you come to Greece with me, Jay, I've got two tickets and it's a three-star hotel from the 3rd August for two weeks. I'd like it for you to come." She didn't hesitate: "Will I need malaria tablets?" He was confused by this response and said he'd find out and that they'd maybe talk about it on Friday when he picked her up. She had known Connor for four months, liked him; he worked in IT Support, they had met in the canteen. He had seen her for several days, wondering if he could speak to her. She was always surrounded by other people. On this particular day, Thursday 17 March, her friend Becky had gone to collect knives and forks and she had been left on her own. He seemed very tall then – she had noticed that. She also noticed that his shoes seemed far too big for his feet, *like boats* her gran would say, they did literally float away from the sides of his feet. He'd come up to her at the table just as Becky came back. "Hi Jay," he had said, "how is it in Finance?" "It's fine," she said, "a bit boring, but I'm getting there, the girls have been very helpful; not sure they all like me though." Connor asked if she needed any extra help. He then said, "If you feel like you need it, do you want to meet for a drink on Friday? I'll be at the Fox at 7.00 p.m." She said that she would. Becky had laughed out loud and pointed at Connor's shoes as he walked away. "Shh," said Jay, "I like him." Since then they had seen each other twice a week, sometimes three times, she'd been to his home, he'd been to hers. He had a Renault Clio which his father had given to him when he was 18. "I'm lucky really," he said, "spoilt rotten, that's me." That was all he'd said about his family. He'd met her mum, "Pleased to meet you Mrs B," he'd said and held out his hand. He looked her straight in the eye as if he had nothing to hide and she liked that about him.

She was 20 when he asked her to go to Zante with him. She told her mum. "Who's paying? It will be expensive, you mark my words." It's Connor's treat," she said. "There is no such thing as treats," her mother had said. Everyone wants something in return. Her grandma was the worst. "Don't go running off with any Arabs. Bring us back 400 Bensons and don't drink anything but bottled water, don't even clean your teeth in it, don't eat no fruit nor salad, if you vomit a lot dunk your head in the sea. Don't let those Muslims get you to eat their meat, wear one of those hats, or blow you up either." Her mother had then added as she turned away, "Don't give anyone your credit card, not even in a bank, ring me every day and don't get pregnant." With her mother's words ringing in her ears she wondered if she had known that she had already slept with Connor. It had not been good; she had regretted it and he knew it, she always did somehow.

He picked her up at 4.10 a.m. outside her house; his friend Martin drove them in his truck, it was on his way round the M25. She clambered into the front seat. It was very dark and very cold and her bare feet in the thonged sandals seemed out of place and she wished now she was wearing her Ugg boots instead. Connor was wearing his football shirt, jeans and for reasons she could not understand, new, even huger boots which made his feet seem larger than ever. He was excited and he cuddled her against him as the truck drew away and into the darkness. "Got your passport and everything then, Jay?" Connor asked. "Got your bikini and your pill," said Martin as he nudged Connor and slapped his thigh. Martin had originally been planning to go to Zante with Connor but he had backed off at the last minute.

At the airport hoards of people were queuing at the desk. Connor held the tickets in one hand with his case and he held her hand with the other, he was sweating and seemed anxious. Jay asked him how many times he had been abroad. "Once with me parents, once with the school and now with you. That'll be the best trip of them all," he said and she kissed him. In the departure lounge Jay looked at his new boots, They had writing down one side and were yellow with huge laces coming out of metal rings. When did you get those boots, Connor? She laughed as she spoke and he looked upset. "Don't you like them then?" "I think you might get a bit hot, that's all," she said, "and maybe not so good in the sand."

On the plane Connor had a beer. "It's only 9 o'clock," she said. "I'm on holiday now Jamie and it's all to play for, it's all to play for," he had said. Jay read her magazine while Connor listened to his iPhone. He moved his feet up and down with the music and sometimes whistled quite loudly. "Can you keep still for a bit? Also your boots are so hard on the floor it's making the woman in front turn round," she said, but Connor closed his eyes and went to sleep.

Once through passport control they waited for their baggage. They seemed to wait for a very long time; other passengers from the flight had their bags; Connor had his, but hers had not arrived. They waited by an area that someone told them was Help Desk, it was signed in odd hieroglyphics. The man was unhelpful and said "No problem" repeatedly. It was impossible to tell him that it was a problem but they gave him their names and the tour-company details. Connor was blasé,

"You can wear my clothes, babe, you look hot in anything." Jay was upset that the holiday had started like this and she began to recall things in her suitcase that she might never see again. She was relieved that her pill was in her handbag; it was, wasn't it?

The tour rep swept them up. "You've kept everyone waiting; now let's get you on the coach." All eyes were on them as they stumbled up the steps of the huge bus that was filled to capacity. They had to sit apart and Jay was sat next to a young boy carrying a large boomerang, Connor was at the back of the coach sitting with a group of girls; she could hear them all laughing. The boy with the boomerang was looking out of the window, she studied his thin legs in his shorts and his enormous boomerang clutched tightly on his lap. The boy's mother spoke to her, "Where you going, pet, which hotel you at?" Jay told her that she didn't know as her boyfriend had arranged it all. "We're at the Beach Shack again the woman said, lovely there you can watch all the men's bums as they go by with their beers, that's what I'm looking forward to, pet."

The coach had been going for some time and it seemed to be getting dark. Finally it lurched to a stop by a hotel. "The Miramar," shouted the rep. Several groups got off and there was now room on the coach to sit with Connor. She wished the family a happy holiday and moved to a window seat but Connor did not catch her eye he was still chatting to the girls.

The tour rep came on the coach and announced there would be a short delay of ten minutes while the driver changed over. Across the coach aisle a young woman with very short dark hair turned and smiled at Jay and started to speak. Within minutes she had told important parts of her life story. Jay found people often told her things, sometimes things she would rather not have known. This girl spoke almost non-stop. "There are two factories 10 minutes from where I live, that's Waterlooville near Portsmouth. My name is Kiki and I live with my mum and stepdad. I've only been back there for six months. Before that I was living with my boyfriend until he cheated on me for the third time." Jay nodded and said she was sorry. Kiki went on, "Mum was okay about me returning, she said it would be company given that Chris my stepfather was usually out. I had always got on well with him, he lived with us since I was three. Chris worked in Portsmouth's Sainsbury's in charge of stock-keeping or something, he moved things around on forklift trucks. He had not been married; he said that before he met and married my mum he had no children. Chris liked photography. He had fallen out, or so he said, with his own family but we never knew why. He just sort of laughed over it whenever the subject came up and then went quiet. Mum worshipped Chris, he was so different from my real dad who was never interested in Mum or in me for that matter and spent his time either asleep or watching football. He was in the pub a lot too, it was hard to know how my mum and he got together at all but they did. Mum used to say it was because his dad had an allotment and that she always trusted gardeners. My dad had never touched a blade of grass let alone a spade so I never would work that out. Grandad died before I was born but everyone said he was a gentleman." Jay turned round to see if she could catch Connor's eye but he seemed to be asleep on the shoulder of one of the girls who was laughing with her friends. Kiki noticed this and asked, "Is that your boyfriend, looks like he won't be for much longer then?" Jay was feeling slightly sick, she turned back and looked out of the window into the Mediterranean darkness, a man was rolling a barrel of beer along the ground.

Kiki went on, "The other day Chris told mum and I that something really bad had happened to him when he was a kid and it was the first time he had spoken about it. He said that it was so bad that if we knew about it we probably wouldn't love him any more. Mum told him that nothing could be that bad and he said that it was, but he then wouldn't say any more. The factory where I work makes tin things, I'm on the assembly line and my friend Roz is five yards from me so we can chat and indeed chat we do. Roz is the sort of girl that everybody speak to, she has got a round face, a big smile and a birthmark across one ear which you can't see because her hair hides it but Roz is convinced that everyone can see it. She's got a little boy, Joe-Joe, and she's a good mum. Her mum looks after Joe-Joe while she's at work. Joe-Joe doesn't have a dad. The only thing Roz will say about him is, 'if I hadn't known him I wouldn't have had Joe-Joe, he was a bent bastard and that's all I want to say about it, Kiki, so don't ask no more, OK love, OK?' I was keen to go on holiday but I didn't have anyone to go with me. I looked up lots of deals and when this one came up I told Mum that I would pay for her if she came with me and she said I can't leave Chris, Kiki, you know I can't. I asked her why she couldn't, she said, I just can't, that's all.

It upset me a bit because the last time Mum and I had been on holiday was well, basically well, never. Not just the two of us, not with Dad, not with Chris and I would have liked that. I've seen families on holiday and they look confident and attractive, I suppose that we wouldn't look like that anyway.

Jay wanted Kiki to stop, the girl never paused for breath. "I do think people will talk to me when I am away, it won't be that awkward when I'm on my own. Some people might ask and some people will just look at me and they might think that I'm a jilted honeymooner, it doesn't bother me, they can think all they like. I am not taking many clothes, you don't need them do you, not if it's hot. The thing I will take though is all my shoes but then they are quite heavy aren't they? I will take a book, not that I do a lot of reading, but it might make me feel less awkward in the restaurant having a book even if I don't open it, it gives you something to focus on. I always think that all the people I met on the plane going out, are they on the plane coming back, but I suppose you don't always meet the same people, do you. I suppose the waiters might hit on me, but then they didn't before when I went to Frankie and Benny's with Roz on her birthday last year. They looked right through me like they could see my knickers. I'm staying on a resort. It looks nice, there's a pool and a bar called Sundowners. I shan't sunbathe that much because I could get cancer, I think it runs in our family. Do you think I talk too much by the way, some people say I do but it's all in me head and sometimes it needs turning out, do you know what I mean?"

Finally a driver stumbled into the seat and they were off again. He looked remarkably like the first driver but Jay was glad to be going again; she craned her neck round to see Connor coming down towards her. Again she heard laughing and shouting from the girls, "See you later then." Connor was flushed and happy as he fell into the seat next to Jay, "Those girls have got some brandy back there," he said. "Nice for you then, need not have come away just for me," Jay said. "Don't be daft," he said and kissed her; he smelt terrible. "Anyway," he added, "they're at our hotel, The Acropolis, so we'll be seeing them."

Five minutes later they were headed towards Reception; she felt ill thinking about her lost suitcase and wondering what she was going to do. The rep was no help at all. "Don't worry," she had said, "it happens all the time and if they don't bring it in three days you can get a voucher and buy some new clothes, not that you need many here it's so hot."

Up in the room Connor spread out on the bed, his huge boots still on his feet, marking the white cotton sheet with mud. "Do take your boots off, Con," she asked. "That's not all I'm taking off," he said, and grabbed hold of her. With his boots still on he was snoring within minutes while she lay smothered by him. Jay disentangled herself from Connor's bad breath and walked to the small balcony, watching the brilliant red sun go down across the bay. The view from the room was amazing. She was beginning to feel better about it all and the room was quite nice, spacious. Jay wanted to let her mum know she had arrived, she wouldn't let on about the suitcase yet, no point. It was then that she looked through her hand bag for her pills. Phew, they were there, but just three days' worth; she had put the other packet in the case, knowing she would take them to delay her period until she was home.

Connor finally was roused from his coma and they explored the hotel with its beautiful trees and scented flowers. It was close to the beach and they wandered about hand in hand. "Did you bring flip-flops, Connor," Jay asked him, "those boots are going to get hot." Connor grabbed her and kissed her – "I will definitely be getting hot all right," he said and laughed.

At the Beach Shack Reception, Vivien asked the clerk if they were in the same shack as before, "Shack 17" she said, "we've had it every year." Rob turned to her, "not that I would know about that. You were here last year, Rob," she said "and you would have been here the year before but what happened?" Rob shrugged his shoulders and slumped down in an armchair. Liam stood next to his mum, he had hold of his little Trunkie and the boomerang. You go and sit with Rob, she said but Liam did not move. Finally the desk clerk said, "Madam you are not in 17; we have a roof repair there but we have 23." "Is it the same as 17?" Vivien asked. "It's a tiny bit smaller," the clerk said, "but you will love it." "What do you mean by smaller?" "Madam, it is just the one room like 17 but smaller, just one bedroom," the clerk said, "plus the bathroom and the kitchen of course; there is one double bed and one single. Come, I show you." He took them out and he started to make his way. "That's not what we asked for." Vivien was put out, "we wanted 17, we've always been in there, I've always been there, Liam loves it, he needs his own bedroom." "We don't have, madam," he said, "we don't have, hotel very full." Rob stood up. "What's going on, you mean to say you haven't got what we have asked for, what I paid for, you haven't got it, chummy, have you?" Vivien did not say that she had paid for the holiday. "I think we have to go and look at it," she said. "I for one am not sharing a room with anyone, they will have to do something different," shouted Rob as they walked off into the night following the man with the keys.

They made their way up past the other shacks which faced the beach, No. 17, it was true, was boarded up, the tarpaulin on the roof, the roof felt just flapping in the wind. No. 23 was not on the beach, it was a row back, but there was still a glimpse of the golden sand and the sea.

The clerk flew the door open in a sweeping elaborate gesture, "see it, lovely madam, it perfect, you will love and complimentary dinner is on Demitris, it no problem for you." "I don't want complimentary dinner," said Rob, "I want to stay in a place that we have paid for, that I have paid for, that has two rooms, one for us and one for him." He gestured with his thumb towards Liam who was standing by the door. "I hope tomorrow we will be able to mend 17, be no problem," said the clerk, "but tonight sir I invite you dinner on us and stay here." Vivien was weary, "thank you very much we will do that." "Well I'm not happy, not happy at all," Rob said and he walked out of the door. Vivien exchanged glances with Liam who looked away. "Go and put your things out on the bed," she said to Liam, "sort out your pyjamas, find your swimming things for tomorrow, I'll be back in a minute, I'll find Rob." Liam opened his Trunkie and sat down on the bed and put his boomerang on the pillow. He noticed there were no blankets, just a thin sheet. He was pleased to be in the same room as his mum; that way he would be able to wake up and see her. He remembered the pool and the waves in the sea and the big breakfasts where he could help himself to milk through an urn-type thing. He wondered what they would be having for dinner and the thought of it then made him feel funny. He wasn't sure that he wanted dinner and he knew that Rob wouldn't let him take boomerang to the table. He kissed boomerang an extra three times. Outside he could hear his mother speaking to Rob.

Rob came into the room, glanced at Liam and went into the bathroom. A few seconds later he said, "I'm off to the bar." "Wait for a minute, we'll all go with you," Mum said. He turned and walked away. "I've put boomy into bed," said Liam, "he's all tucked up." Liam saw that his mother was crying.

Neighbours

1.

First one neighbour is running, shouting, then she is screaming. I can't understand what she is saying or doing. Another neighbour rushes past her carrying a shotgun. There is much noise and five shots are fired. Following much movement towards the back of my neighbour's garden, other people from the forest have come too; they also are running. It is midday and normally there is not a soul about. They all stand around looking to the ground. I throw my hands into the air and say hello several times in Turkish, I then shout out, "Pleased to meet you," it being one of the few phrases I know other than "Mr Brown is an architect from Antalya."

I am told that, unusually, two snakes were found slithering through the grass, dangerous snakes that could kill a person. My neighbour tells me to buy some special chemical powder to put all around the edges of my garden. The next day he hands me a sack of it; it is bright yellow and I spend the day piling it on as instructed, a quarter of an inch thick. It it is hard to understand how anything would deter a snake, perhaps one is already living in my garden or indeed his long friends are planning to join him. I comply; nonetheless my usual open door to the garden is now closed at night.

2.

My friend in London tells me that her new neighbour has said some very strange things to her. He told her first of all, "I am glad you are like me with a total dislike of any degree of physical contact with another human being." My friend was taken aback and responded by saying, oh actually I don't have that problem. He then said, "let me put it this way if you see two men kissing it looks horrific, if you see two women kissing it's truly ghastly, if you see a man and a woman kissing it's stomach-churning, I tend to look away." He then added, "but then I worry what else I am going to see when I look away, I can't stand it, I'm relieved that you feel the same way." He then went in and closed his door.

3.

My neighbour's daughter is 7 years old, I like to talk to her about the games she is playing. She usually plays on her own and I watch her talking to herself, bouncing a ball against the wall and running from one end of her garden to the other. I also see her sometimes climbing onto the roof of her father's shed. "What are you doing," I ask her; she says, "I am pretending to be a chicken." I ask her why; she says, "because I could then get eaten by my mummy and be back in her tummy."

4.

A boy is brought to see me. His father says I have to fix him or he will have to go and live somewhere else as he is making his stepmother ill by his constant demands for attention and angry outbursts.

The boy plays in the sand, tells me how much he misses his brother who died two years ago. I ask him, "What would you wish for if you had a magic wand?" He says, "For people to smile and not to frown when they see me. The lady next door gave me a peach stone to plant in my garden, she said that by the time it had grown into a tree I would forget a lot of things that happened when I was little. Do you think I will?" he asks.

5.

Frank tells me that when his dog dies he will die too. "How do you know this," I ask. "Stands to reason doesn't it," he says, "he'll need me to look after him in heaven." I comment that Frank has been a farmer for over 60 years and has slaughtered animals and seen the births and deaths of thousands of lambs on Romney Marsh. "A dog is different," he says, "part of me, my right hand and anyway I promised him."

Notes Towards Loss

1.

"I don't mind about it but he does. Ben needs to go to sleep first or else he makes a noise that gets to mum so I go outside with him and put him in the buggy.

"Sometimes he screams until he is blue and once he scratched my face but he didn't understand that I had to do it. I had to strap him in. There was a day last week when I hit him a bit, hit him hard because he has to learn things.

"Mum hadn't taken her tablets yet so I made some tea for her and got her to lay down. When mum gets ill I help out more but then she doesn't notice things as she sleeps a lot. When she hears voices I take the radio to Pam's house next door as once she smashed it up. I put the cushions over the telly and the cloth over it as well.

"Our dad's a bastard. Mum said that and that he didn't deserve to have a lad like me. He comes sometimes, says it's not right and then goes away. He did change Ben's nappy and rang the Social. We don't want them poking in here as one time the doctor made her go away and Ben was taken off me. No one knows how to get him off to sleep like me."

2.

"When Steven said I smelt funny and that he wouldn't be my partner in PE I cried a bit and then I ran off into the trees. It was dark there. They didn't find me.

"Miss Bartlett took me in the toilets and washed my face and gave me some shorts. She slipped a banana in the pocket at break but I don't like them much.

"Our mum went mad when that woman came to our house and said we should have sheets on our bed again. She made mum clean up and she brought things with her.

"It was better when we had the light-bulb in our room but Brian smashed it with his shoe from the top bunk when he got sent upstairs. He weed in the corner of our room again and now it's brown on the floor and rotting a bit."

3.

"I like to chat and I know that I shouldn't do it. I'm always following people around I don't like being on my own I know I get in the way and I do want to be good. I am good, but I chat too much, I know that. 'Leave it out,' my mum says, 'for Christ's sake leave it out for a minute.'

"I don't know what I get wrong but then I do. Maybe I am bad that's it, I am not good at things so I don't sleep much, mostly I play in my room.

"When Uncle George lived here I'd sit on his lap a lot; no one said it was wrong, he said it was good.

"But I don't like being on my own and when I don't sleep I listen on the stairs. I heard them say that Uncle George was locked up."

Stunned by the Misery

Across the Rectory Road car park a mother screams at her child in the pushchair she is steering with one hand, while the other hand drags a lurching, sobbing toddler wearing an all-in-one suit. "Hold up that f…..g balloon will you," she says to the infant in the pushchair. The orange balloon on a stick has come close to the ground and the child responds by lifting it higher. The group go past me, cars back into spaces, it's raining, it's murky, people are running to the pay machines, their heads bent.

There is a sudden bang and then silence before a woman's voice screams out, "Now you've burst it, that's the end of that you little shit. Serves you right, it's gone forever." The toddler, in fright, runs across the car park under the wheels of a reversing car.

That evening when she walked back through the park it was busy, the sound of the ring road was like an engine, continually in the background. A man sat on the park bench resting on his knees, wearing shorts, reading the newspaper; he was bald and looked a bit like her dad, or how she imagined he might be. He was wearing trainers and an old England shirt was round his waist; the man looked at his shoes in a distracted sort of way, away from the paper. Now and again he folded it up and put it down on the seat next to him and occasionally rubbed his eyes. A group of schoolgirls were sitting in the shade. She didn't know any of them and there seemed to be a lot of them. Sometimes she would have been scared that she might be hit on by them but today she just sat down on the grass. The man on the bench got up and walked past her; she noticed that he had very white trainers and that his feet were flat, he had tattoos on his arm that she couldn't read. People had told her that she looked like her mum, she couldn't see it herself, certainly she didn't know her dad so she couldn't see any of that. Often she had wondered about him, but being pregnant now things made her wonder differently. Who would the baby look like? Would he or she look like Darren? Could that be changed now? Was it set in stone for ever like most things were? Sooner or later she'd have to tell her mum, sooner or later they'd have to tell Darren's mum and dad, sooner rather than later she knew that Darren would leave her. She wanted Darren more than she wanted the baby. That was the hardest part. The baby was a link to him but with the baby he would be gone, without the baby he might stay. She got up and walked back around the side of the park past the plants with the big sticky out leaves, she liked them, they looked like her Nan's cactus, the ones they were supposed never to have touched. She remembered when she did touch them and the tiny thorns had been in her fingers for weeks, but she never told anybody because she knew what her mum would say, "you were told not to touch them, now look, you never listen, you're like your dad, he never listened either." What would her mum say now about the baby?

She walked back again up the high street and into New Look. Her friend Maeve sometimes worked there. She walked round the shop looking out for Maeve with beautiful pink hair. Maeve always seemed to know about everything but she wasn't there today or at least she couldn't find her. Wherever she looked there were women with children looking worn out, worn down, dragging children along by the hand with another in a pushchair, babies screaming for a feed, sometimes there were grandmas with babies, or were they just mums looking old? She passed Timpson's, the shoe-repairers, they seemed to be selling Christening gifts; "when did shoe repairers sell christening gifts, from now," she thought. Just as she reached Wilkinson's a voice shouted out, "Hi ye." It was Maeve. She looked beautiful as always. Her pink and gold hair hung down her back, she was wearing little white shoes and a very short skirt and a brilliant blue lacy top. "Hi ye," she said, "didn't you hear me?" "I just went into New Look to see if you were there." "I'm on my lunch," said Maeve. "You all right, you want to come with me, I'm just going shopping for my mum in Wilkinson's." "Yeh, all right," she said. She picked up a wire basket and Maeve headed determinedly for the tampon section. She picked up six packets of Night Time Extra. "My mum's in the change," said Maeve, "she has blood everywhere, I don't know what to do to help." "Oh," she said, "Anyway, I need to buy a card for my nephew," said Maeve, and they went off to look at the birthday cards. They came away with a 'Fireman Sam I Am Two'. Maeve said, "He's real cute, I wouldn't mind if he were mine." "Wouldn't you," she said, "wouldn't you really." "No, he's real cute, I look after him quite a bit," said Maeve. "Anyway what you doing down town?" She couldn't answer, she didn't know what to say. "I just wasn't in work today," she said. "Are you sick," said Maeve, "you look sort of odd." "I'm not sick I've just got a lot to think about." "Oh, yeh," said Maeve, "would that be Darren you've got to think about." "That and a few other things," she said, "I wouldn't waste time thinking about Darren," said Maeve, "what is there to think about with Darren, it wouldn't take you long to think about him." Maeve didn't have a regular boyfriend although she could have had anyone she liked, she just couldn't be bothered, it seemed. She liked having fun too much. She always seemed to be busy with other things, things to do with her family. There were a lot of them, Maeve had three brothers and an older sister, they often did things together. She was jealous. It would be good to be part of a big family she thought. Maeve said, "Gotta go back to work now, anyway, what you doing tonight?" "Er, not sure," she said. "I'm going to be down the town," said Maeve. "I might see you then." "Yes, see you," she said and walked off.

Waiting for the bus she started to feel a bit faint. She leaned against the plastic edge of the bus stop seat and luckily the bus came along a few minutes later. Just before she boarded the bus a woman was running along the pavement carrying a lot of bags. It was her mum's friend Janine. She was red, puffed out, overweight, she thought she looked quite grim. She plonked herself on the seat nearest the doorway. She nodded in acknowledgement. "That was a close one," the woman said, "my feet are killing me. It's this heat, everything swells up, don't it, everything's like some heaving lump. How's your mum?" she said. "Oh, she's fine," she said unconvincingly. In fact when she thought about it she didn't really know how her mum was, it seemed ages since she'd even asked her mum or thought about how she was. At the moment she couldn't think of anything but herself and what was inevitably growing inside of her.

Janine opened a packet of chocolate éclairs, "want a sweet?" she said. "Yes please." She took it gladly, she remembered that she hadn't eaten anything all day. "You don't look too right to me, you okay?" "Oh, yeh," she said. "Help me off with this lot." She helped Janine off with the shopping, there was a lot of clanking as she realised that she had at least two bottles of wine and a bottle of whisky in one of the bags; no wonder it was heavy. There was also a 2lb bag of potatoes in the other bag and a huge packet of toilet rolls. She thought about Janine stuffing her face with potatoes and swilling it down with the scotch and the wine and sitting on the toilet many minutes later. That's disgusting she thought, that's quite disgusting. There was a mess in Janine's garden as they walked up to the front door, it was everywhere, there were old milk cartons, bits of cars, a derelict caravan in the driveway that you had to squeeze past to get to the front door. Janine lived here on her own with her three children. The boys were a handful, they were very grim, nobody liked them, except for some reason her mum liked Janine. She thought maybe they'd gone to school together, she'd forgotten now. She dropped the bags on the step. "Thanks love," she said, "tell your mum I was asking after her." She made her way back down the path and stepped in a lot of chewing gum which made a mess of her sandals. It would take her ages to get that off.

The Seat

1.

She tells me that she is sitting here because she has recently stopped work, that she is having a baby in four weeks' time and that her home in Singleton is north facing. The flat has poor light, there is no sunshine, balcony or a patio and she says that she craves the sun. Her partner is also from Albania and she tells me that he has just started, last week, with his own business cleaning cars inside and out in a car park at the back of Tesco's. They want to move but he is worried that he will not make any money. She is going back to work when the baby is three months old and her mum will then look after the child. She tells me, that's what grandmas do, they look after the children. She asked me what I do for work and I tell her. She says, "I don't know how anyone could harm a child but then I suppose I do. I was four when we left Yugoslavia and I saw a lot of things that made me think; I also saw my father shave off my sister's hair because she said that she loved a boy. Then we went to live in Germany and I loved it, the weather was so good, I swam every day. Now we can't go back, it's so expensive, my partner is going back next week. Do you think he will come back for me and the baby?"

2.

He told me that he thought he had felt dizzy and was sitting down just to catch his breath, he thought he would be all right in a minute or two. His fingers were stained with nicotine and I saw that his face was not so old. He told me that he had lived on his own now for 12 years, that his wife had died young. "Too young. She had a heart attack at 35, too much floor scrubbing on top of having the four little'uns, I reckon, but they never said." He said that he had had a girlfriend but they had never lived together, "things are better when you know what's happening, I know what's happening if I live on my own." He took out a cigarette. "I would offer you, love, but I'm saving, saving up for a rainy day so I can blow it all at once if you know what I mean."

"I had pigeons once upon a time, they were classy. I won prizes. Now the only prize I'll win is £10 on the lottery."

He gets to stand up and then falls back down again, "I'm not so well as I thought." A middle-aged woman comes by pushing a trolley. "You chatting the girls up again Brian, Millie's at home waiting for you." The woman turns to me, "he's had four wives, they've all died young, must be what he puts in their tea."

3.

On Monday I was looking out of the window from my office and by the seat a man was being arrested. Three police officers and the man's friend surrounded him while he was handcuffed and his pockets were searched. The contents of his pockets were removed by the police officers who were wearing plastic gloves. The man was swaying from side to side and he seemed drunk, his friend stood by with one leg against the wall with his hands in his pockets, he was moving about in a restless way. The man kept repeatedly shouting out, "Do you know what I mean?" No one seemed to know what he did mean. The police officer spoke to someone on the radio. The handcuffed man was wearing a red jacket, trousers with a big long sign up the side of one leg. The lady from the shop put out some large old plastic sweet jars with a sign saying, free for anyone to take. The contents of the man's pockets were all over the wet ground – a comb, a sweet, a pen, a tissue, a plastic dog and a mobile phone. The man was taken by one policeman, handcuffed, to the police car; he continued to shout out louder, "Do you know what I mean?" The remaining police officer put the man's belongings into a plastic bag. The woman from the sweet shop shouted out after them, "Ashford scum, all of you." She looked up and saw me watching and shook her fists.

Stories from the Contact Centre

One

It was the second Saturday in the month and Philip went to get Danny out of bed early. "Come on, Danny, we've got to get to the shops to see if we can get you those new school shoes and then we're going on to meet mum." Danny reached out for his Gameboy and started playing on it as he tucked down further into the covers. Philip asked him again, "Come on Danny, you've got to get up now, and when I say now I mean now." Danny turned over to face the wall while still playing with his Gameboy. Philip pulled the covers off the bed and found that the bed was wet. "Danny, how many times have I told you, tell me if you've wet the bed." "But I haven't," said Danny. "You have son, you're laying in it, it's all wet, get yourself in the bathroom and I'll strip the bed again, get in the shower and make sure you wash." Danny went off into the bathroom still playing on the Gameboy. Philip stripped the beds and on the way out he stuck a downward sad face on Danny's star chart.

At the shops Danny was helpful, choosing his new shoes without difficulty. After lunch Philip reminded him they were going to see Mum. "I wish you could stay there, Dad, I wish you could just be there when I see Mum." "But you know that I can't," said Philip. "She comes to see you, not me."

As soon as they arrived at the Contact Centre, Philip looked around and saw that Sarah was not there. "She won't be long, let's just wait a little bit." After about five minutes she arrived. Philip saw that she looked more tired than ever. She was carrying two big bags. Philip hoped that she was not going to give Danny any more clothes or toys but had brought something for them to play with today. Danny's eyes lit up when he saw his Mum and he went over to her and she cuddled him. She then started shouting at Philip before he could leave, "Why do you dress him in these clothes, why do you dress him like there is something wrong with him, why do you not dress him in the clothes I bring, eh eh, answer me that?" Philip said, "Let's not have a row about this now, Sarah, he's just wearing his ordinary clothes, these are the clothes he likes to wear." Danny put his hands up to his ears; he really didn't want this. Philip said, "I'll be just waiting upstairs, okay?"

Sarah liked to do jigsaws and over the next two hours they did nothing but a big complicated jigsaw together in the middle of the room. Everyone seemed to look at them. Now and again Sarah would shout out to one of the contact supervisors, "You tell me why my son is so thick." He hated it when she behaved like this and the supervisors spoke to her quietly, calming her down. She always apologised to Danny as she cuddled him, "You know I don't mean it, I just get frustrated." At the end of contact he was relieved but always sad to see her go. He noticed that the scars on her eye from the operations were beginning to heal. It was embarrassing, Danny knew that his mother looked odd, and feeling guilty and remembering made him feel sick. Since she set fire to her hair it had taken him a long time to get used to how she looked nowadays. He hugged her and sometimes he wished that they could stay together like that just the two of them forever, but then he knew that it would be too hard.

Two

The journey down from Preston had taken five hours. Bill had picked them up in the van at 6.30 a.m. He said, "It'll save your legs waiting at the bus stop, they're only every hour and if they've a mind they don't come at all." They were grateful. Jean had packed a flask of coffee, some sandwiches and a piece of cake. She knew how Alfie felt faint very quickly if he didn't eat regularly. He wouldn't manage that, not with the travelling as well. The upset of it was bad enough, to think that they had to book up to see their own grandchildren in a place where other people had to watch them, it wasn't right. They'd never done anything wrong, they loved the kids, they'd never harm them. A bitch of a daughter-in-law had made their lives hell. Jean had known from the moment she saw her that she was trouble, "all front, that's what she is, all front." She remembered Alfie saying, "You can say that again and quite a front it is too on her, if I may say so." Jean had thrown him a look. "You wait and see if I'm not right," she said, "that girl means nothing but harm to our Richard, I can tell it."

When the girls were born Jean had been thrilled with her two little granddaughters who lived three streets away and Marcia would bring the girls over after school at least three times a week. She had a part-time job in the video shop. "It gets me out, mum," she'd say. Richard had a job at the building suppliers and Jean thought they were just an ordinary family like everyone else. Then one Friday afternoon Richard came home. It was unusual; he never had a day off work. "What's the matter?" Jean asked him. "Nothing, can you have the girls for the weekend, I'm taking Marcia away." "Well that's new," said Jean, "but yes, I will." When the girls came that weekend they weren't their usual happy little selves. "Mummy and Daddy have been arguing," said Katie. "Shouting all night, Daddy says Mummy's got a boyfriend." Susie added, "I heard her kissing someone on the phone, she kissed her mobile phone." At the end of the weekend Jean watched as their car drew up outside and Richard got out to collect the girls. "Where's Marcia?" "Mum I need to tell you something," said Richard. "I can't find Marcia, I've been down south this weekend to look for her, she's left me, she's met a bloke from London and she says she's not coming back, what's worse is that she's coming tomorrow to take the girls."

Weeks and months went by and Richard came round for his evening meal now that he was on his own. He heard things, how she was accusing him of being drunk all the time and never helping with the children, him seeing other women, how the girls didn't want to see him. That was two years ago and it had all gone from bad to worse. Things happened that Jean had never even dreamed of knowing about. Katie had said her granddad Alfie had touched her while she was having a bath and that Katie said she never wanted to see granddad again. The police had come and taken Alfie away, it was terrible, it made his diabetes go haywire. Jean thought that the world couldn't get worse; he loved those little girls. She knew that Alfie would never have touched Katie, he was just not that sort of man, but then some days she'd wonder and she'd think back on things she had put away, it made her think twice but she never said. And now they had to go down to see the girls in a Contact Centre in a place where other people could watch what they did, what they said. It had taken two court hearings and them being interviewed to get this far. They would have to make the best of it.

Jean had never been to London; Alfie had, in the lorry, but Jean hadn't thought much of it as they went on the Underground to get through to the other side of London before finding their way down south to the place where the girls were now living with their mum and her fancy new man called Todd. From what Jean heard, Todd took the biscuit. He had a brand new BMW car and he worked as a manager for a cinema complex. They got to the door of the contact centre, Alfie said that he felt a bit funny. Jean had given him his sandwiches and the coffee on the train. "Have a seat," she said, "you'll feel better in a minute, it's all the upset." Once inside he did seem to perk up a bit. The woman in charge made them a cup of tea and told them to wait upstairs where there was a comfortable settee. When the girls came in Jean thought that her heart would break, their stick-like arms and legs were just as they'd always been; they were wearing thin dresses, it was November. The girls were all over her, she never wanted to let them go. They spoke to Alfie but she noticed that neither of them went near him; that wasn't how things used to be. Jean asked if they'd seen their Dad. "We see him every day," said Katie, "of course we see him." It was then that Jean realised they were now calling Todd Dad. "I meant your real Dad," said Jean. "Oh him," said Katie, "no, we don't see him any more, mum says he don't send her no money." At the end of their time with the girls Jean thought again that her heart would break. She watched them walk out the door without turning back to wave, like they always had done in the past.

Three

When Julie told him she was pregnant he was without doubt the happiest man in the world. When she told him two days later that it was twins he went straight to the pub and got plastered. When he came back Julie didn't look too pleased. He explained in a way, as he always did with a sideways lopsided grin. "It's not every day a man gets to be told he's going to be the dad of twins." After the boys were born things changed. Julie got tired and he spent more time at any pub. Things weren't great between them; they went to a counsellor and he promised to stop drinking. Instead he had cans at home. "I'll just have one more while the footie's on," he'd say to Julie. He loved the boys, Robbie and Billy, he'd take them out as proud as anything in the double buggy while Julie could have a clear-up at home. Only once did he take them in the pub; somehow Julie found out. "Do that again, I'll leave you." He worshipped Julie, she'd been the best thing that had ever happened to him and he wasn't about to blow it.

Three years later when Julie started working he looked after the boys more and more, he'd pick them up two nights after nursery school and bring them home, give them their tea and wait for Julie. Just once in a while he'd buy a can or two at the offie. "You've been drinking," she said when she got home. "No I haven't, you're imagining it," he would say. One day Julie came home and said she'd had enough; either she would go or he should go but it would be easier if he went because she would have to look after the boys. He pleaded his case and said he would go to Alcoholics Anonymous, he would stop drinking. Julie said, "It's ten times too often; just go, and take your bottle opener with you." He knew she meant it.

After Julie left everything slid. He lost his job, but he did see the boys. Julie would bring them round regular as clockwork and he loved his time with them but once, or was it twice, he couldn't remember now, he'd had a can or two during the time he'd had with them. Billy had told his mum. The next thing he knew they were all in court and Julie was saying that he was an unfit parent to see them on his own. Now he had to see the boys at the Contact Centre. They always came, never let him down, not like some of the children and some of the stories he heard with the other dads. Julie always made sure the boys came and they always looked spick and span. "How's your mum?" he'd ask the boys. They would tell him; sometimes he didn't want to hear their answer, sometimes he couldn't look when he saw her in the doorway, she looked so beautiful. Once she came over to speak to him, the boys liked that. He touched her arm, it was soft and warm. "You look good," he said. When Julie looked at him she saw that his front teeth were missing. She couldn't repay the compliment. When the boys left the centre with their mum he went into the pub across the road. "A quick half to see me on my way," he would say to the barman, who now knew him as a regular.

Four

The day she found out that Mike was leaving her Barbara told the children, "Your dad's found another family to live with, he doesn't love us any more." Emily, who was 14, told her mum, "I never want to see him again." Robert, who was 10, worshipped his daddy, sat and cried. "I never meant to hurt you, Barbara," said Mike, "I never meant to hurt you, I just never felt like you needed me." Barbara had needed Mike, she'd needed him very much, it's just that she wasn't a person who could show her feelings very easily. It had always been her problem, even the girls at work had said to her, "Loosen up a bit, Barb, liven up, get yourself going." She was just not like that. When she met Mike she thought her world had just started. He saw in her the things that she wanted people to know about her without needing to tell them, and now he had left her, just like her dad had. It was all happening again.

It was two years Mike had been gone now and Emily still refused to see her dad. Robert had been seeing a psychologist, he wasn't doing well at school, he got into trouble. They'd all been to see a therapist, Mike as well. Emily had spat at him in the family therapy session, she was angry. "You've got your nice little family with Carol and your new baby and Carol's children, Rachel and Sally, it's all cosy wosy, you don't need us anymore," she had said. Her father had said nothing; Barbara was, as usual, speechless. Towards the end of the session Emily had turned on her mum and had said, "You should say something, you should stop being so dumb." Those words had hurt her, she knew that Emily was right but she couldn't do anything about it. Now Emily had agreed to see her dad at a Contact Centre and she and Robert went off to see him. When they'd gone Barbara went up and looked in Emily's bedroom; she was sure she was seeing a boy. She was sure she was sleeping with him.

At the Contact Centre Mike broke down when he saw his children. He was so happy. "Don't you bloody start, we have enough with Mum," said Emily. Robert just held his dad's hand. "I didn't leave you," said Mike, "it isn't you I left, just remember that." But Emily wasn't listening, she was looking at her mobile phone; there was a text there for her. She would be seeing him later, and so what that he was a married man with a kid.

Five

The day Mum took them all to the refuge was when a bit of the world ended. He saw it on the news, an aeroplane had gone into a big tower in the middle of America. Everyone was crying, everything had come to an end. It was all there was on the TV, even at the refuge, the lady was talking about how awful it was and what a tragedy and how many people had been killed. He wasn't sure how people had come to be killed but he knew that his dad had done it. He'd seen Dad hitting Mum more times than he could remember; now he slept next to his mum and he could always look after her. Sometimes he heard his mum crying in her sleep. She wasn't awake but she was crying while her eyes were closed and he would shake her to wake her up but she didn't. He didn't know why his mum had to take pills to help her sleep, she seemed to do that fine on her own.

It was a long time before he had his own bedroom in their own house. When he did he didn't like it. He wished he was back next to his mum again. It was a shame because she'd had it decorated out in Liverpool stripes with a Liverpool bedspread. He remembered that his dad supported Arsenal. He knew that his mum had to go to court a lot and a lady had come to talk to him. She asked him about seeing his dad. He didn't want to see him, not after he'd killed all those people, not after he'd hurt his mum, not after he'd made a piece of the world come to an end. Lots of times people came and told him that he had to go to see his dad. His mum told him that she might go to prison if he didn't go. That worried him, who would look after him then. His brother Terry went one day to see Dad but he was sick in the car of the lady who took him. She brought him home. "Your Dad goes to the Contact Centre every week just to wait for you," the lady told him. He could wait all he liked, he wasn't going anywhere near him soon.

Six

After she gave birth to her, the midwife plonked her straight on her chest. "Here we are mummy, now give her a good feed," the midwife had said. "Sit up a bit and I'll help you," but it hadn't worked. The midwife had taken her away, wrapped her in a blue blanket and put her in a see-through cot next to her bed. Melissa hadn't cried, she was a good baby, everyone said that. Bottle feeding went well but she knew that something wasn't quite right between her and Melissa, she didn't really want to look after her. She took her back to the flat and the health visitor said she was doing very well. Once or twice Gary came by to see her, he gave her some money, it was very handy. He peeped in at the cot, "she is well cute," he said, "well cute." "Not so cute at two in the morning," said Amy, you should be here then. "You know I can't be," said Gary and turned on his heel and left.

In a year a lot had happened. The old lady next door had complained to the social that she cried all the time; Melissa never stopped, that was true. She now had a social worker and someone came every day to check on the baby, she knew that they were worried that she might have hit her, they had once thought they had seen bruises on Melissa. Now they were talking about maybe her going to live with foster parents. "Who is the baby's father?" asked the social worker. "Gary," she said. She actually couldn't remember his last name and this made her feel funny. She knew where he lived with his wife and two children and she gave them his address. At the end of the court hearing the Judge said that she could look after Melissa providing she had some help, but that Gary would see Melissa every fortnight.

Here she was on a Saturday morning waiting outside with all the other mothers, with all the other dads, with all the other buggies, with all the other kids inside and hanging on to them. She was surprised that he turned up. "All right, mate," he said. "No, I'm not all right," said Amy, "and I'm not your mate, so wrong on both accounts, Gary." She handed him Melissa and walked off.

At the Contact Centre, Gary tried hard with Melissa, he walked round with her, he got out toys that made a noise, but Melissa would just cry and had her arms out towards the door, the one her mother had walked through. He didn't know what to do.

Seven

He felt stupid buying Easter eggs in January but he would only be seeing his son four times a year, that's what had been agreed, so here he was with two carrier bags, some Christmas presents, some Easter eggs and some clothes that his mother thought that the boy might like. He had been very pleased to marry Donna, he knew that she had only done it for the money so that he could get his immigration status but he had been very grateful. Neither of them had bargained for the fact that they actually ended up quite liking each other. Between them they had produced little Jackie. She made it clear that she wouldn't stay with him. "I don't actually love you," Donna had said, "you knew that right from the start, I never pretended." "In my country sons are special, we don't just walk away from our children," he'd said. She hadn't listened. "If you want to see him you'll have to go through the courts, I don't think it's right, I'm moving on in my life and I don't want you involved, I told you that, I told you right from the start."

The story had been told to the Judge. He understood that Donna was moving abroad, he understood how the couple had come to marry. What was more confusing was how little Jackie had come to be born when Donna had said that she had never liked him. That hadn't made sense but then not everything did; it was ordered that he should have contact with his son four times a year.

Now as he waited he realised a whole hour of the two hours had gone by and no-one had come, she had not kept her promise and he felt stupid sitting there with all the bags. He went up to the lady in her office. "I don't think they are coming," she said, "would you like me to call someone for you?" He hadn't got a number for her. "I don't think so," he said, "I don't have her details." "Maybe you'll have to go back to court," she told him. "Maybe I just can't bring myself to do it, I've got some Easter eggs in here and some clothes my mum sent over, give them to someone you think might need them," he said as he left.

Eight

When Sonny came back from seeing his mum it was always difficult, he couldn't get a word out of him. He and Dawn learnt it was best to let him come round in his own time. Sometimes he'd make the mistake when he picked him up, he'd ask, "how's your mum?" He knew how Ellie was, he knew from looking at her from afar how much weight she'd lost, how agitated she was, her lank hair and her permanently ringing hands. "She's fine," Sonny would say, "She's really good, she's starting a new job next week." Once Dawn had found in his bedroom an advert that he'd drafted for the local newspaper; he was selling his electronic toys, he knew why, to give Ellie money. He knew that Sonny stole from him and gave Ellie his findings. He didn't mind, he would give Ellie money if she really needed it, but he knew exactly where it would go and perhaps Sonny also knew that Ellie would immediately spend anything she had on drugs.

One day when Sonny came back from the Contact Centre he was behaving very oddly. He'd run straight up into his bedroom and didn't come out for a couple of hours. He shouted up the stairs, "You all right, Sonny?" There was no reply. He went into his room. Sonny was asleep but he couldn't wake him up. Dawn came running up, "We need an ambulance."

When his stomach had been pumped out they found that he'd taken heroin. It had almost killed Sonny. He knew where it had come from and that he would never forgive Ellie. When Sonny could speak he said, "I'm sorry, Dad, I found it in her bag and thought if I took it that she wouldn't have to."

PROSE

III

Uncollected Prose

Abandonment Tales 1

1.

That afternoon I got on the bus, the stop was right outside of Nan's house. She was asleep when I left so there was no waving from the window like usual. The bus came straight away, a miracle really. Usually, I'd have to wait for hours, just sitting there in the shelter with the graffiti and cigarette ends. I don't smoke myself anymore, not felt like it somehow; strange, that. The money was in £10 notes and some £20s, there were also a few fivers. It was sure good to be moving but I still felt odd, very odd in fact, a lot of pains everywhere and nowhere. Nan says I get illnesses like she has cups of tea. It'll kill you in the end that chondria of yours, Dulcie, she tells me. My reflection in the window confirmed that I had put on a few pounds lately, not that I've ever been huge, more slender, but Nan's cooking has meant I eat more puddings and potatoes in gravy. Nan's gravy is famous in our family, for being delicious that is. I'd been living at Nan's since Vince moved in with mum; we have a personality clash, mum says. I told her straight out, "Vince hasn't got a personality, mum, he's just a man with nothing, nothing in his head, nothing to give you except deep grief, just pure rage and anger and loathing for everyone who isn't him." It came to a head really, inevitable, he wanted mum to himself, it was clear, and I was in his way. Vince had two boys, Jayden and Stewart; he never saw them. Lucky them is all I can say but to hear him talk you'd think they were Princes William and bloody Harry. Apparently they had perfect manners, never answered back, studied all day and night and ran errands all weekend and cleaned the roof tiles on the house in their spare time. Like I say though, he never saw them, hadn't been allowed to for the last five years – court order. Vince kept the loot he made from his scaffolding in the wardrobe inside his shoes. He told mum he had no money and was on Universal Credit but I knew his game because I followed him twice. So when I left Mum's I took what I could, thinking it could be handy and I'd buy Nan that plant stand she wanted.

Life at Nan's was OK really. I was 15 when I moved in, Granddad had died when I was ten, heart attack, dropped dead as a stone when he was at work forklift driving. He ran into the shelves with the machine, nearly killed his best friend. Nan sort of never got over it really, think she had a stroke because one side of her face is still a bit wonky when she gets tired. I could see she was getting tired a lot lately and I wasn't helping any. I needed to get a job but I didn't know how really because I can't add up, I'm too thick, I can't speak to people, I don't know, because they'll think I'm dumb because my words go all over the place when I'm nervous. The only person who did understand me was Adam. Best not go there really, not now I'm on the bus at last. Adam said he loved me and I believed him until that message came through on his phone from that bitch Angie sending him two letter 'A's in a heart. I asked him, "Who is she, Adam?"; I remember he said, "Girls just find me, Dulcie, I don't go looking for them and anyway nothing is cast in stone, is it, not like we are married or anything, so suck it up." The last I saw of Adam was in Costco, he was buying spaghetti hoops and beer, "Oi ya," he said. I didn't look up.

When I get off the bus I have to find the place, it's getting a bit dark but I can see the signs well enough. The hotel didn't have any lights on anywhere; odd because it wasn't that late. The big doorway had two bells, I rang the top one and then there were the footsteps coming downstairs. A tall man opened the door, he looked like Vince with a sour sort of long face and bony fingers which went up touching his face as he spoke. He knew who I was without asking, "Your room is on the top floor, number 9, and there's tea downstairs if you want it. I'll get Marion to take you through your jobs at 7 tomorrow, don't be late, we are busy." There wasn't much to unpack: my pyjamas, the ones Mum bought me, they had a Christmas tree on the front and reindeers up the back. It's nearly Christmas again now, two weeks' time. I hope Nan found the letter. OK, she knew I'd be going soon anyway. If I get time off I'll go and see her. I sent Mum a text saying I had a job and would be in touch, she sent a text in capitals saying BE CAREFUL OF MEN. I didn't reply. I know Vince is still there because Sammy, my sister, told me. Sammy's got four kids, she lives in Leeds with Brian, he's OK, Brian, looks after Sammy which is all I care about at the end of the day.

I go down for tea, it's a plate of sandwiches and there's a tea bag in a cup. The sandwiches are possibly ham, it's a grey meat and it sticks to the white bread, I leave it there and look for biscuits but there aren't any. My stomach pain is getting worse and my belly keeps sort of writhing round. Sometimes it makes me catch my breath. Back in my room I set out clothes for tomorrow, a towel I brought from Nan's, my bathroom bits, shampoo and toothbrush. I check out the shared bathroom along the landing. My feet stick to something sticky and dark, next time I'll wear shoes. The bath is enormous and stained with rust. The taps don't turn easily but then the water gushes out. Someone downstairs shouts out, was that maybe to me?

I lie on the bed and look at my phone, no messages. Facebook has a photo of my sister's recent cooking. I feel very sick and lie down on the bed. Falling asleep has never been easy for me, I get thoughts about Dad and still wonder whether I'll ever see him again. It's been eight years since he went to the off-licence and never came back. That was the year Mum went into the mental hospital and Sammy looked after me with Gran; she's not been right since, I'd say.

At 2 a.m. I wake up shivering and the sick feeling is there again. I stand by the sink convinced I'll throw up. My stomach is very bloated and the pain is making me scared. Then I am sick and over the next two hours I lost a lot of blood, it came from my bottom and I held onto the sink as I wanted to poo but what came out, sliding down my legs was a baby, a rope from my insides attached to it as well, slimy stuff and everything. She was gasping. I lay on the floor and saw I had pulled the sink off the wall. I don't remember that happening but it's there on the floor with the baby and the blood, so much blood. Nan's towel of course Nan's towel. I use my clothes to wipe up the blood but it's everywhere – up the wall, pools of it. I cut the cord with my nail scissors and the baby is crying a lot, little gasps. I wrap her in Nan's towel. I don't know what to do but I cannot have this baby in here. I try to get up but can barely move. It's 6 a.m., I think I can hear people downstairs. I find my large bag that had the money in it. I put her in the bag and I put £40 in there too, two £20s. She might need it. Somehow I make it down the stairs but I'm shaking. No one has seen me; I get out of the door. I walk around for a few minutes. My pillowcase is stuffed into my knickers to stop the bleeding. I find a door step. It's very cold, December and the winds off the sea in Folkestone are wicked. I put her on the step, the house looks OK – the garden is clean and there are flowers in it.

Back at the hotel I send a text to the manager and tell him I'm ill but will be back tomorrow. He bangs on the door, I tell him I'm sick, maybe Covid, I'll get a test. He goes away. I try to clean up but I can't do it, there's too much of it everywhere. At 4 p.m. the police come and bang on the door. They've got the manager with them and a woman who says she's from Social Services. They tracked the blood back to my room.

They call her Georgina now. It was for the best; I did my best.

Abandonment Tales 2

When I was thirteen Mum said it would be best if I went to boarding school in the UK where my dad lived. She sat me down on the green velvet settee in her bedroom and explained that, now my little brother Hanif is four years old, she could go and work and earn more money for us both but that it wouldn't be right for me to be around the flat any more as she would have a lot of visitors. I knew what that was about and it made me feel sick to the pit of myself knowing what she would be doing. Hanif was going to live with my aunt and I was being packed off.

I had not seen my dad for over a year, all I knew was that he lived in Wimbledon in London, somewhere near Big Ben and he had a job which made him a lot of money and that when I saw him on Facetime his eyes looked red and big and different to what I remembered of him. In the background there were pictures on the walls of cars. I wouldn't mind seeing him more, so that would be a good thing if I lived in London.

Mum said that the school she had chosen was waiting for me, that I would get good grades and learn to play the piano and go to university and become a doctor or a lawyer. I wanted to be a beautician like my auntie. The school had a brochure and I looked at it a lot, the photos were of teenagers that didn't look like me. For one, they were white, and secondly they were all smiling and seemed to like being in school. I didn't smile much or so people told me and I did not like school one bit. In Vietnam, school is very dull, it's strict and we have to wear a red scarf with our white blouses and a grey skirt. I don't like wearing it and my friends and I always take our scarves off on the bus going home. The brochure had a map of the school and I saw that it wasn't in London it was 180 miles from King's Cross, wherever that was.

Mum said she didn't need to come with me to the school, that I could travel on my own as the air hostesses would look after me and make sure I met my dad at the airport. He would then take me to the school and settle me in. All my books and uniform would be at the school. I would come home, back to Vietnam in the holidays and that there were a lot of those.

I did not want to say goodbye to Hanif – he and I were that close. He was a limpet, always on my lap or with his little hand in mine. The day I left for the airport, he came in the car and he wouldn't look at me. He had his favourite dragon car on his lap and was very very still, I remember that. When we got to the airport he was sick on my handbag. Mum pulled my case out of the boot and my auntie took me to check in for my flight. Mum said she had to park the car and drove off; she didn't kiss me goodbye. I never said goodbye to Hanif, I do remember that.

At Heathrow the cabin crew took me to Arrivals and I searched for Dad's face but it wasn't there. First I thought that as I hadn't seen him for a long time that he might look different. I remember crying then and knowing I shouldn't. The cabin person noticed a man holding up my name and he had a woman with him. They were from the school and seemed kind, asking about the journey and telling me about my room and the other girls I would meet. I couldn't take it in really, not at all. They said that Dad had been delayed and would come to the school to see me soon. Three hours later we were at the school, I was tired, I couldn't seem to focus much but I ate some rice and a cheesecake. I had a small room to myself and was told that I shared a bathroom. My case was unpacked for me and I couldn't find my photo of Hanif but then I did, I had wrapped it in my pyjamas. I missed him more than Mum.

It's been almost two years since I came here now and it's not been great. I am in trouble a bit, well, a lot actually. I have detentions most weeks. I struggle with the work. I stole a girl's coat and wrote my own name in it but got found out, I ran away to see Dad twice but didn't find his flat. He's been here five times now and taken me out. Tells me he's working hard to pay the school fees, doesn't say much about his life. I want to ask him about what I saw on Facebook, him holding up a little baby girl to the camera with his big face close up to hers but I haven't, I can't, it's too upsetting. I have been back to Vietnam twice to see Mum and Hanif in two years. She kept telling me she had no money for the fare. Hanif cried when he saw me and I didn't stop holding him. He is six now, a big boy. He wants to come to my school but I don't recommend it one bit. The other girls don't like me and I'm never asked to their homes or anything. Some boys seem to like me or anyway they like what I do to them.

Last week the school threatened to expel me. I took a girl's make-up and hid it under my bed; I also refused to take off my maroon loafers – we have to wear brown but they are only a bit red. I spat at a teacher and refused to turn my skirt down. The school counsellor won't see me any more because I refuse to talk to her or say anything. I don't like her attitude, very over-friendly and always touching my arm. Touching is not what I like, not from strangers. Puts me back in mind to one of mum's friends when I was ten, he touched me, yeah he touched me, touched my knickers under my dress. I did tell Mum about it; she laughed it off, saying that she was paid for that, not me, and that she'd have a word. He still would sit there gawping at me and smiling and nodding when he came. If he touches Hanif I'll have him.

Anyway they can expel me if they like; I am 15 now. I could live with Dad and work and get my own place. I mentioned it to him a while back and he said it might not work out but that he'd have a think. He told me to buck my ideas up at school. Last night I spoke to Hanif: I told him I was going to run away. He told me he'd send his dragon car to get me.

At the Salon

I'm not doing it again even if she is part family. She should count herself lucky because Graham won't have her in the house so my letting her see Gracie is all down to me. Plus I have looked after Travis and Renee even though I never got any thanks for it, not even a Christmas card. No, I'm not doing it again. That other wind-up merchant Candice and her so-called boyfriend Gino, he can take a jump. They came to dinner, right, and everyone had a bottle of wine each and I made frittatas which Graham said were like stones but anyway, they didn't bring a thing –

not a thing. No, I wasn't drunk, I only drank the one bottle which I know is not like me on a Saturday. Their son Mario, he was trying to play with the girls and I knew it wouldn't work out, well he came down stairs into the kitchen, dancing about and I asked him, "What's wrong, Mario, what's wrong," but he said, "I'm just dancing, Vicky, I'm just dancing" – so I thought – fill your boots, Mario, fill your boots. He seemed happy enough. Then when I went upstairs and saw what those kids were doing, well, dancing, my eye, they can all jump I tell you and not high enough for me. That other boy of John's, Ricky, he's a bit on the spectrum isn't he? Have you seen what he does with his, you know what? It's not right, is it – John should tell him don't you think? It's not hygienic, is it, and he could get into a lot of trouble. I'd tell him myself but you don't know with people like that, do you, he might not like it, retaliate etc. Did you want the heated pad under your feet? Isn't it working? I'll turn it up, no you shouldn't get any static from it, no it won't be shorting out. I'll turn it off and on again. OK, yes, I saw that flash too. You don't need it anyway. Are you comfortable?

Family 1

While mum is dying they have an Indian meal. They weren't certain that she was dying at the time but they had a fair idea. She lay on the settee in the front room with a pallor that made them feel uncomfortable. Mum had been in the hospital for five days but had now been discharged because they said she would be more comfortable at home. She had wanted to come home and on arrival immediately lay on the settee and was unable to eat much and only spoke in small gasps. "I think we should have an Indian takeaway today," said Troy. "Chicken tikka or masala?" Gwen asks. I think mum would like okra. Nothing for me, mum said, nothing for me.

After the Indian meal was cleared away they propped mum up so she could see the telly. "Do you think we should call the doctor?" Troy asks. "I don't want a doctor," mum said. "I just want to sit here and watch all of you doing normal things." They both look at mum, "Can we make you more comfortable?" "No, I just want to sit here and watch." As it happened, mum was like that for two more days. They didn't have another Indian meal; they ate things from the freezer, things that mum had made. "What would dad say if he was here?" Troy asked. "I think he would say that we have done our best." Gwen looked out of the window, but did we, did we always do our best or did we wear her out, should we have insisted she had the okra, she liked that didn't she?

At the funeral there were a lot of people, she had been a popular woman.

Family 2

On the plane a couple are talking, between them is a small child, probably three years old. The man says, "So you are going to throw up, I told you when you had that vodka, you are going to throw up, but you are always f…ing drunk; when we land you are going to go to your mother's, you are not coming home with me." The woman is slumped against the window, the child is laying on top of the mother with a blanket over him with just his head above. The man is agitated, large and red-faced, no hair and is drinking vodka from the duty-free bottle. The mother asks, "How much Calpol did you give him?" He says, "Enough". The woman replies, "And now you are poisoning my kid, drugging him up". The man says, "I am just giving him enough so that he sleeps during the flight". The woman says, "I don't know what to do any more". The man says, "I've told you, you are going to your mother's, you are not coming home with us, you are a f…ing drunk". The boy starts to cry, whimpering and then he starts crying loudly, the mother says, pointing to the air hostess, "You see that lady there, that lady with the hat on, I am going to ask her to put you out of the plane door; we're up in the sky, you know what will happen to you then, don't you, you'll die." The boy starts screaming, the mother tries to get up from her seat but staggers back announcing that she is going to throw up.

A few minutes later the woman is sick, the child is screaming and the father gets up and starts wandering about the plane looking for his friends. He finds them, they are only a few seats away, laughing. The mother is being helped by the air stewardess; she is being very sick.

Eventually she stops; the child is now sound asleep and the mother sleeps too. At Gatwick they are standing by the luggage carousel; the man stands apart from the woman and the child is running round in circles. "What's wrong with you now, bloody kid, right mental you are."

Teeth — tricky things

"Put your tooth back in your pocket," she says. "Don't go on at me," he answers, stuffing both hands deeper into his jacket pocket. "If I have told you once I have told you a hundred times looking at it isn't going to make it any better and you'll lose it". Her white bob frames her face that has become somehow larger over the years and, he would say too, a little menacing.

Norman's tooth had fallen away two days ago, it was a front one that had fallen from the Maryland bridge that had solved the lower jaw problem a while ago. He was anxious about the tooth, had put it in some tissue paper in the bottom of his pocket ready for when he saw the dentist in 3 days' time. Norman liked to reassure himself that it was still there.

She often went on at him no matter what he did or what it was. He felt old and inadequate particularly now with the missing tooth. They were out for the day; they had been shopping, he bought her flowers; she liked that, but he had bought the wrong ones. "You know I don't like carnations," she said, "they remind me of garage flowers, the flowers they sell on the forecourt. You could have been a bit more imaginative. Lilies, or something, Norman." "I thought you liked pinks, you liked them when I grew them in the garden in Somerset." Yes, she thought, that was when you had hair, teeth and we had a garden and not a balcony, now I want a bunch of real flowers and a real man.

When he did see the dentist he couldn't find the tooth, he thought it was there, absolutely cast-iron certain but when he turned out the pocket he only found a small piece of grit in the lining. "That's alright," the dentist said, "I can easily make another one but there will be a delay; come back in three weeks and we can put it back in". Three weeks, he was horrified, he couldn't go for three weeks looking like this.

When he got home he told her, she was vitriolic. "Didn't I say you would lose it, I told you to keep that tooth in your pocket and not touch it. Oh, Norman, go on to the balcony and weed the pots." Later, when he was emptying the waste bin in the hall he found the tooth in its paper nest. He knew he hadn't put it there.

Snatches from the sauna

"Her name is Autumn Shaw," he said, swinging his tattooed arms across his narrow chest. "She's the best and the worst thing that ever happened to me. Autumn is her real name and all her bits are her own too." I ask how long they have been together. "Hot in here now, isn't it," he says, shifting his body, fanning his face with a hand. "We've been together for five years now and I love her to bits; we've come here to the pool tonight as Chloe is with her dad for the weekend, first time in a long while." He's right, the sauna is now pretty hot and he moves to the lower seats next to me. The scar on his cheek is livid and deep. "Autumn won't marry me, though I've asked her enough times, I don't know why but there you go." We talk about the coldness of the sea and the people who swim all year. "Not for me," he says, "not for me, but then that's maybe why the army rejected me: too soft." I ask about the scar on his cheek, adding that it must have been painful. "Oh, that," he says, touching it gently with two fingers as in a benediction, "that was Chloe's dad, he did that about two weeks ago." He closes the door carefully as he leaves.

She taps her foot for a while and checks the timer on the wall. "Is this supposed to be good for your skin?" she asks, but doesn't look me in the eye. I reply that I have no idea but that the warmth is good for my bones. "I hate water and stuff in my eyes. This chain is getting hot round my neck." I comment on its apparent weight and size for a gold chain. "Oh yeah, can't leave it in the changing room, I don't trust no one, do you?" A man joins us, sits on the top level; he's huge, like a sumo wrestler, grunts a greeting. "Gosh, you ate all the chips, didn't you?" she quips. The man says he's in training, has to keep his bulk up. "I think you look amazing anyway, pal," she says. On her arm is a tattoo of a bird and the name, Chloe. We sit in silence while she taps her foot in an agitated manner. "I'm too hot now," she says, shifting her body from side to side. I suggest a cold shower like the Scandinavians. She laughs, "You got to be kidding; I don't want to freeze my tits right off, do I?" The door opens; it's her partner. He leans in. "Summer, you coming or what?" "I thought your name was Autumn," I say; "Oh, he always calls me that when he's angry, don't you?" He scowls. "And you can stop looking like that too, chum," he says looking at the sumo on the top floor.

Once they've gone, the sumo tells me he's met the girl before. "Is her name Autumn or Summer?" I ask. "Her name is June Shaw, lives on the estate next to my mum, works as a beautician; nice girl, had Chloe when she was fifteen; the dad's a paedophile they say – it was in the papers. He's just come out, this week I think. June never believed it, said he'd never hurt a fly let alone a child."

Encountering Eugene

The boy was wary, dark eyes, bothered hair, holding a toy, a Transformer, as though his life depended on it. His knuckles firm, white, see-through, like a jelly fish I thought, almost shiny against his green frayed school jersey. His mother spoke first, something had to be done, she couldn't take it again, his violence towards her since his father had up and gone. The boy, Eugene, was rude, beyond anyone's control, now suspended from primary school, he spat at passing cars and people. He ate when he wanted to by raiding the fridge and was up all night on his father's computer and always playing with the Transformer, nothing else. A social worker said going into care was a last resort.

Turning to Eugene I asked if he could show me his Transformer but he swished it out of sight placing it under his jersey as he spat at my chair. He was asked not to do that again as my Transformers had firm views about spitting and so if he wanted to see them he'd have to agree not to spit. His mother told me that her life had been bearable even while the fights with Eugene's dad had been terrible as the boy had not, at least then, been as bad – he had slept at night and at school. She had recently learned that her eldest sister was in fact her mother and who she thought of as her mother was her grandmother. The shock had almost killed her she said. They are Greek Cypriots, these things don't happen in our culture. No one will say who my father is, perhaps it is my grandpa, I now know nothing. I am thinking wildly, but then I never did fit in, always thought something wasn't right, now I know it. I tell her she's had a great deal to manage and life would get back on track. Eugene had studied my three Transformers and turning them into tall creatures he knocked them over one by one, laying his own down under my chair appearing to be at rest.

Eugene saw me alone eight times after that first meeting. His white clenched fists still holding firm but once in a while he showed me a world in sand. A place where a man, a father, drove a horse into the bedroom and carried a boy away while he was asleep. A blue dog ate the bad people and a Transformer killed a grandfather, turning him into wax like a candle. His speech was always brief, coming in darts of fire, like spit, anxious, eager, keen to hit a target. Once he told me he had seen photos of naked people on his father's computer; one of them had been his aunt.

Then, grandma brought Eugene; he held her hand I recall. They are living with me now, it's better for them she said. Eugene nodded. He was at a new school and mum had a job, his dad had not made contact and was thought to be in prison.

Three years later I catch sight of Eugene across a road; I am at the traffic lights. He must be 13 now, his hair is longer and he is in school uniform; he is running to meet someone I think. His shoelaces are undone, he is gripping a bottle.

Another request to see Eugene is made by his mother, Eugene wants to live with his father who has now remarried with twin daughters, he is living in Ireland. Eugene is again vicious towards her and also her mother. Grandpa has died, he's now the only man in the house. Eugene tells me they never wanted him anyway, he just didn't fit it. He laughs when I mention the Transformers, asks where mine are; same place I say and he looks for them. Large loose-limbed teenager, black hair curling down his neck reaching into the box. He's not met the twins, thinks it would be OK to go, nothing for him here, not now, a girl broke his heart. School is shit. He is 16 soon anyway. He agrees to meet Dad here not in Ireland, see the twins maybe.

I'm driving into the supermarket and the tall young man is pulling about 70 or so trolleys on a long rope into a bay; it's Eugene alright. He doesn't see me but then perhaps he actually does as he sort of gives a second turn round of his dark head.

At the station some three years on I see Eugene in a South East railwayman's uniform. He has a whistle in his mouth, he is in charge of my train which is leaving the platform. He has a beard and a mark, a wound to his forehead under the hat brim, it looks recent and angry. Seems he is still local. That would have been four years ago now and I hadn't been on trains that much. Then two days ago I am in hospital, Accident and Emergency, surgery is needed. I'm waiting for a bed, the nurse tells me a porter will collect me. It is 4 a.m., I am cold, tired and in pain. A wheelchair comes crashing round the corner, I hear it banging into the corridor's sides. They say you need a ride missus, he says. It's Eugene alright. He doesn't see me, I'm huddled into my coat, mask on my face. I'll get you there, don't worry, lady, he says and the ride is memorable. His swift darting movements, like fast travelling spit, have not changed, his dark head now under a blue hospital hat. As I get out of the chair I see his white knuckles still clenched on the wheelchair handles, almost iridescent, see-through like jellyfish, I thought.

Popped on hold

When I couldn't wake Shauny up I knew it weren't right.

His head was sort of sidewise like it were twisted.

I shouted for mum to come up but she didn't so I shook Shauny again then I put his chimes on as that makes him laugh. But it didn't, did it.

I felt upset then and I rang Jody my key worker. The receptionist popped me on hold for a long time when I said I couldn't wake Shauny up.

Then an ambulance came. Jaidon had been the last one to change Shauny and the policeman asked him a lot of questions at the hospital.

The doctor couldn't wake Shauny up either and guess what, when I rang the funeral place they popped me on hold as well and it made me sad, reminded me of when I'd rung Jody.

Turkish Adventures

1

The boy with markedly yellow teeth tells me that the bougainvillea is "good for lady, two colour". He jabs at the stem of brilliant pink and clear white; "Beyaz" he adds. Helping me to car he says, "Luck luck luck lady." I'm worried why I need so much of it,

As I plant this beauty I think of him, the roll-down mat in the back of the hut where he sleeps among the plants, his plastic shoes and yellow teeth. The plant slips from its plastic sleeve, the root ball is barely an inch long. It will need a lot of good fortune to survive but it's OK, I have it in mind.

2.

At the barber's shop which is also the electrician's shop which doubles for the grocery store where a man also advertises that he fixes tyres, I point to a photograph of my broken window extractor fan. Excitedly, the girl finds a part that looks like what I need. She holds it in the air but then we see it has no back to it. "Ah," she says, "problem evet." I agree, "Problem evet." She calls on the mobile to someone who tells me in English that the part will come in a week, adding, "Maybe lady, maybe lady, a week".

A week later I visit the shop and show them my photo again. Ah "Yarin," they tell me, "Yarin, tomorrow". The electrician is now shaving a man, it is the local carpenter who waves at me.

When yarin comes I pop in waving my phone photo, the woman is excited again and holds up the entire whole extractor fan. "Evet," I say, "problem yok". The girl points to the barber's empty chair, "Problem," she says. I assume no electrician.

The next day I go to the shop again and the electrician follows me in his car. The fan is installed and works well. "You want shave, lady?" he asks, pointing to my chin.

Milton Keynes UK
Ingram Content Group UK Ltd.
UKHW031906250924
448833UK00001B/44